African Studies
History, Politics, Economics, and Culture

AF757943

Edited by
Molefi Asante
Temple University

A Routledge Series

African Studies

History, Politics, Economics, and Culture

Molefi Asante, *General Editor*

The Athens of West Africa
A History of International Education at Fourah Bay College, Freetown, Sierra Leone
Daniel J. Paracka, Jr.

The Yorùbá Traditional Healers of Nigeria
Mary Olufunmilayo Adekson

The 'Civil Society' Problematique
Deconstructing Civility and Southern Nigeria's Ethnic Radicalization
Adedayo Oluwakayode Adekson

Maat, the Moral Ideal in Ancient Egypt
A Study in Classical African Ethics
Maulana Karenga

Igbo Women and Economic Transformation in Southeastern Nigeria, 1900–1960
Gloria Chuku

Kwame Nkrumah's Politico-Cultural Thought and Policies
An African-Centered Paradigm for the Second Phase of the African Revolution
Kwame Botwe-Asamoah

Non-Traditional Occupations, Empowerment and Women
A Case of Togolese Women
Ayélé Léa Adubra

Contending Political Paradigms in Africa
Rationality and the Politics of Democratization in Kenya and Zambia
Shadrack Wanjala Nasong'o

Law, Morality and International Armed Intervention
The United Nations and ECOWAS in Liberia
Mourtada Déme

The Hidden Debate
The Truth Revealed about the Battle over Affirmative Action in South Africa and the United States
Akil Kokayi Khalfani

Britain, Leftist Nationalists and the Transfer of Power in Nigeria, 1945–1965
Hakeem Ibikunle Tijani

Western-Educated Elites in Kenya, 1900–1963
The African American Factor
Jim C. Harper, II

Africa and IMF Conditionality
The Unevenness of Compliance, 1983–2000
Kwame Akonor

African Cultural Values
Igbo Political Leadership in Colonial Nigeria, 1900–1966
Raphael Chijioke Njoku

A Roadmap for Understanding African Politics
Leadership and Political Integration in Nigeria
Victor Oguejiofor Okafor

Doing Justice Without the State
The Afikpo (Ehugbo) Nigeria Model
O. Oko Elechi

Doing Justice Without the State
The Afikpo (Ehugbo) Nigeria Model

O. Oko Elechi

Routledge
Taylor & Francis Group
NEW YORK AND LONDON

Routledge
Taylor & Francis Group
711 Third Avenue
New York
NY 10017

Routledge
Taylor & Francis Group
2 Park Square
Milton Park, Abingdon
Oxon OX14 4RN

© 2006 by Taylor & Francis Group, LLC
Routledge is an imprint of Taylor & Francis Group, an Informa business

First issued in paperback 2013

International Standard Book Number-13: 978-0-415-64725-0 (Paperback)

No part of this book may be reprinted, reproduced, transmitted, or utilized in any form by any electronic, mechanical, or other means, now known or hereafter invented, including photocopying, microfilming, and recording, or in any information storage or retrieval system, without written permission from the publishers.

Trademark Notice: Product or corporate names may be trademarks or registered trademarks, and are used only for identification and explanation without intent to infringe.

Library of Congress Cataloging-in-Publication Data

Elechi, O. Oko.
Doing justice without the state : the Afikpo (Ehugbo) Nigeria model / O. Oko Elechi.
p. cm. -- (African studies)
Includes bibliographical references and index.
ISBN 0-415-97729-0 (alk. paper)
1. Dispute resolution (Law)--Nigeria--Afikpo. 2. Customary law--Nigeria--Afikpo. I. Title. II. Series: African studies (Routledge (Firm))

KTA3755.E44 2006
303.6'90966945--dc22 2006010759

Visit the Taylor & Francis Web site at
http://www.taylorandfrancis.com

and the Routledge Web site at
http://www.routledge-ny.com

To the
Ever loving memory of late Mama Aliji Uro-Elechi (1925 – 2005)
for your love, support, and inspiration, and for giving so much and expecting so little,
And to Ola, Ogbonnia, Nnenna, Eze and Ugo Elechi, my family, my rock, for their love, support, understanding, patience, and inspiration
And to the
People of Ehugbo (Afikpo).

Table of Contents

List of Figures

Foreword

The Case for Traditional Jurisprudence in a Modern Nigerian Setting

This innovative book makes the case for the continued applicability of a traditional system of settling legal cases at Afikpo, one of over 200 groups of Igbo living in southeastern Nigeria. I have personally known the author for some time, as I was external examiner on his Ph.D. dissertation at Simon Fraser University. Afikpo, his original home, which he writes about here, is familiar to me; since I carried out extensive cultural and social anthropological field research there in 1952–1953 and 1959–1960, with brief return trips since then. Professor Elechi's knowledge of Afikpo language and culture, combined with his training and experience abroad in criminal justice studies, makes him the ideal scholar to present interpretations of an African indigenous legal system and its applicability today. The book is unusual, among studies of the application of the law in African societies and countries, in arguing for the considerable advantage of retaining and supporting traditional legal systems in the modern era, rather than totally replacing them with Western European models, which are often ill-suited to African societies. The latter is the general rule today on the continent. Professor Elechi is writing about what he describes as acephalous societies, an anthropological term, which technically means "headless," but, in fact, refers to those indigenous societies in Africa, of which there are many, which have lacked centralized state controls. An acephalous society generally resolve accusations of law-breaking and conflict through forms of resolution that allow both accuser and accused to go on living together in peace, a necessity in order to prevent the disruption of the small-scale society with its constant face-to-face relationships. While it has always been possible for the guilty party to move away to reduce friction, and this sometimes has occurred, the resolution of the conflict so that both parties can continue to interact with one another, and other members of their society without friction, has been much preferred. This maintains the stability of the society.

Africa's non-centralized societies developed different techniques for dispute-resolution procedures in order to maintain internal peace. In some cases elders of the whole community have handled the matter, and in other disputes the accusation has been settled by the senior members of the families of the two sides involved, who have met to work out a resolution. Again, appointed or elected officials of known wisdom have adjudicated cases. In still other instances religious officials have played roles in the settlement. A non-centralized African society may employ two or more of these devices depending on the nature of the dispute. The point is that after the resolution both parties agree to live together comfortably. The emphasis is on reconciliation. This does not always mean that one party is always fully satisfied, though this is the goal, but that whatever dissatisfaction exists on the part of some persons, it is publicly put aside in terms of their members' relationship to others in the society, including the members of the other group involved in the case.

In the traditional system of adjudication at Afikpo, which I became familiar with by the 1950s, if there was no resolution of a case, if final agreement failed, there was a turn to one of two religious mechanisms to reach finality. The accused, if denying guilt, could swear innocence at an Afikpo spirit shrine. If the person became ill or died within a year he or she was believed guilty of lying, the spirit having caused the harm. If the individual remained healthy he or she was considered to be innocent. A second mechanism was for both sides to consult an Igbo oracle outside of Afikpo, the most popular being *Ibini Okpabe*, located in the town of Aro Chukwu, some fifty miles to the south. The oracle arrived at a decision by apparently mystical means, but in fact, this occurred with the assistance of persons associated with it. The power of the oracle, as a spiritual force was greatly feared at Afikpo, and its decisions were respected. These two seemingly irrational methods of settling cases (in the eyes of Westerners) in fact, often led resolutions that prevented serious community disruption, which would otherwise have occurred due to the failure of settlement at Afikpo. It should be noted that litigants were invariably backed up by a host of family members, age and residential mates, and friends, so that any single case might involve numerous community members. Social schism was prevented, and the local group was preserved through ritual means. Today such legal mechanisms are rarely employed, rather litigants can take cases that are very difficult to resolve in the traditional sector to a government court. However, they often prefer not to, as court decisions are quite unpredictable.

Professor Elechi advocates a system of local-level jurisprudence based on the value and experience of tradition, somewhat modified due to changing social and political circumstances. It is not a static model but allows for reasonable change, while maintaining its basic legal principles. As the author indicates, it does not apply to serious crimes such as murder, armed robbery, arson and violent sexual assaults, but to accusations that are mostly in the field of what in the West are generally called civil law. The more serious crimes are still to be adjudicated by government courts. The author, in fact, argues for the juxtaposition of two legal systems, and their integration within the larger system of law within a modern African state, rather than the complete integration of Afikpo and other non-centralized African societies into a Western legal system at both the microjudicial and the macrojudicial level.

Curiously, that which Professor Elechi prizes, harks back to the British colonial system in Nigeria which instituted a system of indirect rule developed in the early twentieth century, for less serious crimes and accusations, with an emphasis to varying degrees based on indigenous culture, on the use of native law, native police and native courts. Serious crimes were tried in the colonial courts; in Nigeria's this was based on British law and not on indigenous Nigerian legal principles. This bipolar legal system developed since the British lacked the colonial personnel to operate at all legal levels. It required colonial officials, and sometimes anthropologists hired by them, to study and report on "native law and custom." Today, the Nigerian federal and state governments and their lackeys (the army, the police), are in many ways more exploitive of individuals at the local level as were the colonialist. But now the "native," is mostly educated, and has a public voice while this rarely occurred under colonialism. Professor Elechi is a product of this change. The similarity of his approach to colonial legal processes that formerly existed at Afikpo do not mark the author as an apologist for colonialism, as the today's political setting differs markedly.

Part of the author's motivation for the development of his views is his experience and that of others in Nigeria, with the police, who are often corrupt and allow or disallow cases going to courts according to the bribery that they are able to extract from the litigants. And unlike during in the colonial system, there are plenty of Nigerian personnel to man the police and the courts at all level, often strangers to Afikpo. The present system of state and federal government justice in Nigeria is a farce; it is rarely fair, it seldom work well and it often leaves one or both sides involved in a case financially in ruin from the pressure of having to bribe the police, and even a judge, in order to have a hearing, no less a fair one. Professor Elechi's writings contribute to a broader move among Nigerian today to rethink governance in the country, particularly among individuals and groups living in the southern half.

The author's thorough familiarity with Afikpo culture and society makes his assessment of the situation realistic. During the colonial period and until a good many years after post-colonialism began about 1960s, scholars, such as I, writing about the continent's cultures and their social groupings were almost entirely from the West. The situation has changed in recent years, as Africans more and more have become the spokespersons for their own societies. Professor Elechi's book exemplifies this newer trend. He is a sensitive observer and recorder on his own people. Afikpo, the society he writes of, is unusually complex in social groups—age grades, men's societies, title societies, organized matrilineal and patrilineal descent groups, both village and general Afikpo leadership, the presence of descendants of non-Igbo peoples in a largely Igbo cultural environment, and so on. He shows how these and other social elements have meshed in the past into an intricate social system that belies the frequently expressed popular stereotypes in the West that Africans are simple people living in simple societies with social principles of behavior. There has not only been social complexity at Afikpo, but the traditional legal system long ago established clear rules for case settlement procedures and the nature of punishment for particular crimes.

The author's approach is based on his experiences in two worlds—on the one hand university training in Norway and Canada and teaching in the United States with the knowledge acquired in living in these places, and on the one other hand a deep knowledge of his own African culture in which he was brought up in and has kept in contact with. It is his ability skillfully to combine these two orientations, sometimes seemingly at odds with one another, which greatly enriches his writing. His analysis can serve as a model for other African societies undergoing change and modern influences. His book speaks for the value of tradition, even if modified, in the context of modernity.

Simon Ottenberg
Emeritus Professor, Anthropology
University of Washington, Seattle

Preface

The Afikpo indigenous justice system is examined as an alternative system of justice in South-East Nigeria from a restorative, transformative and communitarian principles. Despite the dominance of the Nigerian state criminal justice system in social control, the Afikpo indigenous justice system still holds sway, and is perceived to be more effective and legitimate. The Afikpo model is rooted in the traditions, cultures and customs of the people. Indigenous social and political institutions function as channels for conflict resolution and justice. The processes and principles of conflict resolution are emphasized. The model's continued perceived popularity and legitimacy are discussed, as is the basis for the system's co-existence with the Nigerian State agencies of social control.

A major finding of this study is that the Afikpo model is victim-centered. Restoring the victim's emotional and material losses is the goal of justice. The system recognizes the victims' needs for information and vindication. Victims are empowered and vindicated by all stakeholders acknowledging their suffering and loss. Victims, offenders, and their families, as well as the general community, are involved in defining harm and repair. Offenders and their families are held responsible for the victims' injury and material loss. Offenders are persuaded to pay restitution to victims. They also apologize to the victim, his/her family and the community. In sum, the goal of justice is the reparation of harm done to victims and communities by offenders. Appropriate support is accorded victims and their families by the community. Social control is a community property, therefore necessitating collective effort and responsibility. Its survival and relevance is proof of its popularity, effectiveness and legitimacy. The research findings show that litigants are happier and more satisfied with the justice system as is shown by their cooperation and compliance with the decisions of the tribunal. Acceptance and compliance with the decisions of the tribunal are more likely when the litigants are actively involved and participate in the justice-making process. In the Afikpo indigenous justice system, decisions are reached through a consensus of all stakeholders. The cathartic and educational value of the justice process is reflected in the positive behavioural changes of offenders in particular, and other community members in general.

In addition, the Afikpo conflict resolution model is inclusive and seeks to address the interests of all parties to the conflict. The social solidarity and humane emphasis of the system is reflected in the treatment of offenders. The institutions of social control are formal agents of resocialization, hence providing offenders support through teaching and healing. The offender must first acknowledge the wrong, then, show remorse, shame, and accountability through reparation and expiation.

This study is grounded in theories of restorative, transformative and communitarian justice and other concepts of African justice. Inquiries into state, state/society and postocolonial state theories are undertaken to further illuminate this phenomenon of an alternative conflict resolution model. An inquiry into the Afikpo community's conflict resolution mechanism and processes is also an inquiry into the community's system of governance, social, political and economic institutions and activities. Being an exploratory study, several qualitative research methods were utilized. They include participant observation, oral history, in-person and focus group interviews of 40 men and 15 women.

The Afikpo indigenous justice system is functional, effective, unique, democratic, and allows for the participation of all community residents. This study unveils a different kind of knowledge, which will contribute to the growing body of literature in restorative justice.

It is reiterated that the Afikpo indigenous justice system is unique, effective, and humane.[1] The system is flexible, dynamic, and allows for the democratic participation of villagers. Group interest and social solidarity are the goals of the justice process. Victims, offenders, their families, as well as the general community, are involved in defining harm and repairing harm, and resolutions of conflicts are arrived at through rigorous discussions of all stakeholders. Judgments are based on consensus and derive from available evidence and the opinions of participants.

The book is organized into eight chapters. Chapter One introduces the study and briefly reviews the theories and history of restorative justice. It is reiterated here that the Afikpo indigenous system of conflict resolution functions as an alternative system of conflict resolution. Ultimate power and authority reside with the Nigerian State courts and other officials of the Criminal Justice System. However, the Afikpo indigenous systems of conflict resolution remain the primary avenues for conflict resolution in the community. Although litigants not satisfied with judgments of the traditional courts may seek redress in the State courts. Only State courts have jurisdiction over serious violent crimes like murder, armed robbery, arson and violent sexual assaults and so on. Ironically, most cases of murder in the community are through sorcery and witchcraft, which the state courts do not recognize. Cases of murder through sorcery and witchcraft are brought to the Afikpo indigenous courts, which handle such cases.

Chapter Two of the book reviews some of the major theories of restorative justice. The arguments for restorative justice are reviewed, as well as the benefits of restorative justice approaches to victims, offenders, the community and the criminal justice system. Further review of how the state systems and community's indigenous systems of conflict resolution co-exist, were undertaken. The chapter concludes with a selective exploration of African philosophies of justice.

Chapter Three reviews the custom versus law debate, which is at the heart of restorative justice principles in the African context. Issues of human rights and the status of human rights in pre-colonial Africa are explored. To illustrate that human rights was recognized by pre-colonial African societies, the socio-political organizations of the Ashanti of Ghana and that of the Igbo people of Nigeria are examined. A brief socio-historical inquiry into the concept of human rights is also undertaken.

Chapter Four examines the Nigerian Criminal Justice System in post-colonial Africa. It is argued that corruption is mostly responsible for the ineffectiveness of the Nigerian criminal justice system. The system alienates the people it serves. A brief examination of the operations of the Nigerian Police is undertaken to illustrate the ineffectiveness of post-colonial state criminal justice systems. Post-colonial theories and the dependency theory are reviewed to get insight into why post-colonial states of Africa have failed to perform.

Chapter Five provides an historical overview of Afikpo town to enhance an understanding of the historical basis of the Afikpo system of conflict resolution. Economic activities are important to understanding the system. It is believed the economic system reinforces the communities' egalitarian and cooperative outlook which is essential for the effective functioning of restorative justice systems. There is a State-sponsored customary court in Afikpo intended to bridge the gap between the colonial imposed systems of justice and that of African indigenous systems of conflict resolution. The customary court is examined to understand its relevance in conflict resolution in Afikpo. Owing to certain methodological difficulties, only the structure and process of the courts are examined with respect to the general objective of the book.

Chapter Six examines some major Afikpo indigenous institutions of conflict resolution. These institutions are also major agents of socialization and resocialization. Some of the institutions of conflict resolution are extensions of primary groupings and so tend to apply more mediative techniques in conflict resolution. Some of the institutions of conflict resolution are more formal and apply both mediative and arbitrative approaches. However, all the systems of conflict resolution are, guided more by group interests rather, than the narrow interests of litigants, and decisions are reached by consensus of participants. While every case is examined on its merit and past judgments do not determine cases, past judgments are sometimes used as precedents.

Chapters Seven and Eight present the research findings. Chapter Seven begins with a review of the available literature on African institutions of marriage, family, and divorce to understand how they affect women. To appreciate the status of women in African societies, an understanding of the workings of certain traditional institutions and their effect on the well-being and rights of women are important. Certain African traditional practices such as dowry and female circumcision are considered oppressive to women. These issues are examined in light of this argument, especially since these issues are often the basis of the conflict that come to the traditional courts. Women are focused here because most culturally based systems of justice are perceived to oppress and alienate women. One of the fears expressed by some Canadian Aboriginal women with the proposed devolution of justice to the Aboriginal people was that the transfer of power to customary laws that derive from patriarchal values may not serve the interests of women and children especially as it relates to cases of violence and sexual abuse. Modern Canadian laws they argued were becoming more sensitive to women's issues and therefore better suited to family violence cases.

Chapter Eight presents the responses of the various institutions of conflict resolution to violations of customs and other offenses. To understand the prohibited acts and the responses, a review of the sanctions of other African societies is undertaken. Such crimes as murder, sorcery and magic, theft, adultery, rape and incest, are examined. The position of the victim and offender in the Afikpo indigenous systems of conflict resolution, are further examined. The chapter concludes with an examination of the challenges confronting the Afikpo community model of conflict resolution. It is suggested that demographic changes, the existence of Christian and Moslem groups and economic factors present challenges to the system that need examination.

I have provided at the appendix an overview of the research methods employed in the collection of data for this study. The interest in the processes of data collection is because it further highlights the dynamics of social interaction in the community to have a better appreciation of the culture that informs and sustains this system. The issues of justice and politics are complex, and one research method cannot adequately cover the issues. Several research methods, known as triangulation, were employed in the study. Methods include participant observation, oral and focus group interviews, oral history, and archival research. Prior to the field trip, ethical approval to conduct interviews was obtained from the Simon Fraser University Ethics Review Committee.

Chapter One

Introduction

"Justice cannot be for one side alone, but must be for both"

—Eleanor Roosevelt

"Judgement is not given after hearing one side"

—Igbo proverb

Afikpo is the second biggest city in Ebonyi state, which is situated in South Eastern Nigeria. In 1991, the population of Afikpo was estimated to be 110,000. The administrative headquarters of Afikpo North Local Government Area, prior to colonialism, Afikpo, like most societies in Africa, had a well-defined system of political and social control. This like other aspects of African, democratic socio-political practices, was subjugated by the British colonial authorities when they instituted a central government for Nigeria. Afikpo peoples' resistance to colonial rule and the emergent colonial political and judicial institutions partly explains the survival, and the increasing popularity, of the Afikpo traditional[1] conflict resolution system.

The principles and practices of the Afikpo indigenous justice system is examined from a restorative, transformative and communitarian paradigm. The thrust of this inquiry is on the traditional political and social institutions and their application in recent years. These institutions function as channels for conflict resolution and deviant controls. Emphasis of the study is on the processes and principles of justice making, rather than on the outcomes of the system's response to crime and victimization. The basis of the Igbo peoples' egalitarian world outlook and ability to constantly adapt to changes is inquired into. The Afikpo indigenous institutions of social control are also effective and widely respected major agents of socialization[2] and resocialization, providing teaching and healing support to both victims and offenders, and their families. Teaching is also intended to transform the offender from a non-conforming person to a conforming individual to protect the community. Other objectives of the Igbo socialization and resocialization processes are to inculcate the values of moral uprightness, industry and discipline in the Igbo person (Iro 1985). The Afikpo community conflict resolution system commands nearly total acceptance and participation, and is, widely viewed as legitimate by the community. Further, attempts are made to explain how and why these institutions co-exist with State regulated non-indigenous institutions of conflict resolution.

The Afikpo traditional system of conflict resolution functions essentially as an alternative system of conflict resolution. Nigeria, as part of its colonial heritage, has instituted modern institutions of conflict resolution. The modern Nigerian system of conflict resolution, similar to western juridical systems, makes use of the police, courts, prisons and other governmental agencies of social control. No claim is made that the findings of the research can be generalized beyond the Afikpo community. The nature of the Afikpo resolution system is unique. As a result, this exploratory study tends to fit into what is commonly known within the qualitative research methods as "intrinsic research." Stake defines intrinsic research as a

> . . . specific, unique, bounded system . . . undertaken because one wants better understanding of this particular case. It is not undertaken primarily because the case represents other cases or because it illustrates a particular trait or problem, but because, in all its particularity and ordinariness, this case is of interest (in Denzin/Lincoln (ed.) 1994: 237).

This book derives from my Ph.D. dissertation, which foundation was laid during my undergraduate studies at the University of Oslo. My academic interest in restorative justice started after I heard Professor Nils Christie speak about the subject in one of the Oslo University Institute of Criminology's seminars. Further readings of Nils Christie's works on restorative justice re-affirmed my observation that similar principles guided the Afikpo traditional system of conflict resolution. I was immediately fascinated with the logic of restorative justice, particularly because it seemed to provide the answer to me for why the Nigerian State Criminal Justice System was ineffective and largely ignored by the Afikpo people. The Afikpo traditional system of conflict resolution was chosen for this study because I am familiar with the system and culture of the community. I was born and raised in Afikpo and participated in some of the cultural activities of the community as a child. With time, my involvement in the social and political activities of the community was confined to Church and School activities. The Church and School authorities discouraged us from getting involved in the cultural activities of the community. The indigenous system was believed heathenish and a negative influence on Afikpo youth at the time.

BRIEF HISTORY OF NIGERIA

Nigeria is located in Western Africa, and the geographic coordinates are 10 00 N, 8 00 E. Nigeria is bounded on the West by the Republic of Benin, on the North by Niger and Chad, Cameroon on the East, and the Atlantic Ocean in the South. The political history of modern Nigeria began in 1914 when Lord Lugard amalgamated the protectorates of Northern and Southern Nigeria under British rule. In 1954, the first fully federal constitution was drawn-up, initiating the process to self rule. In 1956 the British colonial authorities granted Western and Eastern Nigeria self-governing status. This self-governing status was accorded to Northern Nigeria in 1959.

Nigeria achieved its full political independence from Britain in 1960. Nigeria promptly adopted a federal constitution, with three semi-autonomous regions, namely the Northern, Western, and Eastern regions, which were dominated by the Hausa/Fulani, the Yoruba, and the Igbo ethnic groups respectively. The three regions and the federal government each operated the Westminster style parliamentary system.

Presently, the geo-political structure of the Federal Republic of Nigeria is made up of 36 states and the Federal Capital Territory, Abuja[3]. According to the 2005 population estimate, the total Nigerian population is 128,771,988. The age structure of the population according to data from the World Factbook on Nigeria is as follows:

> 0–14 years—42.3% (male 27,466,766/female 27,045,092);
> 15–64 years—54.6% (male 35,770,593/female 34,559,414);
> 65 years and above—3.1% (male 1,874,157/female 2,055,966).

The population growth rate is 2.37%; the birth rate is 40.65 births per 1,000 population; the death rate is 17.18 deaths per 1,000 population, according to the 2005 population estimates. Based on the 2005 estimates, the infant mortality rate is 98.8 deaths per 1,000 live births. The life expectancy rate of the entire population is 46.74 years, with males averaging 46.21 years, females 47.29 years.

Nigeria is the most populous African Nation, and potentially one of the wealthiest countries of black Africa. Nigeria is blessed with skilled human and abundant natural resources. Nigeria is also considered the most ethnically diverse society in the world with about 252 identifiable ethnic groups. More than ninety-nine percent of the northern population, are Moslems, who account for more than 50 percent of the total Nigerian population. Christianity is dominant in the South, accounting for about 35 per cent of the country's total population, while adherents of African religion make up the balance.

The Nigerian economy is heavily dependent on oil earnings. Oil production, at about 2 million barrels a day (mn b/d.), account for over 90% of total Nigeria's export earnings. However, oil accounts for only 13.6% of total GDP. This is because the economy is still based on a traditional agricultural and trading economy. Nigeria, once a large net exporter of food, now imports food, owing to the failure of the largely subsistence agricultural sector to keep up with rapid population growth. The dominance of the oil sector in the economy led to the neglect and decline of the agricultural sector.

The area of Nigeria is 923,770 sq.km, with the land mass totaling 910,770 sq.km, and water 13,000 sq.km. About 33% of Nigerian land is arable. The climate in Nigeria varies from equatorial in the south, tropical in the center, to arid in the north. The terrain also varies from southern lowlands, with hills and plateaus prevalent in the center of the country. The southeastern part of Nigeria is mountainous, with flat land in the north.

The literacy rate of Nigeria's population of 15 years and above is 68%. The literacy rate of males is 75.7% and that of females is 60.6%, according to the 2003 estimates.

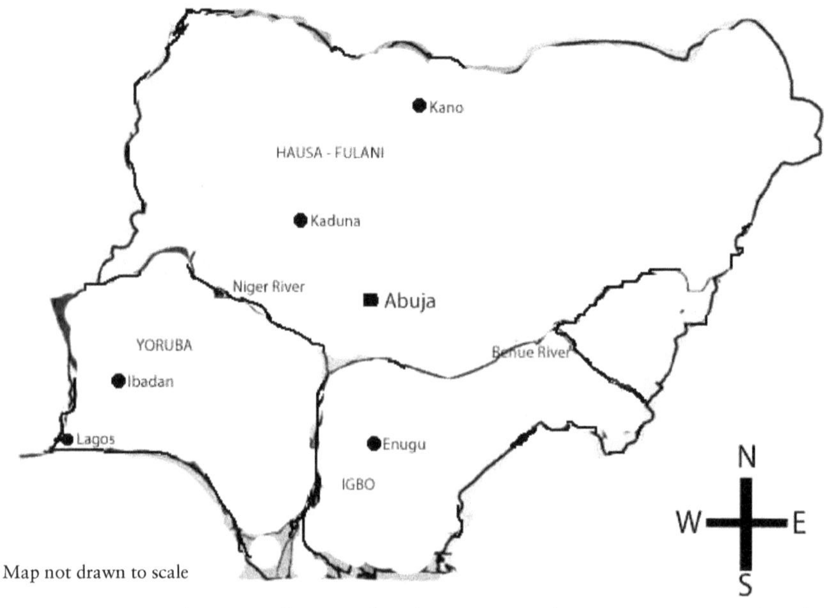

Figure 1.1. Map of Nigeria Showing the Three Major Ethnic Groups – Namely – the Hausa-Fulani, Yoruba and the Igbo.

Map not drawn to scale

Figure 2.1. Map of South East Nigeria Showing Afikpo Town – the Study Area.

OBJECTIVES OF STUDY

The thrust of the study is the examination of the Afikpo indigenous system of conflict resolution in contemporary times. The justice system derives from Afikpo peoples' culture.[4] Inquiry into some aspects of the peoples' culture was undertaken with a view to understanding the basis of the justice system. The culture of a people is central to its world outlook. The culture of a group, according to Roberts (1979: 39) "reflects the extent to which its people will identify with individualist or collectivist values. There is a link between the dominant social values in a society and the likely responses to conflict. This includes the amount of quarreling that is acceptable, the way disputants approach an altercation, as well as the way that third parties are expected to intervene." Included in the inquiry was a critical evaluation and assessment of the traditional political institutions and social organizations that function as channels for peace-making and social controls. The study emphasized the process and principles of conflict resolution.

One major objective of the study comes from my experience growing up in Nigeria where a vast majority of the people find the type of justice offered by the state courts inappropriate for the resolution of their disputes.

There was always an acrimonious relationship between my community and agents of the criminal justice system. For example, it is an offense against the community to report a crime or take a conflict to the state courts or police, until the community had mediated on the matter. A goal of my research has been to address the question: Why have the African indigenous institutions of social control remained relevant in the affairs of the people despite the dominant position of African states in social control? Specifically, my research goal was to discover why the Afikpo system enjoys such wide approval and seeming legitimacy among the Afikpo people. The system's popularity seems to cut across economic and social class boundaries, even among non-indigenous people living in Afikpo. Again, many questions help to understand the continued existence and popularity of the Afikpo indigenous system of conflict resolution. What is the system's concept of justice? Is the system free of the charges of "nothing works," "disguised coercion," and "net widening" associated with other alternative systems of conflict resolution? Why is the government-sponsored alternative conflict resolution unpopular?

Another major objective of the study is to examine major Afikpo traditional institutions, both as agents of social control and resocialization from a restorative, transformative and communitarian justice perspective. Further, inquiries are made into how the community resolution system responds to certain norm violations and conflict in the community. Again, the position and roles of victims and offenders in the system are examined.

It is hoped that findings from this research will inform future Nigerian criminal justice policies. Further, it is difficult not to assume an advocacy role and use one's writings to counter Western views of African justice system as repressive and simplistic, and that African indigenous justice systems are not capable of respecting the rights of women, suspects and other litigants. Furthermore, with the current worldwide interest in restorative justice, it is important to trace restorative justice to its roots in indigenous traditions in Africa, Asia and Native American cultures.

WHAT IS RESTORATIVE JUSTICE?

There is no agreement on what constitutes restorative justice principles and practices. Some refer to restorative justice programs as transformative justice, peacemaking criminology, relational justice, or community justice. The different names reflect the varied visions of their proponents. Marshall (1996) believes we are involved in a restorative justice process when "victims, offenders and other stakeholders meet face-to-face to resolve their conflicts" (Bazemore and Walgrave 1999: 47). Marshall views restorative justice as a diversion, hence only certain cases are suitable for the process. Serious violent cases are not suitable for restorative justice processes. Other restorative justice advocates view the system as involving "a variety of processes or procedures, including those that occur within the formal justice system, aimed at reaching an outcome focused on repair" (Bazemore and Walgrave 1999:47). Others argue that restorative justice must take place in an informal setting and participation must be voluntary. Restorative justice is a negotiative process, where the victim, the offender and the community are primary stake-holders. Adherents of this perspective observe it is possible to transform the state courts to operate in restorative fashion. Participation does not have to be voluntary for participants may be coerced into involvement in the restorative process. Coercion may be applied to achieve reparation to victims or for offenders to do community service. However, "what makes these obligations and processes 'restorative,' rather than retributive or rehabilitative, is the *intent* with which they are imposed and also the *outcome* sought by decision-makers" (Packer 1968 as cited in Bazemore and Walgrave 1999:47). (Italics in original).

The diverse outlooks notwithstanding, what is commonplace is a disenchantment with the current state-administered retributive justice system and the need for alternative ways of responding to conflict, crime and victimization. The criminal justice system is seen as authoritarian, and alienates victims, offenders and the community who are primary stake-holders in the conflict (Christie 1977). Retributive justice systems are considered rigid and obsessed with punishment. Restorative justice system advocates support increased victim and community involvement in sentencing processes and general response to crime. As Marshall (1996:37) points out, restorative justice is defined as a "process whereby the parties with a stake in a particular offense come together to resolve collectively how to deal with the aftermath of the offense and its implications for the future" (cited in Bazemore and Walgrave 1999:47).

As an emerging paradigm, restorative justice views and responds to wrong-doing differently from retributive justice systems. Rather than view crime as an act against the state, a violation of law, an abstract concept, for which the offender is accountable to the state, it views crime as a violation against an individual or group of individuals, and interpersonal relationships. The primary victims are those directly affected by the offense, and the secondary victims are the family members of victims, offenders, witnesses and members of the affected community. As such, accountability is primarily to the victims, and secondarily to the state. Restorative justice represents a paradigmatic shift, which Pranis, et al (2003:10) state are:

1. from coercion to healing;
2. from solely individual to individual and collective accountability;
3. from primary dependence on the state to greater self-reliance within the community; and
4. from justice as "getting even" to justice as "getting well."

Further, distinctions are made between the retributive justice and restorative justice, by focusing on their peculiar processes and objectives. Walgrave (1994), as cited in Weitekamp (1999:75), notes that a retributive justice system responds to crime "within a context of state power." Their focus is on the offense, and the state is empowered to inflict punishment and seek just dessert, while the victim is generally neglected. However, it is noted that the retributive justice system embodies sometimes certain traces of restorative justice objectives. Nevertheless, restoration of the victim or the community is not part of the major goals of retributive justice. Rehabilitative response as an aspect of retributive justice, contends Walgrave (1994) "takes place in the societal context of a welfare state, focuses on the offender, provides treatment to him or her, seeks conforming behavior and ignores the victim as well" (as cited in Weitekamp 1999:75). On the other hand, restorative justice empowers the community and other primary stake-holders in the conflict. Its goal includes repairing or restoring losses, the satisfaction of the parties to the conflict, with the victim seen as central to the whole justice process.

Restorative justice is incomplete, according to Bazemore and Walgrave (1999), if it does not seek to repair the harm caused by the victimization. Essentially, restorative justice must seek to restore the following according to Braithwaite and Parker (1999:106).

- Restore property loss
- Restore injury
- Restore sense of security
- Restore dignity
- Restore sense of empowerment
- Restore deliberative democracy
- Restore harmony based on feeling that justice has been done
- Restore social support."

Restorative justice has a focus on restoring victims, including the community, to the position they were before the conflict as much as possible. In this respect, Bazemore and Walgrave (1999:48) define restorative justice as "every action that is primarily oriented toward doing justice by repairing the harm that has been caused by a crime." From this perspective, crime is defined by its impact on the individual victim and the community, and the fundamental response should be to repair or compensate the victim for the harm caused. The punishment or rehabilitation of the offender should not be a top priority.

Restorative justice theorists and practitioners such as Christie, Braithwaite, and Zehr present restorative justice as a different way of thinking about crime, especially our response to crime and victimization. They recognize crime is a violation of people and relationships. They seek ways of repairing harms to victims while exploring ways to prevent future harm. Restorative justice advocates are mindful that crime creates obligations, which must be made right. Offenders are persuaded to take responsibility for their actions and for the harm they have caused. Offenders' competency is enhanced in the process. Restorative justice seeks redress for victims, and recompense by offenders. Further, efforts are made to reintegrate both the victim and the offender within the community. Restorative justice advocates seek solutions, which promote repair, reconciliation, and reassurance. It is noted that there is sometimes a need for the government to cooperate with the community to achieve these objectives.

Restorative justice, unlike retributive justice, does not view crime primarily as a violation of the state. Crime is viewed rather comprehensively. Rather than defining harm as lawbreaking, restorative justice advocates recognize that offenders harm victims, communities, and even themselves. Justice involves the victim, the offender, and the community. Criminal justice officials may participate in the process but do not dominate the proceedings. Restorative justice success is measured by how much harm that has been repaired or prevented, rather than by how much punishment that is inflicted.

A restorative justice system empowers victims in their search for closure. Victim recovery, through redress, vindication, validation, testimony and healing is emphasized. It is recognized that victim restitution, reparation, safety and fair treatment are key priorities. Restorative justice provides opportunities for the discovery of truth about what happened and the harms that resulted. The cause of the conflict is identified leading to understanding about how to forestall future victimizations. One notable lesson from the South African Truth and Reconciliation Commission following the demise of the Apartheid system and the atrocities committed during that reign of terror, is that the open and honest airing of conflict can lead to understanding, healing and even reconciliation. If the post Apartheid government has insisted on punishing the perpetrators of the Apartheid atrocities, this would have alienated the white minorities and created further antagonism thereby undermining the peace and reconciliation objective necessary for the social, economic and political development of the country.

Restorative justice empowers communities through partnerships in action. Cooperation, inclusive and integrative arrangements strengthen communities' bonds necessary for the control of crime and victimization. Community mediation meetings provide opportunities for the review of community norms and standards. Attending to the needs of victims can prevent deterioration of conflict in the community. It is realized that a victim whose needs are not addressed is a potential offender. Further, efforts are made to reconcile offenders with their victims and the community. Community members develop a renewed appreciation for the contribution of every member of the community. Every member of the community counts, and positive contributions by community members are valued.

BRIEF HISTORY OF RESTORATIVE JUSTICE SYSTEM

The term restorative justice is fairly new, but the concept is as old as humankind. The current interest in restorative justice could be said to have been initiated when "probation officer Mark Yantzi and co-worker Dave Worth first pushed two shaking offenders toward their victims' homes in Elmira, Ontario, in 1974" (Zher 1997:68). This seemingly simple approach had profound effect on the way society thinks and responds to crime and justice. Attention now shifts to the victim, and the victim's needs for compensation, restitution, validation, security, social support and empowerment addressed. Secondly, the offender is persuaded to demonstrate accountability and responsibility to the victim. An aspect of this was offenders' being made to understand the consequences of their actions on the victim. The restorative process encourages offenders to appreciate that their actions harm people and communities, thereby increasing their empathy for victims. As Zehr (1997:68) points out, "as our foreparents knew well, wrong creates obligations; taking responsibility for those obligations is the beginning of genuine accountability." The process of justice-making must include the primary stake-holders, namely, victims, offenders and members of the community.

It is noted that penal law and the retributive/rehabilitative response to crime and victimization is attributable to the advent of feudalism and state systems. There is no record of crime demanding prosecution and formal punishment for its own sake before the twelfth century. As Cayley (1998:124) observes " . . . there were no public prosecutions and no special criminal trials; punishment was the exception and compensation was the rule." This supports the thinking that our willingness to inflict pain varies with our social distance from those who are made to suffer. Prior to that, acephalous societies employed restorative principles in its justice system (Michalowski 1985, as cited in Weitekamp 1999: 75). Broadly speaking, there were two main kinds of human societies—societies without state systems (acephalous), and societies with state systems. Negotiation and restitution to the victim was central to the justice processes of acephalous societies. Families of both the victim and the offender met to resolve their conflict through negotiation, and eventually compensation to the victim. This approach was viewed as more beneficial to the victim and the entire community since it resulted in the quick restoration of peace and order to the community. Punishment was sometimes applied, but that was only as a last result. Otherwise conflicts were generally resolved without a formal legal system, or the state or supra-familial authority.

A major determining factor of the restorative justice system in acephalous societies, according to Michalowski (1985), was that the social organization of the society was diffuse and kin-based. Individuals were strongly bound to the group due to the belief of the community in collective responsibility. The egalitarian and cooperative nature of the societies mitigated against egoistic pursuits of the individual. Order is maintained in acephalous societies though equality and respect. As Manitonquat (Elder of the Assonet Band of the Wampanoag Nation) rightly observes, "it is clear that the way to heal society of its violence . . . and lack of love is to replace the pyramid of domination with the circle of equality and respect" (as cited in Pranis, et al (2003:10). Christie (2004) further describes this type of justice system as *horizontal justice*. The concept of relevance in horizontal justice is broad—without implying lack of standards. It is the interests of the participants and the community that is imperative. The past and future relationships of the participants are factored into the consideration in conflict resolution. The concept of relevance is a matter of value observes Christie. The employment of violence and punishment is counterproductive in an egalitarian society where the relationship of community members are valued and respected. And equality according Christie does not mean everybody in the community having equal status and prestige, but that the realization of the importance and contribution of community members to the well-being and survival of the community is an important factor in conflict resolution. According to Christie (2004:75–76),

> questions of relevance are handled in a radically different way from what happens in the legal system. Relevance is seen as a central concern, but in situations with horizontal justice as one without pre-defined

solutions. Relevance is established through the process itself. Relevance is what the participants find relevant.

To promote conformity and restrain potential deviance, the needs of the victim was addressed, with the offender persuaded to account for his or her conduct. The satisfaction of the parties to the conflict was imperative to preserve the social and economic ties between the victim and offender's group, as was usually the case. A major justification for restorative and restitutive forms of justice was to forestall family feuds that can undermine community peace and harmony. Arguably, other societies also practiced restitutive and restorative justice. A notable example was the early Hebrews that applied restorative and restitutive principles in responding to personal crimes (Gillin 1935:198 as cited in Weitekamp 1999:84). Monetary compensation was also acknowledged as adequate atonement even for homicide in the Western world. Diamond (1935) as cited in Weitekamp (1999:84) states:

> Of fifty to one hundred scattered tribal communities as to which the information available is of undoubted reliability 73 percent called for a pecuniary sanction versus 14 percent [that] called for a certain number of persons to be handed over to the family of the victim as a sanction. This too is actually a fine, though not a monetary one. One hundred percent of the Early and Early Middle Codes, beginning with the Salic code (around 500–600 AD) and lasting through the Anglo-Saxon laws (900–1100 AD), called for pecuniary sanctions for homicide. It was not until the Late Middle and Late Codes that death was established as the exclusive sanction for intentional homicide.

The restitutive and restorative justice practices of early and acephalous societies gave way to retributive justice and the notion that the state or society is the victim of crime much later. As Weitekamp (1999) notes, the crown's usurpation of the justice process was at the end of the 12th century in Europe. This was after King Henry 1 of England (1116–132) ascended the throne. According to Peoples (2000: 5), King Henry 1 upon rising to the throne,

> . . . announced that from now on the King's Peace shall be maintained throughout the kingdom, and anyone who disturbs that peace by committing a crime is committing a crime against the king. The king (state) became the victim of all crimes, and from that point until only recently, the real victim[5] has been forgotten. The real victim suffered

> the loss from a crime, but the king reaped the rewards that came from a conviction (emphasis in original).

However, the civil society did not relinquish their power to resolve their conflicts to the crown without a struggle. The victim and his or her kinship thus lost their rights for compensation by the offender. Geis (1977) aptly describes this time when "Kings established their power and took the conflict-solving process away from the parties involved by creating a firm, state-controlled, criminal justice system" (as cited in Weitekamp 1999:89). The state's initial interest in the conflict between citizens was not to seek resolution, or eradicate crime and victimization, but to use their intervention in the conflict between its citizens as a money making venture and to preserve state hegemony. The state apparently had a different agenda from that of the civil society. Oppenheimer (1913:162) claims that the state charged "a commission for [its] trouble in bringing about a reconciliation between the parties . . ." (as cited in Weitekamp 1999:87). This practice was started by the feudal lords and religious authorities who confiscated the property of the offender without giving anything to the victim. Sometimes the feudal and religious authorities of medieval Europe punished the offender through imprisonment or corporal punishment, with the victim mostly neglected. Conflict resolution became, a money making venture for the political authorities during this period. A good example of this was, provided by Jeffrey (1957:657) who states that:

> Early Germanic justice was based on a folkpeace, a peace of the community. This gave way to the mund. A mund was the right of the King or Lord had to protect a person or area. At first the mund was restricted to special persons and areas; gradually it was extended to include the King's court, army, servants, hundredcourt, and finally the four main highways in England. It was not referred to as the King's peace. The King's Lords, and Bishops now receive the compensation rather than the Kingship group. They had a mund, which had to be protected.

The monopolization of conflict resolution in society by the state was not limited to mediaeval Europe. Michalowski (1985) describes the case of the Zulu nation in Southern Africa. The Zulu were one of the few societies with a hierarchical and centralized authority in Africa. In the Zulu kingdom, the people were viewed as the property of the King. Therefore, the murderer of one of the King's subjects paid compensation to the King, as against the victim's family or clan as was the case in acepahlous societies. This seemed to be the case in most societies when communitarian societies were displaced by hierarchical feudal systems (as cited in Weitekamp 1999:86).

Peoples' disillusionment with the state operated retributive justice system started long ago. Beccaria (1994) characterized the European justice system as corrupt, arbitrary, and serving more the interests of the judges than that of the society. He therefore argued for a more humane, just, democratic and practical justice system. He was strongly opposed to the torture and capital punishment of the ancient regime. Bentham, another contemporary of Beccaria was also opposed to the justice system of their time. He was in particular against the expanded role of the state. Bentham recognized the need for parties to the conflict to be satisfied with the process. He also argued for the loss or injury of the victim to be restored. According to him, "satisfaction is necessary in order to cause the evil . . . to cease, and reestablish everything in the condition it was before the offense; to replace the individual who has suffered in the lawful condition in which he would have been if the law had not been violated" (as cited in Weitekamp 1999:90). Beccaria and Bentham who were considered great reformers of the legal system were also pioneer advocates of restorative justice.

Other nineteenth century advocates of restorative justice included Bonneville de Marsangy, Ferri and Garofalo. Marsangy argued for the offender to compensate the victim for the losses the victim suffered. The state and society should be responsible for the loss of the victim where the offender is unable to compensate the victim for his or her losses in the spirit of the social contract. Marssangy in 1847 argued as follows:

> Now if it is true that there is no real social security without reparation, the conclusion is that this reparation must take place, cost what it will, and as one of the sine qua non conditions of the social contract; and that, in consequence, society must rigorously impose it on the culprit, at the same time and under the same justification that it imposes punishment on him; however, by the same token, we must conclude that [if] there is no known culprit, society itself must assume the responsibility for reparation. . . . It would be easy to show, with arguments of an irresistible logic, that, when the authors of a crime are known or when the condemned persons are insolvent, the State should repair the harm done to the victim (as cited in Weitekamp 1999: 91).

Weitekamp (1999) discusses several conferences organized to press Nation States to reform the Criminal Justice System in line with restorative justice principles. These conferences were held under the auspices of the International Prison Congress which took place in Stockholm 1878; Rome

1885; Petersburg, Russia 1890; and Christiania, Norway 1891. Participants in the conferences identified that the state retributive justice system neglected the victims of crime. The justice system should persuade offenders to compensate the victims of crime. Part of the rights of victims of crime within the social contract should include their protection from harm. As such, the state must take responsibility for the individual's victimization. Garofalo (1914), a major advocate of restorative justice argued that "if offenders were persuaded that . . . they could in no wise evade the obligation to repair the damage [of] which they have been the cause, the ensuing discouragement to the criminal world . . . would be far greater than that produced by temporary curtailment of their liberty" (as cited in Weitekamp 1999:91).

Chapter Two
Restorative Justice: Theoretical Perspectives

> *What has been accomplished? This: we have kept a vision alive; we have held to a great ideal, we have established a continuity, and some day when unity and cooperation come, the importance of all these early steps will be recognized*
>
> —*W. E. B. DuBois*

Tony Marshall, notes restorative justice "is a process whereby all the parties with a stake in a particular offense come together to resolve collectively how to deal with the aftermath of the offense and its implications for the future" (cited in Braithwaite (1998: 3). In a brief to the United Nations, the Friends World Committee for Consultation notes that

> Restorative Justice respects the basic human needs of the victim, the offender and the community. The administration of justice, according to the restorative model, includes the active participation of people directly involved and affected by the criminal activity. Settlements provide redress to the victim and make it possible for the offender to fulfill agreed obligations (cited in Fattah 1998:109).

Bazemore and Umbreit (1997) recognize that restorative justice includes victims, offenders, and the community. There is an acknowledgment that the victims of crime, their families, and the community are harmed and need healing. Moreover, offenders, witnesses, their families and their communities may also suffer consequences of crime. Nils Christie (1976, 1977), a pioneer researcher and advocate of restorative justice, identified victims, offenders, their families and the affected communities as the principal stakeholders in the conflict. From his perspective, that conflict is a *neighborhood property*, and not a private property or the sole preserve of criminal justice professionals.

Ancient ideas inform restorative justice. Restorative justice philosophies have guided the traditional justice systems of New Zealand's Maori (Pratt 1996); North American Indians and aboriginal peoples (Krawll 1994); and the Japanese/Confucian/Buddhist (Haley 1996). Restorative justice principles, according to Van Ness (1986: 64–68), guided the "traditions of justice from the ancient Arab, Greek and Roman civilizations that accepted a restorative approach even to homicide" (cited in Braithwaite 1998: 1). Braithwaite further notes that in ancient [Indian] Hindu societies, based on the principles of restoration, "he who atones is forgiven" (ibid). African indigenous justice structures and operations also incorporate restorative principles. Uchendu (1965), Gluckman (1955), and Nsereko (1992) see African customary justice systems as process-oriented rather than rule-based. They observe that social solidarity is a primary feature of the African judicial system. The community's interests are paramount hence resolution of conflict through consensus is essential to the system. These systems de-emphasize individual rights and employ strenuous efforts to resolve a conflict which the people believe are just and fair.

Amongst the Igbo people of Nigeria, a fair and just judgment must take into account a wider range of facts and interests, without necessarily compromising the facts of the matter in dispute notes Uchendu (1965). Nsereko (1992) observes that African customary legal processes generally focus on the victim. The offender's punishment is secondary to the vindication of the victim and the protection of the victim's rights. Since the system is victim-centered, the process provides opportunities for the victim to express his/her fury, hurt and a sense of loss. The victim gets to understand and appreciate the circumstances surrounding his/her victimization, and may even be able to forgive the offender. Further, the participatory processes of African customary judicial system create opportunities for the primary "conflict property owners," namely the victim, the offender, their families and the community to be involved in defining harm and potential repair and resolution of the conflict. It is believed that when parties to a conflict freely participate in finding solutions to their conflict, the likelihood they will abide by their decisions is higher.

In holding the offender accountable, the offender's healing is facilitated to ensure that offensive behavior is not repeated. Strenuous efforts are made to preserve connections between the offender and community members. When punishments are meted out, they are directed at re-establishing equilibrium and harmony in the community. However, the offender must first acknowledge the wrongs, then shows remorse and shame. An offender is most likely to feel shame when he or she is connected with other stakeholders in the community, and values their love, respect and relationship. Offender's reparation to the victim is part of the expiation process.

One important aspect of restorative justice worth emphasizing is that it is not always the case that the victim has to be compensated in tangible forms. Restitution and atonement for wrongs can be just symbolic. Michalowski (1985) described this process as "ritual satisfaction." This entails some symbolic demonstration of the offender's guilt through public ridicule. Some harm or other punishments can also be publicly imposed. The process is geared towards the satisfaction of all parties to a conflict essential to the restoration of peace and order in the community. This process is said to be very effective because the victim and the offender are both satisfied with the process, as both regain their honor, which was disparaged by the conflict. Reconciliation is accomplished through the process and peace and harmony return to the community. The offender is understood to have paid his or her dues to the community, and the community acknowledges by forgiving him or her. The offender survives the ordeal with the stigma arising from the offense expunged. A good illustration of this phenomenon is the justice system of the Tiwi of North Australia as provided by Hart and Pilling (1962:16):

> No Tiwi father, except in the most unusual cases, ever thought of bestowing an infant daughter upon any male below the age of twenty-five . . . This meant that a youth of twenty-five had his first wife betrothed to him at that age but had to wait another fourteen years or so before she was old enough to leave her father's household and take up residence and marriage duties with him . . . This did not necessarily lead to chastity among men under forty years old and most young wives continued to become pregnant with monotonous regularity, no matter how ancient and senile their husbands were. Since seduction constituted a serious crime the young offender and the old person faced each other in a "deadly" duel. The elder arrived with hunting spears and the younger man usually with no weapon. After a period of publicly humiliating the accused, the elder commenced to throw his spears at the offender who was expected not to retaliate. However, since he was much younger and hence almost invariably in better shape than the older man the offender could dodge the old man's spears indefinitely if he wanted to. However, rather than exacerbate the problem by publicly humiliating the older man, the young seducer having five or ten minutes demonstrated his physical ability to avoid being hit, then showed a proper moral attitude by allowing

> himself to be hit . . . A fairly deep cut on the arm or thigh that bled a lot but healed quickly was the most desirable wound to help the old man inflict, and when the blood gushed from such a wound the crowd yelled approval and the duel was over. The young man had behaved admirably, the old man vindicated his honor, the sanctity of marriage and the Tiwi institution had been upheld, and everyone went home satisfied and full of moral rectitude. Seduction did not pay (as cited in Weitekamp 1999:78).

THE STATE AND SOCIAL CONTROL

Restorative justice ceased to be the primary system of justice-making in society after the state[1] emerged as the dominant power in society. Braithwaite (1998:1) notes that "restorative justice has been the dominant model of criminal justice throughout most of human history for all the world's peoples." Van Ness (1986: 66) observes that "a decisive move away from it came with the Norman conquest of much of Europe at the end of the Dark Ages" (cited in Braithwaite 1998:1). Thereafter, the King, rather than the victim, the victim's family and the community, became the victim of crime. The shift to the community as the victim of crime as against the individual was reinforced with Divine order with the conversion to Christianity of Constantine in 312 A.D. Thereafter, Christianity was legalized within the Roman Empire with the Church and the State uniting to enforce laws. All officially classified deviants were believed to have sinned against God. Deviants were either possessed by the devil or fell from the grace of God. Violations against the individual were now against the community, which became another word for the Empire, or State. Since the State and the Church (God) were one and the same in medieval Europe, they were victims of the individual breaking a law. And the Clergy, "in claiming a special responsibility for the care of souls and a special mission to regulate and reform society, became Europe's first professional class" (Cayley 1998: 127).

Prior to state usurpation of conflict settlement in society, families of both victims and offenders often met to resolve conflicts within the community's normative framework. As Cayley (1998: 127) observes, " . . . the institution of the blood-feud existed, but its operation was limited by laws and customs intended to bring parties in conflict to a settlement." Van Ness (1997) remarks that crime was generally acknowledged as a 'breach of the common welfare,' but not in the form it is today, as a crime against the state. Rather, "crime was viewed principally as an offense against the victim and the victim's family" (p.7). Hartwell (in Templeton (ed.) 1979: 14) refers to this phenomenon as "politicization." He defines politicization "as that now pervasive tendency for making all questions political questions, all issues political issues, all values political values, and all decisions political decisions." Hartwell (1979) further observes that politicization pervades all relationships. Individuals, instead of defining their problems as private and seeking private solutions, now must seek political solutions, resulting in the empowerment of politicians and bureaucrats, at the expense of individuals and civil society. Hartwell (in Templeton (ed.) 1979:14) notes that " . . . where once the private investigation of social problems was important, public inquiry now dominates, and with public inquiry there is almost inevitably public solution (remedial legislation and the establishment of a bureaucracy of enforcement and control)." Hence, state dominance and authority in social control continues to increase. Formal political institutions of society take precedence over the individual, the family and other societal institutions. The emergence and dominance of the state in society explains why "bureaucracy replaced democracy" (ibid.). Further, Aubert (1969); Christie (1976); and Foucault (1977) claim many voices, ideas, and values are subjugated as a result of the state's dominance of social control.

Zehr (1989) notes crime is defined as a violation of the state and its laws. The focus of the retributive/disciplinary justice process is to determine blame and guilt and to decide appropriate pain and punishment to be administered. Punishment is directed towards achieving both specific and general deterrence. While "Justice is sought through a conflict between adversaries in which offender is pitted against the state; rules and intentions outweigh outcomes, and one side wins and the other loses" (p.10–11). Conflict is repositioned between the individual and the state, rather than between the individual parties. The victim of crime is ignored or marginalized, or appears as a witness for the state, while the offender's role is passive. Both the victim's voice and the offender's voices are, represented by proxy professionals.

Mainstream justice system officials are often criticized for not being victim-oriented and as unconcerned with the interests of the community. The problem many have with the state-operated, mainstream justice system is its failure to effectively reduce crime and recidivism. Fuller (1998: 54) aptly sums it up:

> by waging a war on crime, the criminal justice system labels individuals as the enemy and polarizes their behavior into that of the outlaw. That

> is, people are disconnected from the mainstream of lawful society by the criminal justice system, and obstacles are placed in their path as they try to engage in lawful employment, commerce, or social discourse.

The mainstream criminal justice system in an attempt to reform, offenders, uses prisons and psychiatric institutions. There is little dispute that prisons do not reform offenders. Incarcerated offenders are stigmatized, have high rates of recidivism and experience difficulty in re-entering society. The state retributive and rehabilitative justice-systems use coercive, rather, than persuasive approaches. Citing Andrew Karmen (1984:347) Elias (1993: 104–5) concludes that

> the growing interest in informal justice is fostered by several beliefs: that centralized governmental coercion has failed as an instrument of social change; that people must solve their own problems in decentralized, community-controlled forums; that nonstranger conflicts ought to be diverted from the formal adjudication process whenever possible; that both punishment and rehabilitation have failed to "cure" offenders; and that criminal-justice officials and agencies primarily serve the state's interests, or their own, to the detriment of both victims and offenders.

Fattah (1998) argues that government social control mechanisms are ineffective in controlling crime. He states: "historical and empirical evidence provides irrefutable proof that the system of punishment has not worked in the past, is not working at present, and will not work in the future" (1998: 99). To buttress his argument, Fattah (1998) cites the United States as having the highest incarceration rate in the world, and yet has the world's worst crime problems, an indication that punishment is ineffective. Further, Foucault (1977) doubted that punishment as a means to control crime has any utility. Citing Rusche and Kirchheimer's work on punishment, he notes:

> we must first rid ourselves of the illusion that penalty is above all a means of reducing crime . . . We must situate them in their field of operation, in which the punishment of crime is not the sole element; we must show that punitive measures are not simply 'negative' mechanisms that make it possible to repress, to prevent, to exclude, to eliminate; but that they are linked to a whole series of positive and useful effects which it is their task to support (p.25).

For Fattah (1998), punishment is not only negative and ineffective, but also costly. This cost is material, human, and social. The negative effects of punishment are not only felt by the individual offender, but also by the family of the offender who had no hand in the committal of the offense. According to Fattah, when convicted offenders are imprisoned, those who are also hurt and traumatized by punishment are the offenders' children, wives, other relatives and friends. Fattah (1998) adds that punishment, rather than the resolution of the conflict, tends to perpetuate and expand the conflict. When an offender is harshly punished for offending, it creates further animosity and antagonism between the offender and the victim and their families, further widening their differences and hostilities. Again, the punishment of offenders is often tantamount to double victimization. Offenders, he observes, are sometimes victims of our economic, social and political arrangements who are driven to criminality by our unjust economic policies. Fattah (1998), citing Barnett (1977) argues that the 'paradigm of punishment' is in a 'crisis period.' Punishment, he observes, lacks moral status and is also unproductive:

> . . . the alleged absolute justice of repaying evil with evil is in reality an empty sophism since Christian moralists have always preached that an evil is to be put right only by doing good. Barnett concludes by admitting his inability to find any theory which justifies the deliberate, forceful imposition of punishment within or without a system of criminal justice (Fattah 1998: 102).

The contrasts of retributive and restorative justice systems are similar to the differences in state-society relations. The state's approach and agenda for social control are divergent with that of society. The state uses a 'formal' coercive means to resolve conflict. This approach lacks flexibility and dynamism and does not give room for the democratic participation of the community. Acephalous societies, on the other hand, use informal means of conflict resolution. This traditional method applies persuasive and negotiative techniques in social control and conflict resolution. "These two legal systems according to Parnell are in relation to two types of inclusiveness—the former based on power, while the latter is based on principles" (cited in Elechi 1996). Morley (in Templeton (ed.) 1979:61) observes that the "state subjects people, whereas society associates them voluntarily" and that "state and society . . . are naturally and continuously in opposition." In contrast, Morley characterizes society as "more fluid, more flexible, less constitutionalised, and less resolutely disciplinary than the state, which because of its supremacy possesses a power of ostracism far exceeding that of the most exclusive social organization" (ibid.).

Fig. 2.1. The (State) Retributive Justice and Restorative Justice Models-Two Different Views according to Zehr 2002:21. (emphasis in original).

CRIMINAL JUSTICE	RESTORATIVE JUSTICE
• Crime is a violation of the law and state.	• Crime is a violation of people and relationships.
• Violations create guilt.	• Violations create obligations.
• Justice requires the state to determine (guilt) and impose pain (punishment).	• Justice involves victims, offenders, and community members in an effort to put things right.
• Central focus: offenders getting what they deserve.	• Central focus: victim needs and offender responsibility for repairing harm.

THE CASE FOR RESTORATIVE JUSTICE

Christie (1977) proposes restorative justice as a viable framework for doing justice. The restorative justice model is offered as an alternative to the retributive and rehabilitative justice system. The restorative justice system is also conceived as a worthy complement to the centralized state justice system since some serious violent crimes[2] may not be suitable for the restorative justice model. A major argument for restorative justice is the opportunity it creates for the involvement of victims and offenders, both in the definition of harm and the search for possible repair and healing.

The offender's empathy and appreciation of the harm his/her actions caused the victim is also greatly enhanced by his/her involvement in the process of restorative justice. Christie (1976) and Zehr (1997) note that restorative justice is an attempt to view crime beyond law breaking, acknowledging the injury to both the victim(s) and the community, and in certain cases, to the offenders themselves. Restorative justice defines crime by "exploring the rights of the victim, not by examining the behavior of the offender. The rights of society are satisfied, they contend, when the rights of individual victims within it are vindicated through restitution" (Van Ness 1997: 19). Braithwaite (1998), espousing a republican perspective, believes restoration for victims should mean the following: "Restore property loss; restore injury; restore sense of security; restore dignity; restore sense of empowerment; restore deliberative democracy; restore harmony based on a feeling that justice has been done; and restore social support" (1998: 4).

VICTIMS UNDER RESTORATIVE JUSTICE

Christie (1981) believes that when victims participate in the justice process they are afforded the opportunity to express their feelings and also to ask direct questions to the offender as to what motivated the offender's actions. According to Zehr and Umbreit (1982: 66), "Negotiations and confrontation between victim and offender offer real possibilities for meeting victim needs, facilitating restitution, encouraging offender accountability, and easing workloads for probation departments and courts" (cited in Fattah 1998: 108).

Prior to the dominance of the state in social control, the victim, offender, their families, and the community used to resolve conflicts locally. Schafer (1968), as cited in Van Ness (1997:19), refers to this period in Europe as the "golden age of the victim because it was a time in which the victim's interests and freedom of action were given great deference." Christie (1976) further observes that the modern court system of conflict resolution, with lawyers, judges and other professionals playing a greater role tends to alienate the owners of the conflict, namely the victim, the offender, their families and the community from playing any meaningful role in defining harm and potential repair and resolution.

To restore the "glory" of the victim, advocates of victims' rights propose "increasing services to victims in the aftermath of the crime; increasing the likelihood of financial reimbursement for the harm done; and expanding victims' opportunities to intervene during the course of the criminal justice process" (Van Ness 1997: 19–20). Restorative justice systems conceive of crime as a conflict (Christie 1976) that should be restored to their rightful owners, namely, the victim, offender, and the community who should be involved both in defining harm done and repair of the damage. When primary stake-holders in a conflict participate in fashioning out a resolution, chances that they will abide by their decisions is greatly enhanced.

Fattah (1997) acknowledges that the "victim/offender roles are not necessarily antagonistic but are frequently complementary and interchangeable" (Fattah 1997: 151; 1994). The victim and the offender frequently come from the same ethnic and socio-economic background. Who is legally defined as the victim or offender in the interaction is sometimes purely accidental and does not derive from a deliberate plan or intent. The victim's position, therefore, is compromised when criminal law processes are dichotomized such that behaviors are crimes or non-crimes and the participants are either victims or offenders. Situational factors, it must be noted, are very important variables in the etiology of crime. In this regard, Fattah notes that the

> study of victims, their characteristics, their relationship to, and interactions with, the victimizer, their role and their contribution to the genesis of the crime, offers great compromise for transforming etiological criminology from the static, one-sided study of the qualities and attributes of the offender into a dynamic, situational approach that views criminal behavior not as a unilateral action but as the outcome of dynamic processes of interaction (Fattah 1997: 145).

OFFENDERS UNDER RESTORATIVE JUSTICE

Restorative justice creates opportunities for the offender to be involved in the definition of harm and in the repair and resolution of the conflict (Zehr and Mika 1997, Van Ness 1997). Restorative justice processes are geared towards encouraging the offender to acknowledge the wrongness of his/her behavior. According to Zehr and Mika (1997), the offender must be persuaded to appreciate that violations create obligations and liabilities. Offenders' primary obligation is to victims, and the offender and the victim are involved in the definition of harm and repair. Holding the offender accountable is not tantamount to punishing the offender in the restorative justice process. As such, while the persuasion of the offender to make things right may result in some discomfort and inconvenience to the offender, the intention is not to inflict pain, or seek vengeance or revenge. In this respect, restitution to victims has priority over other sanctions and obligations to the state in the form of fines and other retributions. Offenders also attract community support, encouragement and understanding and are treated with due respect in the restorative justice process. Offenders' healing and integration into the community are emphasized. The restorative justice process provides opportunities for the resocialization of offenders to enhance their competence to function effectively in the community. Efforts are made by the community to increase the offender's connection with community members. Again, conscious efforts are made by the community to show disapproval of the conduct of the offender, without disapproving of or banishing the offender. Restorative justice processes are flexible and are tailored towards a particular offender's needs and competencies. Negative punishments such as incapacitation are applied, only as a last resort.

Braithwaite (1991), in *Crime, Shame and Reintegration*, argues for a justice system that supports and treats offenders respectfully and also maintains the offender's connection to the community. To increase the offender's awareness of injury to both the victim and the community, and also enhance the offender's competency to function effectively in the community, a conscious effort must be made not to break the offender's connection with the conventional community members. Braithwaite (1989) calls this process a "ceremony of reintegration." This approach, according to him, differs from the centralized government criminal justice system that tends to castigate and symbolically degrade and stigmatize an offender as part of the processes of punishment for an offense. The reintegrative shaming approach distinguishes between the offender and the offense, thereby disapproving of the act without casting out the offender. In this respect, if the offender expresses remorse and accepts responsibility for his/her actions, the offender may be forgiven and accepted back into the community. He states:

> reintegrative shaming is disapproval extended while a relationship of respect is sustained with the offender. Stigmatization is disrespectful, humiliating shaming where degradation ceremonies are never terminated by gestures of reacceptance of the offender. The offender is branded an evil person and cast out in a permanent, open-ended way. Reintegrative shaming, in contrast, might shame an evil deed, but the offender is cast as a respected person rather than an evil one. Even the shaming of the deed is finite in duration, terminated by ceremonies of forgiveness-apology-repentance (Braithwaite 1991: 4–5).

Underlying the reintegrative shaming concept, according to Moore and McDonald (1995), is the belief that it is not the fear of punishment that forces people to conform to rules. Rather, conformity is dictated by the individual's own conscience, and secondly by the individual's fear of disgrace in the eyes of their significant others. Shame, is the phenomenon that underlies private conscience and public disgrace. Schneider (1977) as cited by Moore and McDonald (1995: 157–158) notes that

> when a feeling of shame is evoked by public exposure of inappropriate behavior, this feeling might be called 'disgrace shame.' When the threat of potential shame warns people not to complete an action that they might have been contemplating, then shame has encouraged discretion. Conscience might, therefore, be called 'discretion shame.'

Exposure to discretion shame, following this argument, does not always bring about unpleasant feelings. It is our internal mechanism of anticipating behaviors that are publicly appropriate based on our bonds with others. The restraints we feel as individuals against behaviors that would be disapproved by significant others they argue, results from discretion shame.

Chamlin and Cochran (1997), using Braithwaite's (1991) notion of 'reintegrative shaming,' argue that communitarian societies are more likely to engage in reintegrative shaming, and experience relatively low rates of crime victimization. Braithwaite (1991:5) describes "reintegrative shaming, as a communicative, dialogic form of shaming that seeks to persuade offenders to disapprove of their own criminal conduct is not equivalent to ridiculing wrongdoers as persons by putting them in the stocks." In this respect, Chamlin and Cochran (1997: 205) state:

> specifically, social systems that foster values that teach their members that they have social and moral obligations to others above and beyond those produced by self-motivated relationships of social exchange (communitarian societies), are most likely to exercise reintegrative shaming.

THE COMMUNITY UNDER RESTORATIVE JUSTICE

Victims and the community are central to the restorative justice process, unlike a retributive justice system that gives key roles only to criminal justice officials and the offender. When there is a conflict, the community is actively involved in the definition of harm and the search for solution. The community thereby takes initiatives in the building of strategies to prevent crime. Hence, the community's competence in conflict resolution and connectedness is enhanced. In furtherance of the restorative justice processes of conflict resolution, Elias (1993: 88), citing Richard Korn, observes:

> [And] this is what works, and what has always worked, among people who care for each other . . . The offense is viewed as a joint responsibility . . . as a symptom that something is drastically wrong—and that something decisive is needed to correct it. . . . [T]he change called for is the transformation of a criminal justice system based on retaliation and disablement to a system based on reconciliation through mutual restitution.

Restorative justice is participatory justice-making. Restorative justice is not a novel initiative it, rather mirrors ancient ways of settling disputes. It creates opportunities for the victim, the offender, their families, and the community, to be involved in defining harm and potential repair. These are the legitimate owners of the conflict and have more at stake in the outcome of the conflict than the state and other criminal justice system professionals. With the community members actively involved in justice making, the well-being and cohesiveness of the community is strengthened and enhanced. The community is able to learn from the conflict and bring into place changes to prevent similar conflicts in future.

Restorative justice as a philosophical framework requires a change of the ways we think and approach crime and criminality. Restorative justice recognizes that some crimes stem from social problems, hence it is relentless in employing dialogue that facilitates the healing of the offender to ensure that the unacceptable behavior is not repeated. Griffiths (1996: 206), speaking of the Canadian Aboriginal traditional justice system, notes:

> community-based, restorative justice initiatives provide non-adversarial forums for responding to criminal behavior, increase community participation in and control over the response to crime, and provide a holistic context within which the causes as well as the consequences of criminal behavior for victims, offenders, and the community can be addressed.

Restorative justice, for Zehr (1997), goes beyond reforming the current system of doing justice. He conceives the restorative justice initiative as a "revolution" and a "reorientation" towards how we think about crime and justice. The search for "new ways" of doing justice results from the failure of the mainstream justice system to effectively reduce crime and recidivism. According to Christie (1976), reforms of the modern criminal justice system will transfer 'conflict to its real owners.' Cohen (1985) believes that the new arrangements will repossess power away from the state to the people (victims, disputants, conflict owners, the local community), doing justice 'outside the law' or 'without the law.' Fattah asserts that the desired system which emphasizes restorative justice is "a viable alternative that is superior in every respect to vengeful, retributive punishments" (Fattah 1994: 65–66). Fattah also argues that restorative justice "respects the basic human needs of the victim, the offender and the community" (ibid.).

Griffiths supports the incorporation of the customary legal system into the State Criminal Justice system. A customary legal system operates on the principle of the "least amount of interference with the rights of the individual and which have, as a primary objective, not a determination of guilt and the imposition of punishment, but the restoration of peace and harmony within the group" (Griffiths 1994: 5). In the same vein, Carter makes a case for an adjudication process "that is more receptive to a wider range of facts than is presently the case" (Carter 1994: 1). Restorative justice systems accomplish this through the relaxation of rules of evidence and other legal procedures. Furthermore, the focus and emphasis of the retributive justice system differs from that of restorative justice system. The three questions below underlie the focus and emphasis of retributive and restorative justice systems according to Zehr (2002:21)

Criminal Justice	Restorative Justice
1. What laws have been broken?	1. Who has been hurt?
2. Who did it?	2. What are their needs?
3. What do they deserve?	3. Whose obligations are these?

African indigenous justice systems apply restorative justice principles in the settlement of disputes. To appreciate the principles and processes of African indigenous judicial system, some understandings of the philosophical underpinnings of African concepts of justice will be appropriate.

African Philosophy of Justice

A brief review of the philosophical underpinnings of African principles of justice is pertinent. The philosophical issues discussed in this section are highly selective and pertain mostly to the issues relevant to the theme of this study. The philosophical discussion is organized around three concepts, namely, religion, communal values and spiritual communalism. Through oral tradition, mythologies (about the supreme being's relationship to man), proverbs and wise sayings, and arts, symbols and crafts, African scholars have delineated African philosophy and religion. Since most precolonial African States had no written text, the world-views of African people were articulated from the lived experiences and practices of African people. African culture and civilization are passed from one generation to the other through story-telling. Gyekye (1987) believes "philosophy is essentially a cultural phenomenon; it is part of the cultural experience and tradition of a people" (as cited in Serequeberhan 1994: 6).

Religion is very central to the life of African people. Every act, thought of the African, expresses religious meanings. There is no one religion to which every African adheres. Every African community or society has its own religious system. However, we can speak of African religions because of the great similarities in the African peoples' religious beliefs, rituals and practices. No individual is credited with founding or reforming any of the African religions. There are no missionaries with the responsibilities to propagate or disseminate the African religions. As Mbiti (1970:1) notes, the "Africans are notoriously religious, and each people has its own religious system with a set of beliefs and practices. Religion permeates into all the departments of life so fully that it is not easy or possible always to isolate it."

Mbiti (1970) and Gyekye (1996) observe that religion manifests in every activity of the African. Religion is not distinguished from the non-religious in the life and thoughts of the African. The line between the sacred and the secular, the spiritual and the material in African society is very thin. There is a religious component in every human activity—be it economic, social and political. Culture is synonymous with religion in Africa. The African is born into the African culture and religion. Religion is therefore a communal, rather than an individual affair. As such, to be a part of the African culture, is to be part of the religion, hence Gyekye (1996: 4) declared that " . . . in the traditional African society there are no atheists or agnostics."

The African religion has no established creeds or systematic principles which everybody must follow. The individual's religious understanding is expressed through his/her behaviors and attitudes, and it is often a function of how they understood or learned it from their forebears. Religion in traditional Africa is a corporate affair and there is no unanimity in its beliefs, ideas and practices. African religion is constantly modifying in tune with economic, social and political exigencies. As Mbiti (1970:4) submits, "religion in African societies is written not on paper but in people's hearts, minds, oral history, rituals and religious personages like the priests, rain-makers, officiating elders and even kings. Everybody is a religious carrier."

The African religion is a practical one concerned with life here on earth. An important aspect of the religious beliefs of the African does not include the longing for paradise in the life hereafter, nor the fear of hell. In African religion, there is no conception of an end to the world or of time. The universe has a beginning, but has no termination. As Mbiti (1970:5) describes:

> [African] traditional religions and philosophy are concerned with man in past and present time. There is no messianic hope or apocalyptic vision with God stepping in at some future moment to bring about a radical reversal of man's normal life. God is not pictured in an ethical/spiritual relationship with man. Man's acts of worship and turning to God are pragmatic and utilitarian rather than spiritual or mystical.

The African religion is human-centered. The human-centredness of African religion is an indication that the human-being is paramount in value and is an end in itself. Morally speaking, the human-being is the foundation of all values. That human-beings are at the center of the universe, does not suggest that other animals, plants and all of nature are expendable. As Kamalu (1990: 14) points out, "human-beings are very much part of the animal kingdom and of nature. It is recognized that human survival depends on the maintenance of an equilibrium or harmony in human-beings' relationship with other life-forms."

In indigenous African religion, God is recognized as the Supreme Being that created heaven and earth. God's media of communication with human-beings are through other natural objects, such as "trees, rocks, rivers, and mountains, and rivers" (Gyekye 1996:6). This does not presuppose nature worship since the belief is that the objects are inhabited by spiritual beings who are intermediaries between God and humans. The belief in mystical power is a major aspect of the African religion. This mystical power is expressed through magic, which could be utilized by people with such endowment for good or evil.

Amongst the Igbo, it is strongly believed that the universe comprises of three elements, namely, the sky, the earth and the world. As Ogbaa (1999: 127) points out, the "pre-Christian traditional religion that the Igbo still practice is organized around four theological concepts, namely, Chukwu, non-human spirits (deities or oracles), ancestors, and chi. Chukwu, the supreme's domain, is the sky. Chukwu created human-beings and the universe, but was far removed from the universe soon after creation. It is believed by the Igbo that "Chukwu is omnipotent and omniscient; yet he is not considered omnipresent" (Ogbaa 1999: 128). Other lesser gods and goddesses are depicted by statues and icons, because they are closer, but Chukwu is not because he is so far away. Apart from being so far away, Chukwu is beyond full human understanding.

Other important elements in Igbo religion include deities and oracles. These are man-made gods and goddesses and are inhabited by non-human spirits. These objects are not worshipped directly. They are sacred because they are the habitation of the spirits, the intermediary between human-beings and Chukwu (Sky God). Other gods and goddesses worshipped in Igbo land include Ala (Ali), Ahiajoku, and Anyanwu. Ala, the earth goddess is considered next in importance to Chukwu (the supreme). Ala is probably more relevant to the life of the Igbo than any other god. Ala is responsible for fertility in humans, animals, the soil and plants. Ala, the spirit of fertility is prayed to for an increase in the fertility of the land and of humans, essential for the survival of the group. It is due to the great reverence the Igbos hold of Ala that lands are not saleable commodities in Igbo land. Should lands be sold at all, certain sacrifices must be made to pacify the earth-goddess before the land sale can be concluded. Ala is also the abode of the living dead (ancestors). The ancestors are not worshipped but occupy a special place in the Igbo religious practice. Ala is the custodian of Igbo laws and customs, and the goddess of group morality.

Offenses such as adultery, murder, incest, and theft, are crimes against the earth-goddess and humankind. These are capital offenses. It is to be emphasized though, that however serious an offense can be in Igbo land, it can be atoned for with a commensurate sacrifice. Should the culprit fail to perform the expiation rites, the earth-goddess must avenge the wrongs against her. As Uchendu (1965: 96) observes, "Death is not considered enough punishment for an Igbo who has offended against Ala. He is denied ground burial, the worst social humiliation for any Igbo." People who die from crimes against the Ala goddess, are not given proper burial, and cannot be ancestors. They cannot reincarnate as human-beings, and if they do, they will come back as trees or animals. Their souls would wonder forever without settling.

The centrality of religion in African peoples' cultural, ethical, moral, and social beliefs is reflected in the works of African scholars. African scholars articulating African philosophy acknowledge the centrality of religion in African socio-economic and political affairs. Nkrumah's work on *Consciencism* argues that matter is the source of all knowledge. It is the modified perspective of African materialism. He acknowledges the interrelationship between matter and mind, but insisting that matter is primary, hence theories and philosophies derive from concrete practical situations. Nkrumah's position contrasts with Western worldviews that postulate matter as being inert or dead. Matter, according to Nkrumah has life, and the spirit is an aspect of matter. It is the spirit that gives matter its energy. His acknowledgment of the role of spirit suggests that his philosophy has religious basis. In this respect, the human being is similar to the universe in that human-being has both spiritual and physical properties, posits Mbiti (1977). In conclusion, Nkrumah (1964:84) states that:

> . . . the primary reality of matter must either deny other categories of being, or else claim that they are one and all reducible . . . to matter. . . . In a materialist philosophy admitting the primary reality of matter, if spirit is accepted as a category of being, non-residual reduction to matter must be claimed.

Africans, according to Gyekye (1996:35), place "great emphasis on communal values." The interest and well-being of the community transcends that of the individual. This does not imply that the interests, rights and well-being of the individual are subjugated. It means the individual actor must always take into consideration the consequences of his or her action on other members of the community. This paradox is eloquently captured by Achebe (2000:14), thus:

> In the worldview of the Igbo the individual is unique; the town is unique. How do they bring the competing claims of these two into some kind of resolution? Their answer is a popular assembly that is small enough for everybody who wishes to be present to do so and to "speak his own mouth," as they like to phrase it.

Cherished communal values in Africa are "sharing, mutual aid, caring for others, interdependence, solidarity, reciprocal obligation, and social harmony," observes Gyekye (1996:35). Gyekye defines community as

> a group of persons linked by interpersonal bonds—which are not necessarily biological—who share common values, interests, and goals. What distinguishes a community from a mere association of individual persons is the sharing of an overall way of life. In the social context of the community, each member acknowledges the existence of common values, obligations, and understandings and feels a loyalty and commitment to the community that is expressed through the desire and willingness to advance its interests (ibid.).

The concept of community is not limited only to the living. An African community includes those that are dead (the ancestors), and those yet to be born. African communal ethics also include other animals, plants and all ecological life and its equilibrium with humankind. Efforts must be made therefore to preserve the environment for the benefit of those living and those yet unborn. As Mbiti (1977:50) notes:

> Although God is the Creator of the universe and man is at the center of that universe, there are other beings with intelligence, besides man. These include divinities, spirits, and the living dead. . . . In one way or another, they are all related to the world of nature: according to some African mythology, some divinities assisted God in the course of ordering the created world; others serve God by taking charge of departments of nature.

Spiritual communalism is another aspect of the concept of community in African philosophy. Onwuachi (1977: 16) argues that African spiritual communalism does not convey the same meanings as Socialism or Welfarism. According to him, African spiritual communalism is an idea that derives from the indigenous African principles of "*live and let live; collective sharing; common concern for one another; sense of belonging together; social justice; economic progress and viability for all;* and *the*

African indigenous political process of participatory democracy" (emphasis in the original). Further, in line with the African spiritual communalism, it is one's age, responsibility and service to the community that are valued. The economic principle and process recognize sharing according to the needs and responsibility of the individual. Whatever economic benefits that accrue to the individual must be shared with the individual's family and community. He states

> Socially, in African spiritual communalism, there is a collectively acknowledged hierarchical order based on *age, responsibility*, and *service* to the people. It is *not class consciousness hierarchy* but rather *service for the people consciousness*. Hence age, wisdom, accomplishment, and responsibility are very important variables (Onwuachi 1977:17). (emphasis in original).

Nyerere (1968), following the African communalism ethics, rejects atheism and a materialistic view of African societies. He insists that African societies are communitarian by 'nature' and are characterized by a profound sense of collective identity eschewing any traits of individualism. A man's livelihood has a meaning only within the context of his family, kinsmen and tribe. His advocation for a socialist Africa derives from these principles, with "UJAMA"—familyhood as its underlying philosophy. He states:

> For when a society is so organized that it cares about its individuals, then, provided he is willing to work, no individual within that society should worry about what will happen to him tomorrow if he does not hoard wealth today. Society should look after him, or his widow, or his orphans. This is exactly what traditional African society succeeded in doing. Both the 'rich' and the 'poor' individual were completely secure in African society. [. . .] That was socialism. That is socialism. (Nyerere 1968 as cited in Hedlund and Lundahl 1989: 21).

African morality has a social and humanistic basis, rather than a religious basis (Gyekye 1996). African moral values derive largely from the people's experience living in the community. It is informed by the people's understanding of what is appropriate in inter-personal relationships. African moral values are not revealed to them by the Supreme-being. Any behavior that is not geared towards the well-being of the individual and the community is considered morally wrong according to African values. Gyekye (1996:57) insists that the basis of African moral values, are social and humanistic, not religious or individualistic. He states:

Such a basis of moral values enjoins a moral system that pursues human well-being. Thus, in African morality, there is an unrelenting preoccupation with human welfare. What is morally good is that which brings about—or is supposed, expected, or known to bring about—human well-being. This means, in a society that appreciates and thrives on harmonious social relationships, that what is morally good is what promotes social welfare, solidarity, and harmony in human relationships.

For a behavior to meet the standard moral values of the African people, it must include the following: "kindness, compassion, generosity, hospitality, faithfulness, truthfulness, concern for others, and the action that brings peace, justice, dignity, respect, and happiness." (Gyekye (1996:58). In moral terms, the individual is conceived of as inherently neither good nor bad. However, the individual is capable of acting in ways that are either good or bad. The individual is rewarded or punished for his or her deeds accordingly in this life, and not in the hereafter, according to Mbiti (1970). Some African societies however, believe one can also be punished for his or her misdeeds in the life hereafter, in line with their belief in reincarnation. According to Mbiti (1970), morality is a corporate affair in African societies. It is recognized that the individual's wrong doing does not only victimize the direct victim and his or her family, but also undermines the community's well-being. The community must also partake in the responsibility for the wrong-doing of its member. The justice principles expounded here will be better appreciated in the next section where African systems of justice are examined.

SYSTEMS OF CONFLICT RESOLUTION IN AFRICA

Both restorative and state based retributive justice systems are in operation in English-speaking Africa, the latter a consequence of colonialism. The restorative justice system is based on African customary law, while the retributive justice system, operated by the state is based on English common law. The state laws remain dominant. African state laws, like their western prototype, are based on adversarial and retributive principles. Rapoport (1975) doubts justice is possible through the adversarial legal system. In his view, the practitioners of the system, with some exceptions, conceive of the system "as a zero-sum game, where any gain by one side is balanced by a corresponding loss on the other" (p.28). He argues that the system is erroneously premised on the same principles as 'free enterprise' that conceive of social justice as based on the "primacy of competition as a guarantee of a priori social equality" (p.29). In a similar study in Cairo, Egypt, Griffiths et al (1989: 41) concluded that the formal justice institutions were ineffective in "addressing the problems of youth in conflict, not only because of a paucity of financial and programmatic resources, but also to the general irrelevance of such structures to Egyptians residing in urban areas." Citing (Koch 1983: 21), this phenomenon they attribute primarily to the impact of urbanization and industrialization, which together create "a pervasive and necessarily harmful alienation of a large segment of the population from a Country's system of justice administration" (ibid.). A similar experience characterizes most post-colonial states in Africa.

NIGERIAN CRIMINAL JUSTICE SYSTEM

Findings from this research indicate that many Nigerians perceive the Nigerian criminal justice system as an instrument of oppression by the government and the elite. Other available records show that the system is authoritarian, corrupt and lack the infrastructure necessary to be effective and efficient. Many find the system to be unnecessarily bureaucratic, and too complex for Nigeria's level of economic and technological development. As an alien system, many question its relevance in the Nigerian context as its principles and practices do not reflect Nigeria's cultures, customs and religions, and also Africa's concept of justice. Stevens (2000:6) has also identified the following as factors limiting African peoples' access to their state justice systems:

- "—most proceedings are subject to considerable delays at all stages, mainly as a result of the sheer number of cases being processed through a limited number of courts.
- For most of the population living in rural areas the distance to the nearest court may be immense.
- The justice administered by the state seldom involves restorative or compensatory awards or sentences. In this it is often out of step with the expectations of the people whose view of justice is based on traditional models.
- The law and procedure practiced in formal courts are both unfamiliar and complicated from the perspective of most citizens."

The Nigerian government has also acknowledged the problems Nigerians have encountered over the years with access to justice. According to a publication of the Federal Republic of Nigeria, the goals of the government reforms intended to enhance access to justice include:

- "to reduce the cost of litigation and broaden access to justice
- To reduce delays so that cases can be decided speedily
- To ensure that litigants have an equal opportunity regardless of their resources, to assert or defend their legal rights
- To make the legal system understandable to those who use it" (Olujimi 2004:6)

The Nigerian legal system is modeled after English Common law like all other Common Wealth Countries. English jurisprudence is based on Judeo-Christian belief system, with God and the Ten Commandments as the sources of law. In the same manner, some Nigerians are opposed to Sharia law, which they argue springs from Islam and Judaism. While the English Common Law has over time become more secular, and consequently drawn a line between morality and law, the Sharia law is yet to differentiate between morals and the law, the state and religious institutions even in contemporary times.

A major difference between customary law and received law in Africa is that the former is "process-oriented," while the latter is "rule-based." According to Armstrong et al (1993: 14), "African systems of justice focus more on the processes of achieving peaceful resolutions of disputes rather than on adherence to rules as the basis of determining disputes." Armstrong and his colleagues contend that the processes of conflict resolution in Africa "de-emphasized rights" but employed strenuous efforts to resolve a conflict which they believed just and fair. In other words, the victim, offender, their families and friends, and the entire community must consider the processes of conflict resolution procedurally fair, and they must be satisfied with the outcome. They observe it is misleading and inappropriate to insist on rights and rules with regards to African conflict resolution systems as it applies in the Western judicial systems. This is understandable considering the kind of cases that come before the customary courts, which in most cases are between blood relations, hence the need for acceptable and lasting reconciliation.

Amongst the Igbo, a fair and just judgment must take into account a wider range of facts and interests, including that of the community, without necessarily compromising the facts of the matter in dispute.

> Igbo legal procedures aim essentially at readjusting social relations. Social justice is more important than the letter of the law . . . The resolution of a case does not have to include a definitive victory for one of the parties involved. Judgment among the Igbo ideally involves a compromise and consensus. They insist that a good judgment 'cuts into the flesh as well as the bone' of the matter under dispute. This implies a

> 'hostile' compromise in which there is neither victor nor vanquished; a reconciliation to the benefit of—or a loss to both parties (Uchendu 1965: 14).

Nsereko (1992: 22) notes that African customary legal processes "focused mainly on the victim rather than on the offender." The goal of justice was to vindicate the victim and protect his/her rights. The imposition of punishment on the offender, was designed to bring about the healing of the victim rather than to punish the offender. In any conflict, rather than punish the offender for punishment sake, the offender was made to pay compensation to the victim. This practice, according to Nsereko (1992), was "intended to restore the victim to the position he was in prior to the commitment of the offense. This was, of course, limited to the extent to which money or property could solve the problem" (p.22). Nsereko (1992) observes compensation goes beyond restitution. It also represents a form of apology and atonement by the offender to the victim. This ritual (some religious practices often accompany many African traditional processes) helps to dissipate the animosity that victimization may engender between both the victim and the offender and their families. The African indigenous judicial process also "facilitated speedy and inexpensive justice to the victim" (Nsereko 1992: 25).

African indigenous judicial processes rarely distinguish between civil and criminal affairs. According to Nsereko (1992: 25), African indigenous judicial processes combined civil and criminal actions in the same proceedings, except in very serious crimes. Otherwise, it was the victim of a crime who undertook the prosecution. Nsereko (1992) observes that indigenous African jurisprudence distinguished between offenses against the community at large that calls for "collective or community reaction and torts or delicts (wrongs against individuals calling only for an individual or personal response)" (p.26). However, it is important to bear in mind that where wrongs against individuals or groups are concerned, African indigenous judicial processes rarely distinguished between civil and criminal cases. Jomo Kenyatta (1938: 226) noted:

> In the Gikuyu society all criminal cases are treated in the same way as civil cases. The chief aim in proceeding was to get compensation for the individual or group against whom the crime was committed. Since there was no imprisonment, the offenders were punished by being made to pay heavy fines to the kiama and compensation to right the wrong done" (cited in Nsereko 1992: 25).

Nsereko (1992) observes that under African customary justice system, victims were cared for by, the community. Victim care is a priority because of strong social solidarity and a prevailing spirit of good neighborliness in the society. It is a serious offense in Afikpo for an adult male not to respond to the distress calls of a kinsman. For a society where very few insure their lives and property, it is community members that come to the rescue of other community members who lose their property through theft and other misfortunes. When a family breadwinner dies or is incapacitated in any way, it is relatives and community members that see it as their obligation to provide for the widow and orphans. African communities grieve with their own who are victims of crime or other misfortunes.

In sum, restorative justice seeks to restore justice-making to its real owners—the victim, the offender, their families and the community. Compassion is bestowed first to the victim and his/her families. The restorative justice process recognizes that compassion is a central element in the healing process. In focusing on the victim, the restorative justice process is first concerned about the harms of wrongdoing, and secondly about the rules that have been broken. Emphasis is placed on restoring the injury, property, the sense of security and dignity of the victim, and the restoration of peace and harmony in the community.

Restorative justice also supports offenders by encouraging offenders to understand and accept responsibility for their actions. Accountability may result in some discomfort to the offender, but not so harsh as to degenerate into further antagonism and animosity. Obligations must also be achievable hence restorative justice processes recognize and respond to community bases of crime. Above all, efforts are made by the community to disapprove of wrongdoing, rather than the wrongdoer. As such, collaboration and reintegration as a process of justice-making is encouraged, rather than coercion and isolation. Underlying this approach is a belief that all human beings are important and are not expendable. Above all, that human-beings are capable of change. Healing must go deep to the center of the problem, to the soul of the person.

Restorative justice is negotiative and democratic; hence it empowers the community to mediate in conflicts. Ideally, restorative justice provides opportunities for dialogue amongst the victim, the offender, their families and friends, and the community. Conflict provides opportunities for stakeholders to examine and bring about changes to the society's social, institutional and economic structure.

OTHER BENEFITS OF RESTORATIVE JUSTICE

Victims are arguably the major beneficiaries of restorative justice systems. Victims have been elevated from their former roles either as "witnesses" or "complainants" to that of clients of the criminal justice system. Victims are active participants in the system. Their rights to information, contribution and involvement in the processes are assured. Restorative justice systems accord respect, security and restitution to victims. Offenders also benefit from restorative justice approaches through their involvement in the process. Offenders found meeting and talking with victims satisfying. Offenders get to learn new values and improve their cognitive skills. Communities also benefit from restorative justice processes. Communities' skill and ability in conflict resolution are enhanced. Community bonds are strengthened through community organizing and learning of new values leading to healthy human relationships.

Other beneficiaries of restorative justice systems are criminal justice system and practitioners. As Solomon, Jr. (1983: 66) points out: "The costs of handling minor crimes in court fall into three categories: expense to the public purse; burdens for the accused, witnesses, and victims; and the consequences of heavy case loads." With restorative justice, public prosecutors can have a reduced caseload. This is because minor cases will be diverted to community dispute resolution with subsequent court time no longer necessary. With victims, offenders and the community involved in the process, recidivism will be reduced, as offenders perceive restorative justice processes as fairer than state retributive criminal justice systems. What is more, offenders get to have a better understanding of the impact of their actions on victims and the community. As such the prosecution, defense, the judiciary and the law enforcement agents experience a significant reduction in their caseloads.

ARGUMENTS AGAINST RESTORATIVE JUSTICE

There are a number of structural problems that impede the realization of restorative justice goals. Harris (1989), for example, observes that restorative justice processes are directed more at individual-level responses, rather than at the socio-economic structure of society. Emphasis is placed on offenders making things right, and their obligations are first to the victim and then to the community, rather than on socio-economic reforms that account for most conflicts. Harris notes:

> . . . getting the offender to repair the damage caused by his or her offense makes it appear as if crime is solely or primarily an individual problem attributable to the weakness, sinfulness, or other deficiencies of individual lawbreakers. It does not address the role of society, of structural and institutional forces that promote crime and conflict (1989: 32).

Harris (1989) adds that the undue focus on individual offender may only make matters worse, and unlikely to resolve long standing 'social divisions and inequities.' According to her, recognizing that the state, the family and the community should accept responsibility for some criminality, is not to dispute the notions of free will and individual responsibility. Informing this view is the realization that those in conflict with the law are disproportionately males, minorities and the poor. Commitment should first be made towards locating the factors that contribute to crime, inequity, injustice and conflict, for its resolution will open the way for true justice-making. Harris (1989:32) states:

> I find it alarming to discuss how what is being proposed takes into account past and ongoing injustices and contributes toward their redress and elimination. Thus the model is an unsatisfactory one for me in that it is not clearly rooted in a commitment to more fundamental social change.

Empowering victims and the community in justice making, according to Harris (1989), will be more detrimental to the offender than obtains in the traditional criminal justice system, unless there is a curtailment in the power and involvement of the state in the restorative justice processes. She notes that " . . . if balance is of concern and if victims are to be granted a more significant role in deciding how best to respond to crime, their greater power should be gained through at least a corresponding reduction in the power and involvement of the state." Harris (1989) further argues that the restorative justice process of making offenders realize that their actions hurt real people and families rather than the system, sounds somewhat paternalistic and disrespectful to offenders.

Other arguments against restorative justice as articulated by Braithwaite (1998: 3) are as follows. Since restorative justice only deals with minor crimes, the majority of crime victims will not benefit from this approach. Since the implementation of restorative justice approaches, there has not been any appreciable reduction in the crime rate. Further arguments against restorative justice processes are that there are real risks of victims being re-victimized by restorative justice practices. The system's practices might also be detrimental to offenders, since it can constitute a "shaming machine" that can further worsen the stigmatization of offenders. The community is central to the application of restorative justice, and there is a real fear that the heterogeneous nature of urban communities may not be culturally appropriate for the restorative justice system. As such, offenders may be further oppressed through the tyranny of the majority, whose power will be difficult to restrain.

There is a fear that restorative justice practices may unduly widen the nets of social control. And the practice can lead to further disadvantages of women, children and racial minorities. Again, in the restorative justice processes, police power may be extended without corresponding accountability. Further, the separation of powers amongst the legislature, the executive and the judicial organs of government may be compromised in the restorative justice process. As well, offenders, and even victims' rights may be violated due to a failure to properly articulate and follow procedural safeguards.

Morris (1999) takes a critical look at the whole idea of restorative justice. She wonders how restorative justice can restore the (social) justice that is non-existent in our society as constituted. According to her, "you **can't restore a community to wholeness that never was whole"** (p.8) (emphasis in original). She argues instead for a "transformative justice." Transformative justice is similar to restorative justice in that it views crime as a violation of people and relationships. It differs from restorative justice in that it focuses on the causes of crime and treats crime as an opportunity to seek healing for the victim and the offender. She states that "transformative justice is a better approach for all parties involved in the triangle of crime: victims, offenders and community. It prioritizes responding to the challenge of crime creatively in a way that transforms the problem of crime into an opportunity" (Morris 1995:70).

In sum, restorative justice approaches hold great promise. Many obstacles however, remain that need to be addressed. To further illuminate the relevant issues in the retributive/restorative justice dichotomy, a review of the law versus custom debate is undertaken in the next section.

Chapter Three

The Custom/Law Debate in the African Context

A review of the custom versus law debate is relevant to the understanding of restorative justice principles. In many respects, the debate further highlights the points of divergence between restorative and retributive justice systems. Maine (1969) and Diamond (1973), pioneer researchers of the living habits and social customs of pre-colonial peoples in Asia and Africa, argue that the customary practices of Asians and Africans are erroneously described as indigenous laws. Supporters of this viewpoint insist that there is a distinction between laws properly so called, capable of creating enforceable rights and duties, and rules and social customs erroneously referred to as laws, which do not necessarily create enforceable rights and duties but may demand moral obedience.

Rather, African customary practices should be classified as 'primeval substitutes for law' (cited in Lloyd 1964:226). The evidence often presented in support of this argument is that African societies lacked centralized governments essential to the formulation and enforcement of laws. William Seagle (1946), a major proponent of this school of thought, notes:

> The dispute whether primitive societies have law or custom, is not merely a dispute over words. Only confusion can result from treating them as interchangeable phenomena. If custom is spontaneous and automatic, law is the product of organized force. Reciprocity is in force in civilized communities, too, but at least nobody confuses social with formal legal relationships (cited in Diamond 1973: 321).

Challenging this perspective are Malinowski (1961) and Elias (1962) who claim that Maine (1907) and Diamond (1973), among other proponents of the former viewpoint, lack sufficient knowledge of the nature of the societies they purport to study, and so were incapable of distinguishing between what were regarded as laws by the societies and customs. This confusion, they observe, arises primarily because the laws they purported to study were, and still are, largely unwritten. Lloyd (1964: 227), in support of this position notes: "the sociological jurists have taught us to see that even in developed communities law exists on more than one level and that to penetrate its mechanisms it is not sufficient to confine our attention exclusively to the sophisticated documentation of legal rules."

A broader view of the definition of law, according to Lloyd (1964), must take into consideration the notion of 'living law' (living law is explained later in this section) as conceived by Ehrlich. In the United States for example, changes in laws have often come through the decisions of the U.S. Supreme Court. Changes in customary laws have sometimes too, come through the settlement of cases in Customary Courts. Interestingly, international law that lacks centralized governments that legislate and enforce international laws is not classified as customary or diplomatic conventions rather than laws. Lloyd (1964:238) notes:

> [Primitive] customs can thus be shown to possess many of the distinctive attributes of law while lacking, for the most part, the vital centralized organs of law and government: namely, a legislator, to create new law by regular process; a court, with compulsory jurisdiction to decide disputes; and an executive organ to ensure compliance with the laws. It therefore becomes apparent why modern writers, such as Kelsen, have argued that *international law* is closely analogous to primitive law as it constitutes a binding normative system relying for enforcement on self-help remedies, but lacks the centralized organs which are the features of developed law (emphasis added).

Diamond (1973; 1978) distinguishes 'the rule of law from the authority of custom.' Diamond disagrees with Paul Bohannan's (1968) characterization of law as 'double institutionalization.' Bohannan's conclusion is based in the understanding that laws developed from custom. Bohannan does not dispute the claim that laws assume a different character and dynamic after developing out of custom. Furthermore, laws lose certain aspects of their customary potency after this development. Bohannan's analysis, Diamond (1978) argues, presupposes "no primacy of the legal order." Diamond again challenges Bohannan's claim that laws develop along with society. For Diamond, the only correct definition of custom is that credited to Paul Radin (1953):

> A custom is, in no sense, a part of our properly functioning culture. It belongs definitely to the past. At best, it is moribund. But customs are an integral part of the life of primitive peoples. There is no compulsive submission to them. They are not followed because the weight of tradition overwhelms a man . . . a custom is obeyed there because it is intimately intertwined with a vast living network of interrelations, arranged in a meticulous and ordered manner" (cited in Diamond 1978: 240).

Diamond (1978) alleges that Bohannan and those who share his perspectives on law and custom tend to confuse morality with legality. Diamond disagrees with Bohannan's portrayal of legal behavior as mirroring moral behavior. Diamond further states that because Bohannan's understanding is based on wrong premises, acts that lack legal sanctions are sometimes interpreted to be socially or morally acceptable. For Diamond, law and custom are easily distinguishable. Customary rules, due to prevailing convention, may be socially sanctionable but do not equate to law that is sanctioned by an organized political force. Diamond (1978: 241), citing Seagle (1946), insists that "law is not definite and certain while custom is vague and uncertain." Diamond, elaborating on this position, states:

> Efforts to legislate conscience by an external political power are the antithesis of custom: customary behavior comprises precisely those aspects of social behavior which are traditional, moral, and religious, which are, in short, conventional and non-legal. Put another way, custom is social morality. The relation between morality and law is, basically, one of contradiction not continuity (1978: 241).

Diamond (1978) contends that the relationship between law and custom must be a historical one, certainly, not a legal one. For him, there tends to be a general agreement amongst most anthropologists that primitive societies are governed by the customary order, while civilized societies are administered by 'legal or technical' order.

Diamond (1978) cites Plato as having made important contributions to the debate on the dichotomy between law and custom. Plato in 'the Republic' observes that the notions of law and custom are in relation to the different forms of social control existing in specific societies in their different stages of development. Further, laws reflect and result from social changes and development. Diamond reinforces his argument with Marxian cultural theories. Marx, according to Diamond, observes that societies governed by customary practices precede societies governed by the legal order. Interestingly, Marx predicts that societies will revert to the customary order in the future when societies cease to have laws as we know them. Laws, according to Marx, will become redundant, and customary order will prevail when societies attain the higher level of evolutionary order. In the customary regime, the laws' functional role become obsolete since laws' 'repressive, punitive and profiteering' functions will not be compatible with the new order. And with the equitable reordering of institutions, all economic and political conflict will be resolved. Marxists define law as mechanisms for social control by the state, often in the interests of the bourgeoisie.

Sir Henry Maine's (1970) contribution to the law and custom debate is instructive. Maine's thesis is influenced by Darwin's theory of evolution. Maine argues that societies' legal systems go through stages. In pre-modern societies, the legal emphasis is on the individual's right and duties, and this is very much determined by the individual's status. Status is based on family relations. The second and final stage of this legal development is the "contract." At this stage, the contract is "personal bargains resulting from individual will" (Trevino 1996: 21).

In ancient Rome, the focus of Maine's study, society was said to be comprised of "aggregation of families." as opposed to modern societies where the society is a "collection of individuals." The line of authority was from the father to the oldest male. The father's power (authority) was said to be absolute. The family was said to be the original stock which develops to become the tribe. The tribe eventually developed into the state. Roman law, in line with this development, changed its focus from the family to the individual. Accounting for the change in focus of the Roman law was the expansion of the sphere of the civil law. The state thereby assumed monopoly of the civil law jurisdiction, which hitherto was under the control of the family. With the family losing control of matters that used to be within its exclusive domain, its authority declined greatly. This phenomenon freed the individual from the stranglehold of the family. Maine (1970: 163–165) summed up the situation:

> The word status may be usefully employed to construct a formula expressing the law of the progress thus indicated . . . All the forms of status taken notice of in the law of persons were derived from . . . the powers and privileges anciently residing in the family. If then we employ status . . . to signify these personal conditions . . . we may say that the movement of the progressive societies has hitherto been a movement from *Status to Contract* [emphasis in original].

Accordingly, Diamond (1978) and Maine (1889; 1897) concede that law and custom perform the same functions, that of regulating social behavior, but that law and custom differ in their characteristics. Maine states: "custom [is] spontaneous, traditional, personal, commonly known, corporate relatively unchanging—is the modality of primitive society; law is the instrument of civilization, of political society sanctioned by organized force, presumably above society at large, and buttressing a new set of social interests" (as cited in Diamond 1978: 243).

Maine insists law "is symptomatic of the emergence of the state" (ibid.). Common features of the civil power are the bureaucracy and sovereign, and dominant class. They appropriate the surplus goods and labor for the benefit of those not directly engaged in production. The state also usurps the power and authority traditionally exercised by the families, clans and villages. Again, like Jeremy Bentham, Maine argues that "property and law are born together and die together" (ibid.). The emergence of the state also marks the "passage from status to contract, from kinship to the territorial principle, from extended familial controls to public law, etc." (ibid.). Other significant aspects of the emergence of the state, is the codification of customs and the reinforcement of the punitive function of custom. Maine therefore concludes that "the customs of the sovereign were laws, the ceremonies of the kin groups were customs" [and] . . ."that what the sovereign permits, he commands" (Maine 1970: 249).

Challenging the views espoused by Maine and others that African customary laws do not meet legal criteria, Elias (1962) posits that African customary laws have the same quality as Western legal systems. He argues that those who think otherwise based their understanding on erroneous premises. According to him, the basis of this information was from the following four primary sources:

THE MISSIONARIES AND ADMINISTRATIVE OFFICERS

Christian Missionaries were one of the earliest European groups to come to Africa. Their conceptualization of Africa is important because of their impact on academic discourse. Elias (1962) notes that missionaries, like Maine, believe law, morality and religion all developed from a single source, the Judeo Christian religious ethical beliefs. In line with their belief systems, African culture does not discriminate between customs and rituals and other pagan practices. Christianity and Western Civilization was one and the same thing. To illustrate this point, Elias writes of a former Kenyan District Officer, Sir T. Morison, who once wrote: "I soon found myself struggling with graver questions of policy, the questions which go down to the root of tropical administration. Should we override native customs, some of which are in conflict with our Western standard of ethics?" (Elias 1962:

26). Elias notes that Morison had little difficulties resolving this dilemma. He believed that it was his duty to replace the pagan customs of Africa with higher law. Elias observes that some Missionaries actually believed the "manners and customs of the English middle class were part of the Sermon on the Mount" (ibid.).

Elias (1962) observes that the Administrative Officers' perception of African customary law was similar to that of the Missionaries. The Administrative Officers were representatives of the colonial authorities in Africa, as such, it was their responsibility to apply the colonial laws. In applying the colonial laws, they were expected to pay heed to the prevailing African customary rules. Their study of African culture was to be informed by anthropological theories. Elias notes that the Administrative Officers were generally skeptical of anthropological and sociological theories. They gave more weight to their field experience, which was based primarily on testimonies or interviews of African traditional chiefs or opinion leaders. The weakness of this approach, according to Elias, is that "the ignorant African is shy of giving his real reasons to the supercilious white man; he may be laughed at, he will not be believed; this is the sort of subject the white man does not understand, so he may as well give an explanation that he can take in" (Elias 1962: 26).

This point requires further elaboration because the notion of customary law is a colonial construction dating back to the nineteenth century. The notion of laws as a matter of formal Bills and Acts of Parliament or Decrees and Edicts is also new to African societies. As such, it is imperative to address the issue from its origin. The notion of customary law came with colonialism. When Africa was integrated into the world capitalist economy through colonialism, the effect on African social and economic system was enormous. Customary law developed through the "interaction between the colonial administration and the various African political and social systems" notes Rwezaura (1992: 3) as cited in Armstrong, et al (1993: 13). Rwezaura further points out that the development and transformation of customary law during the colonial period occurred through a process in which

> . . . custom and tradition became a means by which the local rulers and family heads bargained with the colonial state for retaining a part of their political power in their communities while individuals especially women and young people appealed to the colonial state to lighten some of their burdens, under tradition through the deployment of liberal values such as natural justice and equity (ibid.).

The Administrative Officers based their knowledge of customary laws on the evidence proved in the native courts. In the native courts, elders, warrant chiefs and other court officials were often asked to give evidence in matters concerning African customs. These individuals who came to the native courts to give evidence were often considered experts on African customs. From proceedings or situations such as these, colonial officials, missionaries and European anthropologists drew up their lists of African customary rules. There are arguments that customary laws emanating from such sources are bound to be influenced by either the individuals giving the evidence or by those who wrote, based on their observance of customary practices. An example of this was, given by Rwezaura (1992: 5):

> what the elders and other witnesses gave as evidence of customary law was [a] distorted and rigid version of customary law designed to express their idea of what the law should be and not what it really was . . . their versions were greatly influenced by the elders' anger and frustration at the loss of political power and challenges they were facing at the time from women and young men (cited in Armstrong, et al (1993: 14).

Furthermore, the recorders of the court proceedings, who were often Europeans, tended to classify the court processes in the terminology with which they were familiar. Processing customary laws in colonial courts was an aversion of a sort. Customary law is process-oriented, while colonial legal systems were based on rules. African legal systems' emphasis is on the process of bringing about peaceful resolutions to a conflict rather than on using rules as the basis for resolving the conflict. As Armstrong et al (1993: 14) note:

> Customary dispute resolution processes de-emphasized rights and sought to achieve solutions to social disputes which were considered just and fair. Thus in relation to customary law it was misleading and inappropriate to talk of rights and rules. However the preoccupation of Western courts with ascertaining rules of substantive customary law where, in fact, none existed resulted in the construction of rules which were often neither customary nor equitable.

Precedence is an integral part of colonial court systems; as such, previous decisions of the courts influenced subsequent cases. Armstrong et al (1993) observe that precedent cases were uncritically cited as evidence of the applicable custom in subsequent cases. It happened that such versions of customary law were accorded authoritative status and applied even to different ethnic groups who had different customary practices.

Other sources of customary laws were from decrees by state bodies such as chiefs and native authorities. Colonial authorities, note Armstrong et al, governed the African peoples through decrees. Decrees were also used to regulate and systematize the diverse sources and content of living (law)[1] custom. The initiative was often from the colonial authorities through their agencies for indirect rule, such as the chiefs and other traditional leaders. The customary laws arising from this were made to serve the interests of the colonial authorities, even if they were, formulated by the traditional rulers.

Armstrong et al (1993) observe that the practice during the colonial period was to separate the systems through the choice of law rules and the jurisdiction of courts. There is more interaction between customary law and received and/or general law in politically independent states. The Constitution of most neo-colonial African states is to provide for courts applying customary laws. The customary courts must, however, apply laws that "are not repugnant to natural justice, equity and or good conscience." However, the nature of the justice, equity or good conscience is often not defined. Armstrong et al note that "The most troubling aspect of this is the question, whose justice, sense of equity, morality or conscience are these to be tested against?" (1993: 17).

Armstrong et al identify two forms of customary laws applied by neo-colonial African states. First, the lower courts, they observe, are more responsive to changing patterns of the living customary law, and are therefore inclined to apply it. Second, the higher courts, they argue, are rather slow to change, and are likely to invoke old colonial precedents, which generally deny women rights. The preceding highlights the contemporary role of customary law in African states.

Another weakness of the Administrative Officers' approach to the understanding of African law was their overemphasis on the punishment of criminals. As representatives of the state, they were involved in the administration of the criminal justice and this may have affected their understanding of African customary law. Their perspective of African law was that it was "all criminal and that because certain criminal offenses are recognized and punished by English law in ways often different from those of African law, the two systems are necessarily poles apart in all other respects" (Elias 1962: 26).

THE ANTHROPOLOGISTS

Elias (1962) notes that, on the whole, anthropologists working in Africa seemed better informed about African indigenous judicial systems than their Lawyer, Missionary and Administrative Officer counterparts. Nonetheless, some of the anthropologists were hampered by their limited knowledge in law. They based their understanding of African customary law on what little they knew about Anglo-Saxon legal concepts. Some of these anthropologists argued that law was non existent in African societies, insisting that 'custom is king' in Africa. They argued that in Africa, rules of social conduct cannot be differentiated into law and custom and that in any case Africans themselves do not make such distinctions.

Elias (1962) observes that while he may find the views of these anthropologists problematic, such views were not as extreme and negative as some of the British lawyers who had never studied African customary laws. One such lawyer, Mr. R. T. Paget, K.C., M.P., in 1951 had this to say about African customary laws: "Thought in tribal society is governed not by logic but by fetish. To the tribe, trial by fetish is just and trial by reason is unjust . . . It is futile to seek reason in tribal justice, as it is not rational" (Elias 1962: 28).

This view was by no means unanimous. Green (1948: 78), a British anthropologist who studied the Igbo society of Nigeria, argued that the African does differentiate between law and custom. She states: "We shall see when we consider the judicial function that in this society law is distinguishable from custom in the sense that it is enforced, directly or indirectly by the community, and that this distinction is recognized by the people." Supporting this viewpoint is Sir Donald Cameron who, at some point, was the colonial Governor of Tanganyika (today's Tanzania) and Nigeria. In 1937, he argued that anthropologists who believe Africans were incapable of differentiating custom from law were missing the point and that proponents of such viewpoints were confusing ceremonial practices with other obligations that carry the force of law. He used the following example to buttress his argument. He states: "dances and drumming at a Native wedding are the invariable custom, but they are not, like the payment of a dowry, essential in Native law to the validity of the marriage" (cited in Elias 1962: 29).

THE JUDICIAL OFFICIAL

The colonial judicial officers working in Africa seemed to have a better appreciation of the African judicial system. Sir James Marshall's views on the matter are very significant. He was, at one time, Chief Justice of the Gold Coast (present day Ghana) and Nigeria. His views are based on his experience as the colonial Judicial Assessor of Native Chiefs. Writing in 1886, Marshall observed that the African peoples' administration of justice was very efficient, (Elias (1962: 35). He also argued that African customary law, from his personal experiences, clearly differentiated laws from custom. He found the African customary laws better suited to the socio-economic condition of Africa, and he felt that the continued application of this system of law would be in the best interest of the African people. He also warned against the application of English jurisprudence in Africa, insisting that it would not be feasible and had the potential of undermining the political authority of the African peoples.

The Privy Council Report of 1919 also supported the advanced status of African Customary law. The Council reported, " . . . there are indigenous peoples whose legal conceptions, though differently developed, are hardly less precise than our own. When once they have been studied and understood they are no less enforceable than rights arising under English law" (Elias 1962: 35). It was noted that there were 'tribes' in Africa whose social organizations were not so developed and, as such, their legal systems fail to meet the standard of the English judicial system. It is not everyone who shares the glowing tribute often paid to the English jurisprudence hence, it assumed the standard against which all other judicial systems must be measured. In 1951 Lord Porter in the House of Lords proceedings was reported to have stated: "The common law is a historical development rather than a logical whole, and the fact that a particular doctrine does not logically accord with another or others is no ground for its rejection" (Elias 1962: 28). Support for this viewpoint was provided by Holmes (1948):

> . . . the actual life of the law has not been logic; it has been experience. The felt necessities of the time, the prevalent moral and political theories, intuitions of public policy, avowed or unconscious, even the prejudices which judges share with their fellow-men, have had a good deal more to do than the syllogism in determining the rules by which law shall be governed (ibid.).

Malinowski (1961), Gluckman (1955), and Elias (1962) are three of the prominent critics of the view that in pre-colonial Africa, custom was law. That there is spontaneous obedience to custom; and where law exists at all, it is predominantly criminal law. As Hartland stated: [in primitive societies] "the core of legislation is a series of taboos . . . that almost all early codes consists of prohibitions" (Malinowski 1961: 56–57). He added that there is no mechanism for enforcing these rules. Malinowski associates these views mostly with the writings of Durkheim, Sir Henry Maine, Prof. Hobhouse, Dr. Lowie and Mr. Sidney Hartland. Malinowski's (1961) critique of the foregoing statements are based on his anthropological studies in Melanesia and he cites the observations of Hobhouse (1915) about pre-colonial African societies:

> such societies, of course, have their customs, which are doubtless felt as binding by their members, but if we mean by law a body of rules enforced by an authority independent of personal ties of kinship and friendship, such institution is not compatible with their social organization (Malinowski 1961:12).

Malinowski argues that Hobhouse's viewpoint, as expressed above, is in line with the Anglo-Saxon definition of law as a "body of rules enforced by an authority independent of personal ties." This definition of law he argues is narrow for it fails to incorporate other relevant elements. He argues that the definition, for instance, fails to recognize that every society has its rewards and punitive systems which is reflective of their values and prevailing socio-economic conditions.

Further, Dr. Lowie is credited with saying "that generally speaking, the unwritten laws of customary usage are obeyed far more willingly than our written codes, or rather they are obeyed spontaneously" (cited in Malinowski 1961: 13). Malinowski (1961), reacting to Lowie's statement, wonders which society would function unless its people obeyed its laws "willingly" and "spontaneously." Civilized or otherwise, he insists, the average person in any society obeys the law not only because of the fear of punishment or the threat of coercion. He argues that in every society that there are "laws, taboos and obligations" which everybody, or almost everybody, obeys without hesitation, and this he attributes to moral and sentimental reasons, but he would not characterize such respect for laws as "spontaneous." He believes that what induces people to obey laws are a complex amalgam of psychological and social factors, but such points were always overlooked by commentators such as Lowie. Why would rules be made if they would not be broken, he ponders. Why does the inquiry not focus on the intent of the rules and sanctions and the motives for its violation and respect, he asks. Malinowski believes the confusion derives from the fact that the commentators on the culture of precolonial Africa have been mostly Westerners who evaluate these systems from what is prevalent in their societies. The apparent absence in pre-colonial Africa of central authority to enforce rules, the absence of criminal codes, courts and other enforcement agencies, very much influenced the views of these commentators. He concludes, based on his study, that "the savages have a class of obligatory rules, not endowed with any mystical character, not set forth in 'the name of God,' not enforced by any supernatural sanction but provided with a purely social binding force" (ibid.).

Elias (1962) contributes to the debate by offering the following definition of law: "the law of a given society is the body of rules which are recognized as obligatory by its members" (p.55). Elias believes his definition of law is the most appropriate because his definition of law recognizes that people must defer to law according to their social imperatives. He observes that in every society there is a normative order to which the vast majority of its members adhere. Hence, he argues that the "determinant of the ethos of the community is its [society's] social imperative" (ibid.).

Elias insists his definition of law is devoid of the problems associated with John Austin's 1885[2] definition of law. Austin conceived of law solely "as the act of a sovereign or of a sovereign legislature, or as a system of categories, or even as a species of control imposed from above" (ibid.). The Austinian conception of law overlooked that there is no universal political organization or social philosophy that all societies subscribe to. Elias argues that the Austinian definition of law is intended to discriminate between "primitive" and "civilized" societies. Elias acknowledges that the level of social and political development of a given society has a bearing on the character of the law, but he objects to using such a consideration as a basis for the determination of law. Elias concludes that "if order, regularity and a sense of social obligation are essential attributes of law, in Western no less than in non-Western societies, our definition can fairly well claim to satisfy these" (ibid.). Further, the processes of determining customary rules are not very different from that of law. This position is supported by Dundas (1915), describing the traditional legal processes of the Bantu people of East Africa:

> Customary law is the experiences of generations which successively have cast this and that aside, tried many methods and found them to fail, until at last some course remained open which proved itself the most workable and acceptable, not because it met merely one requirement, but because it fitted into all other circumstances. *Therefore it is a deeply-thought-out code, and the experience and intellect of generations have worked to make it one link in a chain of usages and ideas.* For the law as approved by custom is but part of the mechanism of society (as cited in Elias 1962: 189), (emphasis in original).

Gluckman (1955) in Aubert (ed.) (1969) studied the judicial process among, the, Barotse of Northern Rhodesia (today's Zambia). The Barotse was one of the few centralized states in traditional Africa. He argued that the functions and objectives of the traditional courts are the same as in any other place, including that of the 'highly developed societies.' The central objectives of the Lozi jurisprudence, Gluckman asserts, is the "regulation of established and the creation of new relationships, the protection and maintenance of certain norms of behavior, the readjustment of disturbed social relationships, and the punishing of offenders against certain rules" (p.163). The doctrine of Lozi jurisprudence is also similar to the legal systems of other societies. Such basic legal doctrines are "right and duty and injury; the concept of the reasonable man; the distinctions between statute and custom; and between statute and equity or justice; responsibility, negligence, and guilt; ownership and trespass; etc." (ibid.).

The judges of the African traditional courts, according to Gluckman, in resolving conflicts, took into consideration the nature of the relationships out of which the disputes emanate. As such, the judges often go beyond the narrow issue of law to consider, for instance, the history of the relationships between the litigants. The courts exercise both administrative and legal functions, as such they have the power to convert a "civil suit" to a "criminal hearing" if that will serve the best interest of the generality of the public. The court's concept of relevance is rather extensive; consequently, the nature of the relationship existing between the litigants is given much weight. The courts distinguish between relationships between "blood-kin" and that between "fellow-villagers." For disputes between husband and wife, which in comparison with the latter is more ephemeral, the focus of the judges could be the "relevant facts." The range of relevance could even be reduced much further if the dispute is between strangers. This is just as well, for the African is very "litigious" and could go to court for various reasons, even when he/she is aware that the case would not be decided in his/her favor. Gluckman notes:

> the litigants in coming to court have appealed for a public hearing of their grievances, and these are examined against the norms of behavior expected of people. The judges therefore upbraid all the parties where they have departed from these norms: Judgments are sermons on filial, parental, and brotherly love (1969: 157).

Litigants are aware that the judges are capable of drawing a line between legal and moral rules. The judges are empowered to protect and enforce legal rules. They cannot enforce moral rules. However, the judges will frown at a litigant who insists on legal rights as against seeking "justice." People easily differentiate between legal and moral victories.

Moore (1978) and Pospisil's (1978) contribution to the law versus custom debate question the portrayal of law as a system that is rational, logical and consistent and derived from abstract norms and the will of the sovereign, without any internal contradictions. Moore insists laws are replete with ambiguities, inconsistencies, gaps and are ridden with internal contradictions. Laws are also open to manipulation. She argues that there are two reasons why no legal system can claim to be rational and systematic, and . . ."one is the piecemeal historical process by which legal systems are constructed. . . . The other is the not fully controllable aggregate effect of the multiplicity of reglementary sources and arenas of action" (Moore 1978: 3).

Pospisil (1978) categorizes laws into two—customary and authoritarian, and these exist in both complex and primitive societies. The differences between the two are quantitative rather than qualitative. Customary laws according to Pospisil pertain to rules which are neither written nor codified, and have been in usage since time immemorial. Members of the community have internalized commitment to the rules. People who violate customary rules have a tendency to feel guilt or shame hence he posits that "conformity to a customary law is achieved mainly through an internal psychological mechanism rather than through external pressure, punishments, or threats" (Pospisil 1978: 64). On the other hand authoritarian laws are found in hierarchical societies. The laws are impositions on the people by external power often against the will of the majority. Compliance to the laws is therefore achieved through coercion.

Hoebel (1967) insists that every society has laws regulating the people's behavior. All laws have certain essential elements in common which are, the laws proper frame of reference. All laws are geared towards the regulation of human conduct, and as such have a social basis. If any distinction is to be made, we should speak in terms of primitive law, archaic law and modern law reflecting the laws in preliterate, ancient, and modern societies respectively. Hoebel (1967) disagrees with the Austinian definition of law and posits that the law Austin defined does not obtain in any known society. He insists laws derive from people's experience rather than logic. Legal norms like any other social norms are products of experience and selection. No law exists in a vacuum. Every law is aimed at preventing or redressing a particular mischief or harm to society. Every society, primitive or civilized has their legal system, which has its peculiar jural postulates. Otis Lee's (1946) legal theory sums up the Hoebelian argument.

1. Every culture, society, and in fact every group, no matter how restricted, represents a limited selection from the total of human potentialities, individual and collective.

2. The selection tends to be made in accordance with certain dominant values (postulates) basic to the group.
3. It follows that every stable group exemplifies a more or less complete and coherent pattern, structure, or system of relationships. "The quality of a society will vary with the quality of its basic values . . . with their suitability to its needs and circumstances; and with the consistency and thoroughness with which they are worked out" (as cited in Hoebel 1967: 17).

African Customary Laws and Human Rights

African indigenous systems of conflict resolution are used to examine African perspectives on justice, human rights, and social control. As noted in the section that reviewed the debate on law and custom, the objective is not to resolve the issues raised by observers, but rather to review the key issues in the debate. It is noted that issues of custom, law, human rights status and definition remain a dynamic and continuous one. The issues that the concepts address seem universal, in the sense that some of the values which form the basis of human rights are shared by different societies, even if there are variations in conception and practice due to differences in culture and level of technological development. In this respect, many would agree with Gyekye (1996) that traditional African societies had their own conceptions of human rights. According to Gyekye, the concept of human rights in traditional African society is situated in notions of human dignity and integrity. Everyone is important and makes meaningful contributions to community well-being. The social and political institutions of traditional Africa gave a foundation for the practice and expression of human rights, and the protection of the individual's rights, such as

> the right to freedom of speech, the right to political participation, including the right to remove rulers, the right to practice one's own religion, the right to food and protection against hunger, the right to the use of lineage land and thus the right to work, the right to own private property, the right to receive a fair trial and thus to receive justice . . .

The concept of human rights, according to Freeman (1995:25), affirms two fundamental principles of Western liberalism. The first is that the human individual is the most fundamental moral unit. The second is that all human individuals are morally equal. These two principles express a commitment to egalitarian individualism.

The state as the duty-bearer, according to Freeman, is obliged to respect and protect the human rights of individuals within its polity. The state, according to the French Revolution of 1789, notes Mahmud (1993), is a political association whose objective is the 'conservation of the natural and inalienable rights of man.' Hence, human rights, according to, Cranston (1973) is regarded as a "twentieth century concept for what was referred to as natural rights or the rights of man" (cited in Motala 1989: 374). The concept of human rights addresses fundamental human needs, regardless of race, sex or culture, and as such is universal.

Lauren (1998), however, argues that concerns for human rights are as old as humanity. Philosophers have, for centuries, been concerned with the nature of humanity, interpersonal relationships, and the position of individuals as members of groups. Inquiries into the meaning of social justice, the relationship between the governors and the governed, and the roles of political authorities in the protection and promotion of individual and group rights are undertaken in this endeavor. As Lauren (1998:11) points out,

> . . . philosophical positions expressing respect for the dignity of each person, protection of individuals, ethical behavior toward others, social justice, and law or rules above arbitrary power can be found in other areas ranging from the Middle East and Africa to pre-Columbian civilizations in the Americas.

All societies have grappled with these human rights issues. In ancient China for example, the philosopher Mo Zi, who founded the Mohist school of moral philosophy, explored the responsibility of the individual to other members of his/her community. His writings emphasized self-sacrifice and duty, not only to one's family members, but to humanity as a whole. Further, Mencius, motivated by the teachings of Confucianism, explored the concept of human nature. Man, he argued, is inherently good. Man's goodness though needs nourishment for it to flourish. In this regard, he came up with the idea of the mandate of Heaven, which emphasized accountability and benevolence on the part of the leadership. Where the well-being of the people is not served by the political leadership, the dynasty's mandate was withdrawn. Rebellion by the people was a justified course of action if the governors failed to live up to the expectation of the people and failed to relinquish power. It is the concern of the individual's rights vis-à-vis the community's political leadership that led Mencius to proclaim that the "individual is of infinite value, institutions and conventions come next, and the person of the ruler is of least significance" (cited in Lauren 1998:10). Further supporting the supremacy of individual rights over that of the government, Hsun-tzu, another Chinese philosopher, stated that "In order to relieve anxiety and eradicate strife, nothing is as effective as the institution of corporate life based on a clear recognition of individual rights" (ibid.).

King Hammurabi of ancient Babylon, in acknowledgment of the individual's inherent rights, emphasized the principles of the rule of law and equality before the law in the nation's legal codes. His office not only promoted the individual's rights, but was also the chief custodian of the peoples' rights. Anyone whose rights have been violated was encouraged by King Hammurabi to seek redress from his office and the law. He admonished thus: "let the oppressed man . . . come into the presence of my statue . . to seek equal protection of the law" (cited in Lauren 1998:10). Lauren contends that in early Sanskrit writings from the Indian subcontinent, it was the government's responsibility to cater for the well-being of the citizenry. As such, "no one in his dominion should [be allowed to] suffer . . . either because of poverty or of any deliberate action on the part of others" (ibid.). This position highlights also the economic rights of the individual in society. Asoka, a third century B.C. Indian leader, decreed that all members of his community should enjoy extensive rights, including that of freedom of worship.

Guru Gobind Singh, the Sikh leader, had a broader vision of human rights. He advocated the emancipation of all oppressed people everywhere, and was strongly opposed to discrimination based on caste, enjoining his people "to recognize all the human race as one" (Lauren 1998:11). In a like manner, Sultan Farrukh Hablul Matin, inspired by the human rights visions of Cyrus the Great of the Persian Empire who lived more than two thousand years ago, wrote:

> For he, it was who, with supreme insight,
> Launched an Empire based not on physical might
> But on the vision of a family of nations
> Linked by bands of Humanity, truth, and right
> (cited in Lauren 1998:11)

Cyrus the Great's visions of "a family of nations" seemed to have anticipated an association of Nations for the protection of human rights like the United Nations.

A tenth century Islamic philosopher, Al-Farabi, according to Lauren (1998) espoused his vision of human rights in his book "*The Outlook of the People of the City of Virtue.*" He envisioned a society of morals where the individual lived in peace, harmony and love with other members of his/her community. As anticipated, ancient African societies had their own perspective of human rights. The relationship between the individual and his/

her political authority was clearly defined, and these ideas and values are found in proverbs and folk lores. The Akan tribe of Ghana, conscious of the dangers of power and inequality in society espoused equality and sensitivity to the rights of others. They warned that "One should not oppress with one's size or might" (Lauren 1998: 11). The Burundi people believed in the equality of all people, and this is expressed through their proverb that "Imana [God] creates men and draws no distinction between them" (ibid.). Human rights are inherent, and leaders, without solicitation, should grant it to all without prejudice. An ancient Djerma-Songhai maxim insists, "You should not [have to] solicit what is yours by right."

THE UNITED NATIONS AND HUMAN RIGHTS

> *Human rights were not a free gift. They were only won by long, hard struggle. This struggle, with all the efforts and sacrifices that it demanded, was inevitable: respect for individual rights, when it passes from theory to practice, entails conflict with certain interests and the abolition of certain privileges. Men and women everywhere should be familiar with the dramatic incidents—well-known and obscure—of a conquest which has been largely achieved through the heroism of the noblest of their fellows*
>
> —*UNESCO*

Human rights are both a cultural and value laden concept, which symbolizes rights, which a person is entitled to for no reason other than his or her humanity. The concept of human rights assumed international status with the emergence of the United Nations[3] Universal Declaration of Human Rights on December 10th, 1948, whose objective is to act "as a common standard of achievement for all peoples" (cited in Alderson 1984: 9). The United Nations Declaration of Human Rights consists of two major parts. The first part, also known as the first generation of rights, protects the individual's civil and political rights, which include the right to life, freedom from torture and inhuman treatment, the right to liberty and security, equality before the law, and freedom of thought. The Covenant on Economic, Social and Cultural Rights is referred to as the second generation of rights. According to the UN Bill of Human Rights, the second generation rights protects such rights as the right to work, the right to favorable conditions of work, the right to social security, the right to education, and the highest attainable standard of physical and mental health. The focus of the first and second generation of rights is on the individual as a human being with inalienable rights, and with integrity and dignity. Moskowitz observes:

> Because there is but a single definition of man, so there can be but a single measure of man . . . Its dimensions are the fixed drives of human nature and all the elemental pleasures and pains of the flesh; the human spirit, with all its intuitions, feelings, fantasies and impulses, which seek the good, the true and the beautiful; and the power of the human mind, which is the basis of man's claim to dignity and worth, to freedom and justice (cited in Mahmud 1993: 487).

THE AFRICAN CHARTER OF HUMAN AND PEOPLES' RIGHTS

The African Charter[4] of Human and Peoples' Rights highlights the cultural value of human rights. It is a regional initiative for the promotion of human rights that is relevant to Africa. The African Charter reflects an African world outlook, legal philosophy and African collective development needs. It is referred to as the third generation rights. Its emphasis is on the protection of national rights, rather than individual rights. As such, the rights listed for protection by the Charter include the rights to self-determination, liberation, and equality of all peoples; the right to international peace and security; the right to use one's resources; the right to development; the right to satisfactory environment and the right of national minorities. The justification for the preference of national to individual rights, and to development, according to Robertson (1982), is because

> the economic development of underdeveloped countries is necessary for their social well-being and political stability, without which they cannot ensure effectively the civil, political, economic, social, and cultural rights announced in the major international texts and that therefore the "right to development" is a human right (cited in Mahmud 1993: 488).

Another important principle of the African Charter is that it imposes duties upon the individual towards the State and community, in line with the African communal ethics.

HUMAN RIGHTS IN PRE-COLONIAL AFRICA

There are claims that pre-colonial Africa had no concept of human rights, and so could not practice human rights. Human rights are only achievable through liberal regimes, since they are product of Western culture. These views are ascribed to Maine (1889) who argues that in pre-colonial Africa, rules of social conduct could not be differentiated into law and custom, hence the rules were oppressive. Further, Durkheim (1966) argues that there are ideally two types of society, namely, mechanical and organic. In societies characterized by mechanical solidarity, members of the society are highly integrated through their cultural and functional similarities. Mechanical solidarity prevailed in pre-industrial societies, and religion and law worked together, with little or no differentiation between the two. Mechanical solidarity societies as Durkheim described them were closest to acephalous societies, while his organic solidarity describes European societies with centralized state systems. Above all, Durkheim insisted that the law that prevailed in societies characterized by mechanical solidarity was basically repressive. Contemporary human rights parlance, therefore, implies a lack of human rights in pre-colonial Africa.

Donnely (1984) argues that the concept of human rights was non-existent in pre-colonial Africa. He states, "recognition of human rights simply was not the way of traditional Africa, with obvious and important consequences for political practices" (p.308). Earlier, he argued that, "even in many cases where Africans had personal rights vis-à-vis their governments, these rights were not based on one's humanity per se, but on membership in the community, status or some other ascriptive characteristics" (p.304). In this respect, according to Donnely (1984), human rights, is a Western invention. To justify his claim, he distinguishes human rights from human dignity. He defines human rights as a right, which is inherent in an individual for the simple reason of his/her humanity. On the other hand, human dignity obtains in situations where the rights of the individual are dependent upon his/her membership of a particular community, hence ascriptive status.

Gyekye (1996), Motala (1989) and Busia Jr. (1994) note that the concept of human rights was not alien to pre-colonial Africa, and that human rights was deeply rooted in African cultural values. Gyekye (1996), drawing from his Akan (of Ghana) culture, observes that the African conceives of the individual as endowed with dignity, and believed in the sanctity of human life. To underscore the belief that all human beings are equal, which are ends in themselves, Gyekye cites an Akan maxim that "all human beings are children of God; no one is a child of the earth" (1996: 150). Gyekye notes that the African believes in human dignity, which is an expression of the natural and moral rights of the individual. The individual's right must be appreciated within a communal context. This is because the group or community rights or interests generally override that of the individual. However, the individual's membership in a community does not rob the individual of his or her dignity, and by extension, the individual's rights.

Further, Mutua (1995) argues that the emphasis on individual rights in Western societies is connected to their peculiar historical experience, which Africa lacks. As such, the pursuit of individual rights is neither natural nor universal. The emergence and dominance of the state in social control in Western societies atomized and alienated the individual both from society and the state, hence the need to seek its protection. On the other hand, African states developed differently, for it was imposed through colonialism on ethno-political communities. Cover notes, "The rise of the modern nation state in Europe and its monopoly of violence and instruments of coercion gave birth to a culture of rights to counterbalance the invasive and abusive state" (cited in Mutua 1995: 342).

John Locke in his *Two Treatises of Government* reiterates the social contract whereby individuals in society concede some of their rights and powers to a sovereign in return for their protection. Mutua (1995:342) notes that this power is conditional and dependent on the state's duty to "protect individual rights and freedoms from invasion and to secure their more effective guarantee" (cited from Donnely 1990:34). When governments fail to protect individual rights, they lose their legitimacy. As such, the emphasis on individual rights by Western societies derive from European history and world outlook, hence they view human rights corpus merely as "an instrument for individual claims against the state" (Mutua 1995: 341).

Motala (1996) counters that in traditional Africa, as well as in modern Africa, the individual was neither autonomous nor alienated. The individual was always a member of an extended family or community. Membership of the extended family or community bestowed the individual with rights and duties. According to M'Baye and Ndiaye (1982), "within the framework of the group, the individual enjoyed freedom of expression, freedom of religion, freedom of movement, freedom of association, the right to work, and the right to education" (cited in Motala 1989: 381). However, according to Motala, failure to conform to the norms of society could jeopardize the rights of the individual. This could occur because, as Marashinge notes, freedom of thought, speech and beliefs were considered communal rights. Other conditions for enjoying these rights were guided by the "principle of respect," according to Marashinge. Respect involved respect for oneself and for others. Respect for others varied according to age, ability, and sex. Respect for others was "very much a part of the normative structure of the legal system, and determined the extent to which freedom of speech could be expressed," according to Marashinge (cited in Motala 1989: 382). Motala justifies the limitation on freedom of speech as similar to what obtains in all societies—it is not absolute.

In traditional African societies, according to Gyekye (1996) and Motala (1989), the individual's right to food was respected and protected. Everyone had access to land, since land was owned both privately and communally. Everyone was encouraged to work, and idleness carried a social stigma. African societies being gerontocratic, the elders are the custodians of the community wealth. The elders, as custodians of the community land, administered the land to the best interest of the lineage or community. Old age is deferred to in recognition of the contribution and wisdom of the elders. Besides, everyone will get old and enjoy the same status. However, it is important to note that the elder does not own or control the community land, but only held it in trust for the lineage or community. An abuse of the position could result in replacement and or denial of other privileges. Again, land is not a marketable commodity, and so the individual had the right to use the land for the production of food and development for residential purposes only.

Notably, Gyekye (1996) and Motala (1989) observe that traditional African societies were democratic and egalitarian, and allowed for the participation of all adults in the decision-making process. Even in communities with chiefs, decisions are reached only after full consultation with community members. All participating adults were free to express their opinions on issues before decisions can be reached. Again, all decisions were reached through a consensus. No one is punished for holding opposing views on issues, and no attempt is made to suppress any voice. In some cases, decisions on issues are deferred until all the constituting members or groups of the community are represented. Sithole aptly sums it up: "Things are never settled until everyone has had something to say. African traditional council allows the free expression of all shades of opinions. *Any man has full right to express his mind on public questions*" (cited in Gyekye 1996: 153 (emphasis in original).

Gyekye (1996) further observes that the individual can assert his or her civil and political rights against violation by the state. This was a recognition by African peoples: that people entrusted with power are capable of abusing it. As such, assertion of political rights, have sometimes led to the removal of autocratic or corrupt leaders from office. This practice is geared towards safeguarding the individual's dignity, which is generally referred to as African humanism, according to Motala (1989). In this regard, "torture, killings, and other abuses would be objectionable in terms of Africa's own traditional standards of human rights" (Motala 1996:387). Human rights, therefore, is not purely a Western invention. Neither did the concept of human rights originate from any part of the world, or from liberal democracy, as postulated in some quarters. Arguably, all peoples of the world do not assent to the same basic values and beliefs, but what is certain is that every society has been concerned with the notion of social justice, the relationship between the individual and his/her political authorities. As Roberts and Merrills (1992) point out, "the struggle for human rights is as old as [world] history itself, because it concerns the need to protect the individual against the abuse of power by the monarch, the tyrant, or the state" (cited in Lauren 1998:11–12).

SOCIAL/POLITICAL ORGANIZATIONS IN PRE-COLONIAL AFRICA

To further appreciate the mechanisms of social control and the status of human rights in pre-colonial Africa, some understanding of the nature of the prevailing social organizations is imperative. Informing this approach is the conception of human rights, which many have described as a "negotiated package." In other words, it is a process whereby the ruled bargain with rulers over rights and the extent of the powers of the sovereign. Basically, human rights, is about limited government. Human rights is concerned with the relationship between people and their political authority. It raises questions about the responsibility of the political authority with respect to the protection of the individual and the scope of the claims that the individual can make from his/her sovereign. In sum, " . . . it is protections against arbitrary deprivations of life and liberty; it, therefore, includes notions of due process (i.e., fair trial, right to confront witnesses and present evidence, appeal, etc.)" (Pena 1994: 212). Further, Lauren (1998:11) asserts that "the issue of human rights addresses age-old and universal questions about the relationship between individuals and their larger society, and thus is one that has been raised across time and across cultures."

To evaluate the extent to which human rights were recognized or violated in pre-colonial Africa will entail inquiring into the mechanisms of rulership. The social history of Africa falls into three classical periods: the pre-colonial, colonial, and post-colonial. To evaluate human rights status in pre-colonial Africa, some understanding of the political organization of pre-colonial African societies is important. Or as Marxian theorists would put it, the examination of law presupposes questions of state, ideology and the class struggle.

Elias (1962) categorized African pre-colonial political organization into two broad groups. African societies in the first group had a centralized political authority, "administrative machinery" or "judicial institution." Societies in this group are generally heterogeneous according to Elias, but defer to one political superior, usually the "Paramount Chief" or the

"King-in-Council." Societies in this group are the Zulu, the Ngwato, the Bemba, the Bayankole and the Kede. These societies comprise several ethnic groups, which explained the necessity for the use of force to hold them together. There are class distinctions based on wealth, privilege, and status and the "incidence of organized force which is the principal sanction in a society based upon cultural and economic heterogeneity" (p.11). Elias found that the Zulus and Bemba kingdoms are exceptions to this rule, for they are culturally homogenous.

THE ASHANTI OF GHANA

The Ashantis of Ghana are a good example of societies with a hierarchical political arrangement. According to Busia Jr. (1994), the social organization of the Ashanti is based on kinship and lineage networks. The political body was centered around the kinship system and the heads of the various lineages. The Ashantis operated a federal system of government that comprised about twenty-two chiefs (petty kings). The political authority rested on the king, together with the other paramount chiefs who constitute the "Ashanteman" council. The head of the council remained the king, whose headquarters is in Kumasi. The council, as the major authority, had power to maintain law and order. It also had the authority to declare war and also enter into treaties with other tribal groups. Each member of the council had a different role. Next to the King who had executive powers is the Prime Minister. Each of the other councilors managed a portfolio like finance, public relations, and so on. Two other offices worthy of note are the head of all the women within the federal system known as the "Queen-mother" and the head of the youth whose office has no political significance.

The King-in-council held court to try both civil and criminal cases. The cases brought before the king were of two kinds, namely the public and private. Homicide and treason, for example, are tried in the King's supreme court. Other cases like adultery, slander, and assaults, are handled as private cases within the lineage units.

The office of the King is an elective one. Eligibility, however, is limited to members of the royal family. The Prime Minister acts in the event that the incumbent dies, abdicates his office or is deposed from power. The Queen-mother, as the head of the royal family, is constitutionally empowered to nominate a candidate for the office of the king.

Busia (1951), according to Busia Jr. (1994), observes that the King did not rule for life, and that he remained in office for as long as he enjoys the good will of his people. Any of the King's subjects has constitutional rights to institute impeachment proceedings against the king. The case succeeds if the applicant is able to convince the majority of the councilors that the king has breached his oath of office. However, if the case fails, the applicant could pay with his life.

THE IGBOS OF NIGERIA

In the second category are African societies with a decentralized political authority. Societies in this group include the Logoli, the Tallensi, the Nuer and the Igbos.[5] The system had certain internal mechanisms for the maintenance of law and order, and also for the enforcement of political decisions. The Igbo people of Nigeria are a good example. The Igbos had no political arrangement that could be called a federation, a confederacy or state. When there is a case or matter that affects the whole village groups, representatives of the villages meet in a general assembly. Jones (1965:5) notes that no village "could be bound by a law or decision made at a meeting in the absence of its representatives" (cited in Uchendu 1965: 45). All persons, including the villages, had equal rights and privileges. Decisions reached at these general meetings were through consensus, which was essential as sanctions against recalcitrant persons or groups were rarely forcefully enforced. All had a voice in these meetings, even though the elders, especially the ruling age grade, wielded a lot of influence. At the village level, however, what obtains can be considered a direct democracy. All adults, including men and women, are represented. It is important to point out that the talks are, dominated by men. Women talk only when they are directly involved, either as witnesses, plaintiffs or defendants. The set-up is aptly summed up by, Uchendu (1965: 46).

> The picture of the Igbo political community which emerges from these settings is one that is territorially small enough to make direct democracy possible at the village level as well as representative assembly at the village-group level; and in which there are leaders rather than rulers, and political cohesion is achieved by rules rather than by laws [sic] and by consensus rather than by dictation.

In Igbo society, the middle-age grades make up the Council of Elders, and they are the major authority in the town and constitute the traditional government. The society is relatively egalitarian, as such, the chances of an individual's rights being violated is minimal. Again, most social and political activities are carried out either through the age grade, family groupings and the lineage, so that the individual's rights are better protected. The powers of the elders are well defined and limited with sufficient breaks such that the individual's rights are not encroached upon.

Depending on the task at hand, a capable individual could emerge to direct the course of events. Such an individual, as against collective leadership of the elders, only lasts for the duration of the event. For example, in Afikpo there have been cases where hippopotamuses were terrorizing villagers, sometimes leading to their evacuation. In one occasion, a brave man organized other men to attack and kill the beast. The community honored the individual with the title of the "hippo killer." An individual leader can also emerge in times of war or other emergencies. Basden acknowledging the collective leadership of Igbo people posits:

> In times of emergency a dominating character automatically came to the front, and the people accepted him as leader until the trouble ceased. He then reverted to his former position in common with other citizens. Nor were any hereditary rights attached to the erstwhile leadership; the basic principle of no ruling families in Iboland remained inviolate. Where such prerogatives are beginning to appear, they are the fruit of modern innovations; they are really contraventions of native laws and customs (cited in Amadi (1982:96).

DISCUSSION

Maurice Cranston defines human rights as "universal moral rights, something of which all men everywhere, at all times ought to have and something of which no one may be deprived without grave affront to justice" (cited in Motala 1989: 376). Cranston believes human nature is essentially the same hence he insists human rights are universal. The concept of human rights as we have it today, he observes, is a twentieth century creation. It derives from what was earlier "referred to as natural right or the rights of man" (ibid.). Lauren argues the concept of human rights is not a Western creation. Neither is, human rights a twentieth century creation. Lauren posits:

> early ideas about general human rights thus did not originate exclusively in one location like the West or even with any particular form of government like liberal democracy, but were shared throughout the ages by visionaries from many cultures in many lands who expressed themselves in different ways (1998:11).

Alderson (1984) traces the origin of human rights to 1215 when the English King John signed into law a document known as the Magna

Carta. The notion of human rights was expanded and strengthened by the 1689 Bill of Rights which was drawn up to form the basis of parliamentary democracy in England at the end of the Civil War. This was preceded, according to Anderson, by the 1640 and 1679 Habeaus Corpus Acts which drew up a legal remedy against "arbitrary detention or imprisonment." These documents are said to have influenced the American Declaration of Independence of 1776, and the French Declarations of the Rights of Man of 1789 and 1793. The concept of human rights also follows the rule of law doctrine that states that all men are equal before the law.

Eze (1984) observes that all societies recognize human rights. Yet, its manner of conceptualization may vary across different cultural settings. He asserts that pre-colonial Africa had a system of law which is similar to the systems of law in Western states. Eze cautions that

> . . . in most traditional African societies the law existed outside the framework of a state in the modern sense. Obedience to the law was maintained through custom and religion as well as established patterns of sanction. These pre-colonial African societies had a high level of organization in which political, economic, and social control was maintained (cited in Motala 1989:379).

We also note from the Ashanti legal system, as outlined above, that there was a clear differentiation between public and private offenses. Writing about the Ashanti, Ratrray (1929) notes that murder and rape, for instance, came under public offense. The significance of this in human rights terms is that the political authorities of the Ashanti society recognized the individual's right to life. Elias (1962), in support, notes that not even the lives of the so-called slaves could be taken at will. Elias further observes that an individual does not lose his right to life because of his or her membership in a particular family, clan or lineage. The convicted murderer faces the punitive sanctions of the law. No other member of his or her family, clan or lineage is punished in his or her place. This is an indication that a certain level of individualism was recognized by the society. As noted above, an individual could institute impeachment proceedings against a King. If it is proved that the King breached his oath of office, then the King's deposition will be effected. Even the claim that women and outsiders within the African cultural and political systems had no rights have been refuted by the fact that a woman occupied one of the highest office in the Ashanti Kingdom. Rattray (1929) cites an instance when a woman held the overall power in the Ashanti federation. Elias (1962) further observes that foreigners were allowed almost all rights except that of holding a political office.

He insists that pre-colonial African societies were even more accommodating of immigrants than some of our so-called liberal states. In sum, Wai (1979) states:

> in the traditional setting Africans had the right to remove chiefs who acted arbitrarily or ruled dictatorially in complete disregard of 'constitutional checks.' . . . Africans participated in the process of decision-making through recognized channels and institutions. Discussion and those who dissented from the majority opinion were not punished . . . there was clear conception of freedom of expression and of association (p.116–7).

Kaunda (former President of Zambia) contends that the African conception of human rights was humanist in orientation. Kaunda describes African humanism as follows:

> The tribal community was a mutual society. It was organized to satisfy the basic human needs of all its members . . . individualism was discouraged . . . Human need was the supreme criterion of behavior . . . social harmony was a vital necessity . . . Chief and tribal elders . . . adjudicated between conflicting parties . . . and took whatever action was necessary to strengthen the fabric of social life (cited in Motala 1989: 381).

Nahum (1982) declares that African humanism gave rise to humanitarian laws in Africa. In war, for instance, complete destruction was not allowed. There were unwritten rules that regulated war practices. An instance of this is that battles lasted between sunrise and sundown, and no wars were to be fought during ploughing and harvesting seasons. Again, only men were involved in war, and maltreatment of enemy casualties and prisoners of war was not allowed (ibid.).

The Igbo societies as described above were relatively egalitarian, democratic and had a remarkable sense of justice. As such, all members of the community participated in the decision-making process. In Igboland, land was either owned by the community or the, lineage; as such, there was no "leisured class of land owners" (Motala 1996). Everybody had equal access to the land and was expected to cultivate the land and produce food for him/her self and the family. Lands could only be leased, not sold.

Another reason cited by Donnely and Howard, according to Mutua (1995), for the non-existence of human rights in pre-colonial Africa was that the individual in certain circumstances was never left alone, for that value is central to the concept of human rights. Mutua, in response, observes that

Donnely's and Howard's position lack internal consistency and displays ethnocentrism and moral arrogance. Mutua insists that human dignity, the basis of human rights, is inherent in all societies. That human beings are accorded special status worthy of protection, which distinguishes humans from animals, attests to that. Fernyhough (1993), in support, notes,

> Thus Donnelly and Howard contend that in pre-colonial Africa, as in most non-Western and preindustrial societies, forms of social and political organization rendered the means to attain human dignity primarily through duties and obligations, often expressed in a communally oriented social idiom and realized within a redistributive economy. Yet both reject with unwarranted emphasis the notion that in the search for guarantees to uphold human life and dignity precolonial Africans formulated or correlated such claims to protection in terms of human rights (cited in Mutua 1995:358).

In traditional Africa, as in all societies, there are sometimes contradictions between the ideal and the practice, as it relates to human rights. There were cultural practices that denied individuals or groups human dignity and human rights. Hobley (1971) talks of trial by fire or water ordeal by the Akamba people. A suspect could, in the fire ordeal, be asked to lick a red-hot sword to prove his or her innocence (cited in Mutua 1995). In Akan society, according to Wiredu, a common citizen's life could be taken when a chief died. The justification for this practice was that the chief needed somebody to attend to him in his journey to the land of the dead (Mutua 1995). Mutua, also citing Wiredu, notes that women were denied access to decision-making political institutions in the Akan society. The gendered division of labor meant that women were responsible for childcare and housework, while men handled security and governance of the community. Again, non-adults or minors were not allowed voices in the public sphere. Mutua, however, reminds us that every culture carried the burden of this "duality of the good and the bad" (p.354).

To conclude, it is reiterated that the issue of human rights did not originate from any single nation, geographical area or people. Human rights are not a product of only one political system either, including that of liberal democracy. Human rights questions are about the relationship between the individual and the larger society or political authorities. Philosophers of all societies were concerned about the nature and outcome of this relationship, despite the beliefs and values of the people concerned. Issues of human rights underlie other issues, such as the notion of social justice and individual liberty and well-being. Human rights, therefore, is not a

Western concept. As Lauren (1998:120) points out, "What the West did provide, however, was not a monopoly of ideas on the subject but rather much greater opportunities for visions such as these to receive fuller consideration, articulation, and eventual implementation." Having laid out the theoretical framework of the study, I now undertake the discussion of the findings in the following chapters.

Chapter Four
Nigeria in Post-Colonial Africa

> *We have to go back to our traditional ways of solving our problems, traditional ways of working together. Otherwise, Boosaaso [a port in war-torn Somalia] would not have peace.*
>
> —*General Mohamed Abshir, Boosaaso's de facto administrator in The Washington Post, 3 March 1996, A29 as cited in (Ayittey 1999:85).*

INTRODUCTION

Nigerian people are disenchanted with the Nigerian government criminal justice system. It is not only in the area of social control that the post-colonial government of Nigeria is ineffective and unpopular. The post-colonial government of Nigeria has failed in its function as a government. This failure has partly motivated this study of the Afikpo indigenous systems of social control. This chapter therefore examines the Nigerian criminal justice system. Findings of the research support the argument the Nigerian criminal justice system is ineffective and corrupt. Some of the theories that explain why the Nigerian criminal justice system is ineffective and corrupt, such as postcolonial and dependency theories, are examined in this light.

As earlier indicated, the centralization and bureaucratization of Western social control systems occurred between the eighteenth and nineteenth centuries. As part of this development, the state became the dominant agent of social control. The prison also emerged as the dominant form of punishment. Positivist approaches to scientific inquiries expanded the role of professionals whose task it was to classify deviants into different categories. Boosted by scientific knowledge, the new experts segregated the deviants into mental hospitals, penitentiaries, reformatories. There was also a marked increase in the role of law and lawyers in the justice system.

This social control system was exported to Africa by European colonial authorities. Incidentally, the imposition of European models of social control on Africa occurred at a time when Western people were becoming disillusioned with the justice system. As Clifford (1974: 185) points out:

> Africa has inherited its approach to the treatment of crime from its colonial era. Some prisons now standing were erected in the nineteenth century and the legal systems followed the colonizers as surely as Roman Laws went with the Legions. Similarly, treatment systems were European in origin and made few concessions to tribal tradition . . . [T]he importation of foreign treatment measures for offenders was often blind to the better and more effective arrangements locally available.

Indictments against the system are that State courts in an attempt to reform offenders remand them in prisons and psychiatry institutions. Records show that criminals deteriorate, are stigmatized, learn 'argot' language, with a consequent increase in recidivism and difficulty in reintegration into the society. As such, by the middle of the twentieth century, a movement calling for the reversal of the ideological and institutional foundations of the prevailing social control system emerged (Cohen 1985). According to Cohen, partly motivating these attacks on the justice system are the "destructuring impulse" which was very popular in the 60s. Part of the agenda of this movement was the search for alternative or complementary methods of conflict resolution.

In Africa, the services provided by the state justice system are poor or nonexistent in some places. This partly accounts for the renewed interest in the African indigenous systems of conflict resolution. However, it is not only in the area of social control that the colonially derived system has failed African people. African indigenous healthcare delivery, for example is becoming more relevant and popular. As Olowu and Erero (1996) rightly observe:

> This renewed interest is based, in part, on the fact that these institutions have proven to be resilient. In addition, they are more effectively institutionalized and Africans rely upon them to provide required goods and services in the face of the failure of the formal, colonial-based structures. Such goods and services include: security, roads, bridges, schools, post offices, mechanisms for conflict resolution, common-pool resources management and credit provision, to mention a few.

THE NIGERIAN JUDICIAL SYSTEM

Nigeria's legal system is based on English Common law, the 1999 Constitution, Islamic and African customary laws. According to the 1999 Nigerian Constitution, the Judiciary is a separate and independent arm of

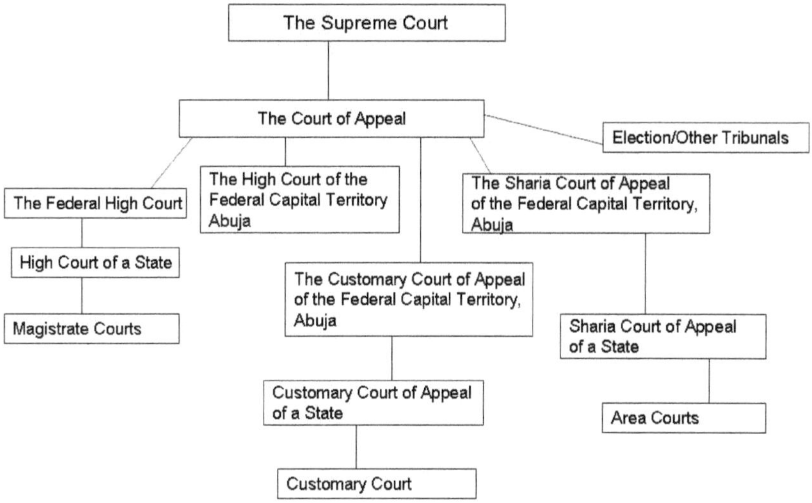

Figure 4.1. Hierarchy of the Nigerian Judicial System. Diagram showing the hierarchy of the Nigerian Judicial System

the Government. Described below is the hierarchy of the court chambers of the Nigerian Judicial System in order of superiority.

The Supreme Court of Nigeria

The Supreme Court of Nigeria consists of the Chief Justice of Nigeria and not more than twenty-one justices of the Supreme Court. The number of Supreme Court justices shall be determined by an Act of the National Assembly. The Supreme Court is the highest and final appellate court of the land. The Supreme Court's primary function is the hearing of appeals from the junior courts of the land. Cases can also emanate from the Supreme Court. The Supreme Court has original jurisdiction in conflicts between the Federal Government and a State or States, or cases between two or more States. Supreme Court judges are, appointed by the President of the Federal Government of Nigeria, on the recommendation of the National Judicial Council. The persons recommended for appointment to the Supreme Court by the National Judicial Council are drawn from the list of persons provided by the Federal Judicial Service Commission. The appointments however must be, confirmed by the Senate.

The Court of Appeal

The Court of Appeal consists of the President of the Court of Appeal and not less than forty-nine members of the court. There is a constitutional provision for the appointment of at least three courts of appeal justices that are learned in Islamic personal law and three justices that are learned in Customary law. The actual numbers of justices, schooled in both Islamic and Customary laws are as to be determined by the National Assembly.

The Federal High Court

The Constitution provides for the establishment of a Federal High Court in all the States of the Federation. Until 1979, this Court was known as the Revenue Court. The Federal High Court is, headed by a Chief Judge, and consists of such number of judges as may be prescribed by an Act of the National Assembly. The Court is duly constituted to hear a case if there is present at least one judge of the court. The court has jurisdiction concerning the revenue of the Federal Government. It also has jurisdiction in civil and criminal cases pertaining to taxation, customs and excise duties, currency, banking and foreign exchange, etc.

The High Court of the Federal Capital Territory, Abuja

The Constitution provides for the establishment of a High Court of the Federal Capital Territory, Abuja. The Court shall consist of a Chief Judge and such number of Judges as may be prescribed by an Act of the National Assembly. The Court has jurisdiction to "hear and determine any civil proceedings in which the existence or extent of a legal right, power, duty, liability, priviledge, interest, obligation or claim is in issue or to hear and determine any criminal proceedings involving or relating to any penalty, forfeiture, punishment or other liability in respect of an offence committed by any person" (1999 Nigerian Constitution, p.98).

The Sharia Court of Appeal of the Federal Capital Territory, Abuja

There shall be provided a Sharia Court of Appeal of the Federal Capital Territory, Abuja. The Court shall hear appeals from civil proceedings involving matters of Islamic personal law. The Court shall consist of–

A. a Grand Kadi of the Sharia Court of Appeal, and
B. such number of Kadis of the Sharia Court of Appeal as may be prescribed by an Act of the National Assembly.

Appointments to the office of the Grand Kadi or Kadi of the Sharia Court of Appeal of, the Federal Capital Territory shall be made by the President on the recommendation of the National Judicial Council. The appointments require the confirmation of the Senate. To qualify to hold the office of the Grand Kadi or Kadi, of the Sharia Court of Appeal of the Federal

Capital Territory, the person must be a legal practitioner of at least ten years standing. In addition, the person must have an Islamic law degree with twelve years experience from an institution recognized by the National Judicial Council. A distinguished Islamic scholarship or considerable experience in the practice of Islamic law can be accepted in lieu of Islamic law degree.

The Customary Court of Appeal of the Federal Capital Territory, Abuja

The 1999 Constitution provides for the establishment of the Customary Court of Appeal of the Federal Capital Territory, Abuja. The Court in addition to its supervisory role hears appeals in civil proceedings concerning issues of Customary law. The Court shall be presided over by a President and such number of Judges as may be prescribed by an Act of the National Assembly. The President and Judges of the Customary Court of Appeal of the Federal Capital Territory shall, be appointed by the President on the recommendation of the National Judicial Council. To qualify for the office of President or Judges of the Customary Court of Appeal of the Federal Capital Territory, Abuja, the person must be a legal practitioner in Nigeria of not less than ten years standing. In addition, the person must have in the opinion of the National Judicial Council a considerable knowledge and experience in the practice of Customary Law.

The State High Court

The State High Court is, headed by the Chief Judge of the State and such number of judges that the law of the State may prescribe. The Court is deemed duly constituted when one of the State High Court judges is sitting. The State High Courts have jurisdiction in all criminal and civil cases that occur in the state. As an appellate court, it hears cases emanating from the Magistrate or District courts. The State Court also plays a supervisory role for other inferior courts in the state.

The Sharia Court of Appeal of a State

The Sharia Court of Appeal of a State is an appellate court. It has no original jurisdiction on any matter. The Court hears cases appealed from the Area Courts. The Court handles cases pertaining to Moslem law. The Constitution provides for states interested in the Moslem faith to establish such. As a result, it is found mostly in the Northern States of the federation, with a predominantly Moslem population.

A Customary Court of Appeal of a State

The Customary Court of Appeal of a State, like the Sharia Court of Appeal of a State, has no original jurisdiction on any matter. The Court performs appellate and supervisory functions to the Customary Courts. The establishment of the Court by the states is optional, according to the 1999 Constitution. As such, only states interested in customary matters have such courts. Hence, the courts are found mostly in the Southern states of Nigeria.

Magistrate Courts

The Magistrate Court is a court of first instance. There are various grades of magistrate courts located in the Local Government Areas of the federation. They handle both civil and criminal cases. Appeals from the Magistrate Courts go to the State High Courts.

CORRUPTION IN THE NIGERIAN CRIMINAL JUSTICE SYSTEM (THE POLICE)

Corruption pervades the entire Nigerian Criminal Justice System, but the Police are singled out here for examination because of its central position in social control. Available records show that corruption within the Nigerian Police Force is not just about a few bad apples in the police, but that the system is corrupt from the most senior police office to the patrol officers. For example, in November 2005, the Nigeria's former police chief, Tafa Balogun pled guilty to graft and was sentenced to six months imprisonment. He also agreed to forfeit the sum of Seventeen billion naira to the government in the controversial plea deal. Many Nigerians doubt the punishment fits the crime. As further proof that corruption, abuse of power, torture and extra judicial killing is prevalent within the Nigerian police, on December 2, 2005, Reuters Nigeria reported that

> The Nigerian government has apologized to the families of six people who were shot dead by police and offered them 3 million naira ($22,600) each, setting a precedent in a country where police brutality is a fact of life. The five men and one woman were shot dead in the poor Apo neighborhood of the capital Abuja on June 8. Police initially said that they were armed robbers caught in the act, but an inquiry established that they were unarmed (2005 Reuters Limited—http://www.nairaland.com/nigeria/topic-3247.0.html)

The Minister of Police Affairs, Broderick Bozimo who announced the compensation to the victims also apologized to the families of the victims and to all Nigerians. The officers involved in this extra-judicial killing of innocent Nigerians were high ranking police officers, including a deputy police commissioner. The same report also noted that the Police in their own publication acknowledged that they killed 3,100 suspected armed robbers in 2003 alone. Barely a week after the above report, by December 15, 2005, sixteen Nigerian police officers were paraded in Abuja for alleged armed robbery and economic sabotage according to news reports (see Nigerian Vanguard Newspapers of December 16, 2005). The Nigerian president, Olusegun Obasanjo and the Inspector General of Police have in separate public statements acknowledged that the Nigerian Police routinely torture suspects, engage in extra-judicial killings and also aid and abet armed robbery (see the Nigerian Tribune of December 15, 2005—http://www.tribune.com.ng/151205/news07.htm) for the statement credited to Mr. Sunday Ehindero, the Inspector General of Police and Camilius Eboh, Reuters South Africa—http://za.today.reuters.com/news/NewsArticle.aspx?type=topNews) for the statement credited to President Olusegun Obasanjo.

The image many Nigerians have of the Nigerian police is that of a "lazy, corrupt, inefficient, bribe-taking, money-extorting officer who connives at crimes 'if the price is right' (Okereke 1993: 113). There are good reasons to justify this public's perception of the police. Peil (1991: 136) said that in 1987 alone, 105 policemen were arrested for crimes including armed robbery, murder and rape. One of the policemen was a Divisional Police Officer (DPO) who was caught sharing the loot with robbers.

Peil (1991) further says that the Nigerian Police's unpopularity derives from a well-established reputation for corruption, which the police excuse, saying it is the product of a corrupt society. She says that there are many cases of collaboration with criminals, molesting of innocent citizens, unlawful arrest and acceptance of bribes. An avenue for bribery is the unpopular road blocks, ostensibly to control traffic violations.

The defense by the Nigerian Police that corruption is not peculiar to them is valid. Many commentators have variously described corruption as endemic and widespread in Nigeria. Adeyemi (1992: 83) notes that corruption has "been recognized as a major problem in the developing world, where it has become a cankerworm, reaching the dimensions of an epidemic in the body politic of the various nations of Africa." Mohammad, in support, observes: "My impression is that the police in this country are no more corrupt than, let us say, veterinary or forest assistants, or land settlement officers, or indeed customs and pay officers. The police are singled out for excessive criticisms only because their sphere of influence is much wider than that of any of these other public servants" (Okereke 1993: 113).

Adeyemi observes that successive Nigerian governments have continually expressed alarm at the situation and have repeatedly expressed their intentions to combat corruption. It seems all efforts by successive governments in Nigeria to control corruption have failed, since the problem persists. The reason for this failure will be made clearer when the dependent state theory is examined later in the study.

There is no record on the extent of corruption by the police. Corruption in Nigeria is an offense with very low reportability. This is hardly surprising considering the nature of corruption and the fact that the Nigerian Police, the institution where complaints are supposed to be lodged, is generally perceived as an embodiment of corruption. Akinnola's study supports Adeyemi's observation. He states:

> . . . the greatest constraint in the capacity of the police (in Nigeria) to enforce the law is their own greed and corruption. Check points established for enforcing the law have been turned into toll gates, the prosecution of offenders is deliberately stalled or sabotaged, once money has changed hands, and indeed in some cases, criminals somehow get to know the identities of those who report them to the police (cited in Okereke 1993: 119).

The pertinent question to ask at this stage is why is corruption endemic and widespread among the Nigerian Police? Or in any case, why is there so much corruption in Nigeria? First and foremost, the government of Nigeria seems to lack the political will to confront corruption and other aspects of the abuse of power in a systematic, organized and consistent fashion. So far, all attempts to control corruption have often been sporadic, or done in a fire-brigade manner.

Since corruption could not be said to be, enforced in Nigeria, those caught during the few times it is controlled consider themselves unlucky, rather than guilty of an offense. The non-enforcement of corruption also gives the wrong signal of governmental approval of the act. Some even claim that the government expects the police to supplement their low wages with the money collected through bribery and extortion. This thinking is fueled by the practice of senior police officers' posting of favored subordinate staff to positions where the opportunity for graft is greater.

Controlling corruption and power abuse, even with the best of intentions, is a very difficult task. Sutherland (1949) identified legalism, that is, the legalistic definition of criminality as a major impediment to the control of corruption. The courts, can only interpret an act as criminal if the act matches with the criminal code definition. The courts, in prosecuting an offender, require some evidence. This is not always available since those in a position to give evidence are often parties to the crime. Besides, bribery and corruption are carried out in such a manner that it is often difficult to prove.

Another factor hampering the control of corruption and the abuse of power, according to Sutherland (1949), is the public attitude that tends to discourage punishment. Thus, punishment should be applied only to the very dangerous offenders. Sutherland argues that the laws regulating corruption do not conform with that of societal sentiments. As a result, there is no organized resentment against corruption by the public. Again, people involved in corrupt behavior are often educated and seemingly reasonable people who do not fit the stereotype associated with criminals.

In Nigeria, the control of corruption is even compounded by the fact that everyone is involved so to speak. And this on its own poses conceptual questions for *criminology* as a discipline. Summer asks:

> If everyone commits a crime, what's left of the concept of the criminal personality? If what counts as crime is much dependent upon the political power to criminalise and the financial power to bribe the police, what is left of the concepts of crime and criminal behavior? What relevance for scientific work would official criminal statistics have? How could one take a sample of prisoners as a sample of criminals? (cited in Kameir/Kursany 1985: 9).

The feeling that everyone is involved in corruption discourages people from reporting corrupt practices to the Criminal Justice System. The Criminal Justice System is considered by many to be an embodiment of corruption. Hence, the general attitude is "why report corruption to corruption?" (Adeyemi 1992: 85).

The foregoing explains why victims of crime in Nigeria lack confidence in the Nigerian criminal justice system, especially the Police. Victims of crime feel doubly victimized by the Police. Their rights are routinely violated. Victims are regularly harassed, hounded and made to pay a ransom before their cases receive formal attention by the Police. The Police are further accused of brutality and corruption.

Factors that further undermine the effectiveness of the Nigerian Police include: a dearth of qualified professionals; poorly motivated staff; and government underfunding. Again, the Police is yet to lose its image as a colonial instrument of oppression. Hence, Nigerians generally perceive the Police as an imposition, and elite and governmental instrument of oppression. The Police therefore lack legitimacy, which partly accounts for their ineffectiveness and powerlessness. To support the claim that the Nigerian Police are inefficient and lack the public's support, a recent survey shows that only about 0.4% of stolen property is recovered by the Police in Nigeria (Montlcos 1997). Further, according to the study, the Police frequently collude with criminals, and "most of the goods they seize are secretly resold to fences or to their owners" (p.2). Further evidence that victims of crime in Nigeria are doubly victimized by, agents of the, criminal justice system, according to the survey, is that the Police generally fail to respond to victim(s) complaints. An indication of this neglect, according to a recent survey, is that "most people had reported violent crimes in which they were victims or witnesses to their local Police station, but nearly 60% said that nothing was done" (Montclos 1997: 3).

It is important, however, to note that many Nigerians lack a basic understanding of the operations of the Police. For example, victims of armed robbery and theft fail to understand why they never recover their property from suspects in the event that the property is, used by the Police as evidence. These cases can be open for years, frequently resulting in goods that are destroyed due to negligent handling and bad storage. Corruption can be implied in that valuable possessions of victims completely disappear from Police custody. Again, victims do not receive any support and encouragement from the Police. Victims, for instance, have to provide their own transportation to and from courts during the trial.

The treatment of victims of crime in Nigeria falls short of the United Nations' standards. The United Nations general Assembly on November 29, 1985 adopted the "Declaration of Basic Principles of Justice for Victims of Crime and Abuse of Power." The Declaration recommends that victims be treated with compassion, respect and dignity. Victims are also to be accorded access to mechanisms of justice and to prompt redress, and remedies such as restitution, compensation and "necessary material, medical, psychological and social assistance and support" provided (p.4). The Declaration calls on societies to acknowledge that victims of crime suffer injury and trauma, and incur financial loss resulting from inability to work and/or hospitalization. The Declaration defines victims as

> persons who, individually or collectively, have suffered harm, including physical or mental injury, emotional suffering, economic loss or substantial impairment of their fundamental rights, through acts or omissions that do not yet constitute violations of national criminal laws but of internationally recognized norms relating to human rights (p.6).

POSTCOLONIAL AFRICA

A major thesis of this study is that the survival and success of the Afikpo system of conflict resolution derives from its legitimacy and authority among Afikpo people. Ekeh's 1975 thesis on the two publics in Africa provides a plausible explanation for this phenomenon. Ekeh notes that one of the consequences of colonialism, apart from the imposition on Africa of foreign languages, morals, religion, laws, political structures and systems of education, are the emergence of two publics in Africa. Western countries, Ekeh observes, have one public. As such, the West can distinguish between the private and the public realm. However, in the West, "the private realm and the public realm have a common *moral* foundation. Generalized morality in society informs both the private realm and the public realm" (p.92). Judeo-Christian values provide the moral foundation of both the private and the public realms of Western societies.

On the other hand, in postcolonial Africa there are two publics. Ekeh calls them the 'primordial' public and the 'civic' public. In the *primordial public*, the individual's behavior is determined by considerations for primary relationships and ties, such as peer, family and kinship groupings. The *civic public* is, characterized by the state and its paraphernalia. The military, police and the bureaucracy all came with the colonial state.

The state is generally regarded as the major agent of modernization. It is pertinent to note that in Europe the State emerged after a protracted struggle amongst the feudal lords, the monarchy, the priests and the mercantile powers. In Africa, the States were imposed by the Colonial powers. The major issue here is that the two publics have different 'moral linkages to the private realm,' unlike what prevails in the West. Ekeh notes that, "the primordial public is moral and operates on the same moral imperatives as the private realm. . . . The civic public in Africa is amoral and lacks the generalized moral imperatives operative in the private realm and in the primordial public" (Ekeh 1975: 92). The African, according to Ekeh, is caught between these two publics. The difficulty arising from this is the Africans' . . ."simultaneous adaptation to two mentally contraposing orders. One solution to this problem formulated by the educated African is to define one of these orders in moral terms and the other in amoral terms" (p.100). As such, the African who evades his/her tax, and those that steal from the civic public are valorized. Ekeh further observes that "while many Africans bend over backwards to benefit and sustain their primordial publics, they seek to gain from the civic public" (p.107). Ekeh opines that the African derives immense benefit from the primordial public, hence he/she feels morally obliged to be loyal to it. Such benefits are not always in material terms. The African "gains back intangible, immaterial benefits in the form of identity or psychological security" (ibid.). The significance of Ekeh's 'two publics' thesis will be better appreciated when we examine the Dependent State Theories. A major claim of this study is that corruption partly accounts for Nigerian peoples' disenchantment with the modern Nigerian Criminal Justice System.

DEPENDENCY THEORY AND THE UNDERDEVELOPMENT OF SUB-SAHARAN AFRICA

The dependent state theories throw some light on the character and performance of the postcolonial Nigerian state. The neo-colonial states of Africa and Asia are often characterized as dependent states. This is because these states depend to a large extent on the more powerful industrialized countries for their economic and political survival. Santos defines dependency as a "situation in which the economy of certain countries is conditioned by the development and expansion of another economy to which the former is subjected" (Magstadt 1991: 426). Dependency, according to Santos, goes beyond the economic and political realms. It affects both the social and psychological attitudes and behaviors of both the dominant and dependent countries alike. The concept describes a relationship that is not equal or reciprocal.

One common feature of the dependent states, especially those in sub-Saharan Africa, is that they are politically unstable. Nigeria, like most new states in post-colonial Africa, has in the past four decades been characterized by democratic attempts and military interventions. In Nigeria, the latest known military coup was in December 1997. This coup, according to government sources, was discovered and foiled before the plotters could execute it. This was the ninth coup attempt in Nigeria since its independence from Britain in 1960. Five coups succeeded in toppling the governments. The military has ruled Nigeria for about seventy percent of the time in its forty-five years year existence as a postcolonial nation.

Dependency theory best explains the underdevelopment[1] of the neo-colonial states of Africa, Asia, Latin America and the Caribbean Countries. Ferraro (1997) credits the theory to Raul Prebisch, the Director of the United Nations Economic Commission for Latin America in the late 1950s. The dependency theory challenges the neoclassical socioeconomic theories that argue that economic growth, especially that which was occurring in the Western World, is beneficial to the rest of the world, following the "trickle-down" economics thesis. This argument, however, recognizes that the economic benefits may not be equally distributed. The proponents of the dependency theory observe that economic growth in the Western Countries does not lead to economic growth in the neo-colonial states. Dependency also describes the kind of relationship existing between the industrialized countries and the neo-colonial states, which is neither an equal nor reciprocal relationship. The power structure and institutions of the dependent states are controlled from outside. Carnoy (1984: 173) postulates:

> . . . whether the dependent state is characterized by parliamentary democracy or authoritarian regimes, it is, above all, a bourgeois state and represents capitalist hegemony. . . . The dominant capitalist class is not necessarily located in the nation, and, it is argued, the dynamic of the dependent state, whether democratic or authoritarian, lies outside the national territory.

Furthermore, Cockcroft et al (1972: xviii) observe that "the so called 'national' and 'progressive' bourgeoisie in Latin America is neither nationalist nor progressive—it is a dependent, comprador bourgeoisie." They represent the interests of the investors from the dominant states. As such, their economic activities impoverish the masses and undermine the society's potential for development. Following the dependency thesis, the world is described as constituting two sets, namely, dominant/dependent, center/periphery or metropolitan/satellite. Again, the Dependency theory, according to Macionis et al (1997: 299), "is a model of economic and social development that explains global inequality in terms of the historical exploitation of poor societies by rich ones."

Structural and Cultural Dependency

Mazrui (1974) identifies two dimensions of dependency, namely structural and cultural dependency. Structural dependency refers to the organization of the world economy that favors the Organization of Economic Co-operation and Development (OECD) Countries, while marginalizing and disadvantaging the dependent states. The emerging situation is one where the economy of the dependent states is determined by the conditions of the OECD economy. Cultural dependency, according to Mazrui, is a phenomenon which "affects two areas of human behavior especially: social stratification and motivation" (1974: 17).

Modernization theory

The dependency theory further provides alternative socio-economic development reasoning to the neoclassical or modernization theory. Macionis et al (1997: 294) define modernization theory as a "model of economic and social development that explains global inequality in terms of differing levels of technological development among societies." The modernization theory also emerged in the 1950s at the height of the modernization and industrialization debate. Hale (1990) believes that the theory derives from Spencer's societal evolution thesis. Here, societies are seen as "integrated social systems, where a change in one part will necessarily require adjustments in all other parts" (p. 456). For science and technology to develop, transformations in religious, political and family structures must occur. Transformation explains economic advancement in Western Countries, hence, modernization theorists argue that it is *affluence* not *poverty* that needs explanation, since the world until quite recently was characterized by material deprivation.

Furthermore, modernization theory explains poverty in the neo-colonial states as resulting from a "cultural lag," that is, cultural practices that are not conducive to technological innovation. Widespread corruption, nepotism and other familistic values characterize their societies and governments, and these practices hamper development, for political appointments are based on ascriptive criteria rather than on merit. Familism is said to stifle personal initiative, and is associated with a high birth rate. Again, underdevelopment in the neo-colonial states are explained by the "culture of poverty thesis." The culture of poverty thesis argues that the poorer nations' cultural values and practices constitute impediments to change and development. Also suggested as, hampering socio-economic development are "limited world views and low empathy, familism, mutual distrust in interpersonal relations, dependence on and hostility to government authority, perceived limited good, fatalism, limited aspirations, and lack of deferred gratification" (Hale 1990: 458). Based on the aforementioned the modernization theory insists that for the neo-colonial states to develop, they must pursue rational, liberal socio-economic policies that utilize modern economic techniques.

Hall (1987: 104), in support of the modernization theory, questions the dependency theory claim that the "core" of the dominant state determined the development in the "periphery." According to his line of thought, trade figures do not support the claim that the dominant states always exploit the dependent states. To buttress his argument, he cites the economic success story of Southeast Asia. He insists that much of the changes for development and modernization must be generated within the country. Evidence that purports to support Hall's claim is South Korea's level of economic development, which in the 1950s, was the same as that of India, Kenya and Nigeria. In support, Callaghy (1993: 185) notes that "in 1950, Korea had a GNP per capita of US$146, while Kenya and Nigeria managed US$129 and US$150 respectively. By 1993, South Korea's per capita GNP had grown to US$7,660, while Nigeria's and Kenya's were a mere US$340 each" (cited in Haynes 1997: 56).

Haynes' (1997) explanation for the disparity in economic development among some third-world countries challenges Hall's (1987) assumptions. Among the reasons that account for why South Korea's per capita GNP grew 18 times more than that of Kenya and Nigeria within a 40 year period was that South Korea

> received 6 percent of global aid in 1960, when its population was less than 1 percent of that of the Third World. Aid was used to build up local industry, while the approval signified by relatively large resource transfers from Western donors encouraged foreign investors to risk long term commitments (p.56).

Another contributing factor to South Korea's economic success, according to Haynes (1997), is that the national government was competent and managed to sustain economic growth. In other words, international support and the legitimacy and competency of a local government could transform a country from an underdeveloped to developing country.

Cockcroft et al (1972) also do not see the validity in the modernization theory as espoused by Hall (1987). Cockcroft et al (1972: xxvii) observe that the liberal economic policies that were applied in some of the dependent states resulted in the socio-economic empowerment for the few at the expense of the majority. Hence, they doubt there is any merit in the modernization theory argument. They note that the "very diffusion of such mistaken strategies of development is a function of the socioeconomic system in which the strategies are developed."

Dependency theorists further reject the premises of underdevelopment in the neo-colonial states, as advanced by the proponents of the modernization theory. According to this line of thought, the duplication of the development process followed by Western Countries is not possible, since historical time is not linear. Besides, the so-called industrialized societies' development was mostly based on their exploitation of world trade due to their military and technological advantage over other countries. In this respect, Frank (1972: 11) wonders why "resource-poor but unsatellitized Japan (was) able to industrialize so quickly at the end of the century while resource-rich Latin American countries and Russia were not able to do so." Frank's explanation comes from his second "hypothesis (that) suggests that the fundamental reason is that Japan was not satellitized either during the Tokugawa or the Meji period and therefore did not have its development structurally limited as did the countries which were so satellitized" (ibid.).

Dependency theory also challenges modernization theory's assumption that neo-colonial states' lack of institutions and cultural practices conducive to development is responsible for the undevelopment of neo-colonial countries. Rather, it is the neo-colonial states' relationship with the developed worlds that underdeveloped them. Carnoy (citing Fernando Enrique Cardoso and Enzo Faletto 1969) states:

> . . . between the developed and underdeveloped economies there not only exists a simple difference of stage or state of the productive system but also of function or position inside the same international economic structure of production and distribution . . . [This is] a structure defined by relations of domination (1974: 53).

Again, Ferraro 1997 (citing Andre Gunder Frank (1972) observes that the capitalist[2] system imposed a rigid international division of labor on the world economy. Validating this international economic division of labor is the "comparative advantage thesis," which argues that countries concentrate on the economic activities in which they have a comparative advantage. In this respect,

> the dependent states supply cheap minerals, agricultural commodities, and cheap labor, and also serve as the repositories of surplus capital, obsolescent technologies, and manufactured goods. These functions orient the economies of the dependent state toward the outside: money, goods, and services do flow into dependent states, but the allocation of these resources are determined by the economic interests of the dominant states, and not by the economic interests of the dependent state (p. 3).

For dependent states to develop, according to Cockcroft et al (1972: xxix), they have to break their stranglehold by the dominant states. They observe:

> the only remedy against the causes as well as the symptoms of underdevelopment lies in the revolutionary destruction of capitalism and the introduction of socialist development. Strategically, in terms of our analysis, the principal enemy in this struggle is imperialism, but tactically in Latin America the immediate enemy is the native bourgeoisie.

Slavery

Africa's underdevelopment is attributed to the negative effects of slavery, colonialism and neo-colonialism. Slavery and colonialism, without question, are momentous historical forces with the greatest influence on African culture and development. Both slavery and colonialism degraded and exploited African peoples, and this left a lasting negative effect on the African peoples' psyche, economy and culture. The African continent's major contact with the Europeans occurred in about 1444 A.D. Slavery was one outcome of this contact. In the 400 years that slavery lasted, about three hundred million Africans were shipped overseas as slaves. It is estimated that about 130 million Africans perished at sea en route to the western-hemisphere.

The enslaved were often the young and healthy and of sound physique. Arguably, these were people capable of having children and of doing productive work. Africa's population is said to have stagnated considerably as a result. Slavery undermined the ground for economic development, in the sense that Africa lost its most productive labor force for centuries. Instead, this crucial labor force was, exploited by the Europeans for their own economic development. The implications of such a sparse population in development terms cannot be overemphasized. It is widely believed that low population densities limit the possibilities of demand-induced inventions normally attributable to population pressure on resources. By 1870, slavery was formally abolished. It is arguable that following the advent of industrialization the abolition of slavery came about, since machines replaced the need for slave labor.

Colonialism

In 1884, during the Berlin Conference, Europeans partitioned Africa among themselves. The partitioning of Africa did not take into consideration the existing ethnic, cultural and historical differences. Some explanations for political instability in Africa have a strong correlation with this historical fact. Following this partitioning, Africa entered into another period of direct political and economic control by the Europeans. Another negative effect of colonialism on Africa was the restructuring of the political economy of the continent to meet the needs of European countries. Adedeji "indicts colonialism for changing Africa's agricultural priorities from food production for local consumption to export crops like cocoa, coffee, and tea—for which prices are set by demand in foreign markets" (cited in Magstadt 1991: 426).

Colonialism disturbed the natural process of state formation, created alien social structures and institutions, and introduced new relations of production. States in Africa were artificially created. In contrast, states in Western Europe developed through a different process. Wathig and Kursany (1985: 12) note:

> political developments were preceded by the crystallization of an industrial bourgeoisie. The dominance of this class occurred after its success over a protracted conflict with the feudalist class which had a radically different economic base, lying in landed property.

Again, colonial authorities were not interested in developing the colonies. Chandra (1980) notes that "the colonial State follows, in the long run, anti-industrialization and anti-development policies. And it does so precisely because it is guided by the 'national situation' not of the colony but of the metropolis" (cited in Carnoy 1984: 176). Even when the colonial authorities attempted to lay plans for development and modernization, they failed because colonial powers "scarcely acknowledged (African) cultural traditions and indigenous political predispositions" (Diamond 1989: 6).

Neo-colonialism

With the advent of independence in most of the African states, neo-colonialism replaced colonialism. Colonialism and neo-colonialism chained Africa's political economy to the international capitalist system. The result of neo-colonialism among others is the rather harsh international economic system that is unfavorable to African development. According to Carnoy (1984: 192),

> The dependent State, for Frank and the other world system analysts, is different from metropole States because it is organized in significant part to meet the needs of a powerful international bourgeoisie and because local bourgeoisie are relatively weak. It is inherently less democratic because it is much more difficult for Third World bourgeoisie to establish hegemony and thus for bourgeois democratic regimes to be legitimate.

To illustrate this, Frank (1972: 13) asserts that the most underdeveloped societies are often those "which had the closest ties to the metropolis in the past. They are the regions which are the greatest exporters of primary products to and the biggest sources of capital for the world metropolis and which are abandoned by the metropolis when for one reason or another business fell off."

Colonialism is to blame for the numerous conflicts in Africa, which Magstadt (1991: 420) characterizes as a war-torn region. Magstadt points out that "The persistence of armed conflict, both domestic and international, has been a stubborn fact of life for many sub-Saharan countries since the early years of independence in the 1950s. Hardly a country in the region has not been involved in a civil war or a border war." It is appropriate to state that war is a major factor impeding Africa's development efforts. These wars result from the pitting together of different, incompatible ethnic groups by colonialism. The cold war between the United States of America and the former Soviet Union also created its own wars in the African continent. President Bill Clinton of the United States, during his 11day visit to Africa in March 1998, acknowledged as much.

> U.S. President Bill Clinton has apologized for American actions during the Cold War that dragged Africa into a conflict that was not its own. . . . American competition with the Soviet Union had led it to "crush the aspirations" of people in Africa, where the weapons poured in by both sides caused conflicts yet to be resolved (Tunbridge 1998: p.A16).

And, indeed, most of the wars fought in Africa are fought with the arms supplied mostly by the superpowers and other European countries with vested interests in Africa.

African Political Elites

Another major argument of the dependency theory is that the political class in Africa, have no economic base outside the state. The capitalist class was yet to develop before colonialism. The neo-colonial state of Africa, according to Diamond (1989), owns or controls the vast share of wealth outside the subsistence economy. Diamond describes African states as *statist,* in that they control virtually all the means of economic production and distribution. In Nigeria, for example, the 1978 indeginisation decree gave the federal government all rights over oil and other mineral resources. And with oil accounting for over 90% of Nigeria's import earnings, Nigerian governments have become the dominant employer of labor in mining, agriculture, and even industry and services. Because the political class have no economic base of their own, the state becomes their source of economic acquisition. They cannot survive without the state. The political class is dependent on the state for their economic well-being, and this generates a feeling of insecurity.

> Because of their insecurity, the political class placed a high premium on power. They accumulated power by all means, did everything to secure it and to prevent others from getting it. As rulership became permanent, politics became Hobbesian: power was pursued by all means and kept by all means and the struggle for power became the overriding concern (Ake 1989: 52).

Experiences from Africa indicate that when the state controls both the economic and political powers, it fosters political instability and corruption.

To exacerbate this problem, African political leadership is not answerable to its own people. Their accountability is rather to the Western Countries and Multi-national Corporations whose financial aid is required to keep the government functional.

Arguments against Dependency theory

Arguments against dependency theories suggest that Africa's underdevelopment cannot be blamed entirely on slavery and colonialism. People holding such views argue that some African cultures and traditions are not compatible with capitalist development. An instance of this view is that Africans tend to be family-oriented. Individualism is greatly discouraged. For instance, the Oromos and the Amharas of Ethiopia are very self-conscious about how other members of the community perceive them. Individualism and over-ambition incur social stigma. Failure to comply with this norm can lead to isolation.

> To ignore this norm is to be ostracized as greedy or as an overachiever. This social ethic is prescribed in maxims: "He dies alone who eats alone," and "Death in a crowd is glory." In principle the morality of cooperating and sharing is good, but in practice the taboo on individualism both constrains competition and stifles aspirations (Magstadt 1991: 425).

Hale's (1990) response to this argument is that it is underdevelopment that reinforces such attitudes. Poverty also compels families to have more children to compensate for high death rates. Poverty is also responsible for the peoples' preference for male children and other familistic proclivities.

Yet another argument for Africa's underdevelopment is that African socio-political elites are accused of corruption and abuse of power. They are said to lack the vision and the competence necessary to lead Africa out of its marginalized position. Mazrui's (1974: 17) reaction to this criticism is that the interests of elites in both developed and developing world are meshed together. The elites of the dependent states have been, culturally conditioned by the West, and this affects their motivations, incentives and aversions. As such, it is not in their interest to break the structures of dependency.

To conclude, the dependency theory explains Africa's economic underperformance. The dependency theory argues that Africa's historical relationship with the Europeans adversely affected its development chances. The effect of slavery on the African Continent goes beyond the human loss. The psychological significance of slavery on the African people is yet to be resolved. Further, colonialism also tied Africa's economy to the international capitalist system. The structure of the international economic system favors the rich countries at Africa's expense. Colonialism brought together otherwise incompatible ethnic groups in one state, which gave rise to tribalism and cultural rivalries, making governance a nightmare here too. African peoples' outlooks are said to be guided by ethnic rather than national interests, which weaken potency for social control, and undermines national sociopolitical mobilization. African leadership is accused of incompetence, ineptitude, and corruption. The dependency theory finds that inevitable, owing to the structural constraints imposed by the international economic system.

In the examination of the Nigerian criminal justice system, it was noted that the system is corrupt and ineffective. It alienates the people, especially victims of crime. The section further explored the basis for the system's failing. We noted especially that the policies that informed the operations of the criminal justice system were not influenced by the environment. Again, the dearth of qualified professionals and poorly motivated staff are factors that undermine criminal justice system's effectiveness. We shall in the next section examine the Afikpo traditional justice system. The section begins with a review of the history of the Afikpo society and people to understand the basis of the system of justice.

Chapter Five

Historical Overview of Afikpo Town

I think that a historian's chief interest is in character and in circumstances. His concern is to discover the hopes, fears, anticipations and intentions of the individuals and nations he is writing about

—*Donald G. Creighton* -

There is no history of mankind, there are only many histories of all kinds of aspects of human life

—*Karl Popper* -

THE BRIEF HISTORY OF AFIKPO TOWN

Afikpo is the anglicized version of the word Ehugbo.[1] Afikpo town is the headquarters of the Afikpo North Local Government Area. It is presently in Ebonyi state, one of 36 states of the Federal Republic of Nigeria. Afikpo belongs to the Igbo ethnic group that inhabit the South Eastern area of Nigeria. The population of Afikpo is about 110,000, according to the 1991 Nigerian Census. Afikpo is located on 6 degrees north latitude and 8 degrees east longitude. It occupies an area of about 64 square miles (164 sq. km.). Afikpo is a hilly area despite occupying a region low in altitude, which rises 350 feet above sea level. It is a transitional area between open grassland and tropical forest and has an average annual rainfall of seventy-seven inches (198 cm.). Afikpo is bounded on the North by the Igbo-speaking peoples of Amaseri and Akpoha; on the South by the non-Igbo speaking peoples of Ebom, Ediba and Ikumoro; Erei on the South-West; Igbo on the East (non-Igbo speaking); and Edda group of villages (Igbo-speaking) on the West. Afikpo is one of the few Igbo speaking people's surrounded by non-Igbo speaking peoples' along the western bank of the Cross River.

Ottenberg (1971) observes that the history of Afikpo could be divided into four periods. The first historical period is the time before slavery when

Afikpo was linked to the coastal areas. This was sometime between the seventeen and eighteenth century. Not much is known about the people who inhabited Afikpo at this time. Ottenberg (1971) believes the population density of Afikpo during this period must have been low, and consisted of a small settlement of farmers. The people occupying Afikpo seemed to have lived in small groups with no indication of any form of centralized administrative set up in the area. According to Ottenberg (1971: 24), "the government may have been based on a simply uterine organization, with some centralizing agricultural rites. The people were apparently of a non-Igbo background and related to ethnic groups of the Cross River type." These people lived off hunting and fishing, and there is no indication that they traded with other people or traveled long distances.

There are findings that indicate that the Afikpo civilization existed as far back as the Neolithic age. Aja (1988) cites archeological findings by Prof. D. D. Hartle in 1966 that state that pottery production in Afikpo dates back to about 2935 BC. Further review of the archeological findings by Dr. B.W. Andah and Dr. F. N. Anozie date the pottery findings in Afikpo to sometime between 4,000–5,000 BC. This pottery antiquity in Afikpo according to Aja (1988) is the oldest pottery find in West Africa. There is a rock shelter at Afikpo that was first inhabited about five thousand years ago. Some writing forms known as Nsibidi or Nsibiri were in use in Afikpo and its environs during this time. According to Isichei (1983: 333), "Nsibidi was a form of ideographic writing, which worked on the same principles as Chinese, and was closely linked to the Ekpe relationship. A similar independent, system has been very fully documented for the Bambara of Mali." These writings were in the form of tattoos on human body, paintings or incisions on calabashes, stems, house walls, and drawings on the ground. The writings even though with some variations were in use in the communities adjoining Afikpo, such as Abiriba, Bende, Igbere, Edda and Aro. Other non-Igbo speaking towns in the region such as the Efik, the Ekoi, the Boki, Ogoja, Obubra and Ikom practiced also the Nsibidi signs.

The second period of Afikpo history, according to Ottenberg (1971), was during the slave trade, which lasted several hundred years up to the beginning of colonial rule. This period witnessed the immigration of people of Igbo descent into Afikpo. These Igbo-speaking people came from around Okposi and Okigwe areas and settled in several villages (Ottenberg 1971). During this time, villages grew larger and more concentrated. Hunting gave way to more farming activities as the people became more settled and organized for the defense of the area. Later, people from Arochukwu, another Igbo speaking people 50 miles south of Afikpo migrated to Afikpo via Ohafia and Edda village groups in large numbers. The migrants from

Arochukwu were mostly farmers and slave traders who dispersed into the Afikpo villages and settled. According to Ottenberg, the Aros were "tied to a complex internal network of slave trading in southeastern Nigeria which was dominated by the Arochukwu oracle, *ibini ukpabi,* employed in resolving difficult legal matters and in other problems" (1971:24). The Aro immigrants played extensive dominant political and judicial roles during this time in Afikpo.

Attempts at tracing the original inhabitants of Afikpo have yielded mixed results. But what seems certain is that these people were not Igbo speakers. A massive migration of Igbo speaking people from the north forced some of the original inhabitants of Afikpo to relocate and yet a substantial number remained and settled amongst the new comers. Ottenberg (1971) observes that Afikpo is an area of immigration rather than emigration. It is however, remarkable that despite the diverse origin of the inhabitants of Afikpo, that today Afikpo is a fully homogenous people and fully acculturated notes Ottenberg. According to him, Afikpo cultural features reflect that of neighboring Igbos and non-Igbos alike. An instance of this is the tradition governing farmland use which further supports the belief that Afikpo has been an area of immigration rather than emigration. He states:

> The origin of about two-fifths of the major patrilineages is probably through direct settlement of outside groups, in which Igbo predominate, especially the Aro. Afikpo is thus a complex amalgam of different cultures and languages in which the Igbo overlay, especially from Aro, has become the predominant one through time and has served as a unifying political and cultural force. While it is not easy to put matters together from the traditional histories, it seems evident that there were at least several different indigenous peoples at Afikpo before the Igbo invasions, much as there are today numerous small cultural and linguistic groupings east of the Cross River (1971: 47).

This account seems consistent with a famous Afikpo legend that credits Igbo Ukwu Omaka as the original founder of Afikpo. Aja (1988) claims Igbo Ukwu Omaka hails from Arochukwu. Igbo Ukwu's other kinsmen who migrated with him were said to have founded also Edda, Amaseri and Afikpo, and this took place about the 17th Century according to Aja. By this time, the people occupying Afikpo were non-Igbo speaking people known as the Egu, the Nkalu and Ebiri. The legend also describes another distinct group called the Ohaodu. The invasion of Igbo Omaka and his entourage forced the original inhabitants of Afikpo to disperse to places around Abakaliki, Nkalegu, Ezza-egu, Nkwoegu, Ikwo, Effium and other parts of the Cross River. The names of these towns reflect the names of the original inhabitants of Afikpo. Professor Afigbo (1981:13–15), a renowned Nigerian historian's account supports this thinking. He notes: "the traditions of the Eastern and North-Eastern Igbo including Afikpo, are rich in accounts of fierce encounters with various sections of the Benue-Congo speaking peoples who appear in their traditions as the Egu, Nkalu and Igbo" (cited in Aja 1988: 2).

Igbo Ukwu Omaka, the founder of Afikpo, introduced democratic rule in Afikpo. According to Aja (1988) Igbo Ukwu Omaka governed Afikpo through the Council of Elders. All members of the Council of Elders had equal say and vote, and decisions were arrived at through a consensus. It is important to note however, that democracy seems to prevail in most Igbo societies, and so was not peculiar to Afikpo. Igbo Ukwu Omaka migrated from Arochukwu where a variant of leadership of elders obtains. On this, Ottenberg (1971: xiv) notes: "the general view of Igbo life is that it is highly egalitarian, relatively classless, democratic, and based on decision-making through the openly arrived at consensus of group of persons."

Afikpo democratic processes were briefly disrupted with the arrival of Alika Obini, the leader of a powerful fetish juju cult sometime in the 19th century. Ottenberg (1971) and Aja (1988) observe that later migrants from Arochukwu inherited the juju shrine, called Otosi, from Alika obini. This group of people constituted themselves into a ruling group, called Amadi (the ruling people). Ottenberg notes that the "Aro patrilineages called Amadi, held a special and powerful shrine, Otosi, to which they sold rights of use to some other Afikpo, who then also became Amadi and were linked into the Aro system" (1971:24). The Amadi became very powerful politically through the control of slave trade. With control of the slave market, they were able to control other commodities such as "guns, gunpowder, cloth, iron, brass and copper rods" (ibid.) with which they exchanged slaves. They organized other Afikpo people to invade neighboring towns to obtain slaves for trade. Soon, they became also the dominant medicine men and constituted themselves to resolve conflicts in Afikpo. They charged fees for offering their services to resolve cases. Those found guilty of offenses who could not pay the fines they imposed were either enslaved by them or sold into slavery. According to Ottenberg, "persons found guilty of crimes they adjudicated paid heavy fines to them or were sold into slavery" (1971: 26). Ottenberg observes that the Amadi did not apply consensus as a means of resolving conflicts. Their judgments were rapid and final without any avenue for appeal. Fear and intimidation became the order of things. They had no respect for the democratic processes of Afikpo. Ottenberg notes

> The use of force was a characteristic feature of everyday life, whether by Amadi or other Afikpo. Revenge for killing was swift; thieves might be buried alive or cut up with a machete on the spot. Children and adults were kidnapped and sold into slavery for personal remuneration. A person's goats or other property were seized if he appeared to have committed an offense; only if he protested might a brief trial be held. Women went to the farms in groups under the protection of males (1971:26).

The leadership by force and the abuse of the judicial processes by the Amadi was a deviation from the democratic tradition of Afikpo. The Amadi therefore were resented and resisted by the Afikpo people. But it was the British colonial authorities that put an end to the Amadi tyranny.

The third stage of Afikpo history dates from 1902 when the British finally conquered Afikpo and imposed their authority on the area. Afikpo became a major colonial administrative center in 1905, when Afikpo was made the headquarters of the Cross River Division. The colonial authorities ruled through Afikpo people who were appointed Warrant Chiefs. The Warrant Chief system was disbanded in 1930 through out the entire country when it was discovered they were corrupt and autocratic. The British became the major authority in Afikpo and bringing with them Christianity and western education. According to Ottenberg (1971:29), "by the mid-1930s, then, we have a strong movement toward a two-caste system. At the top are the small handful of British administrators and Presbyterian or Catholic Missionaries at Afikpo." The British colonial authorities did not hesitate to impose their political, religious, educational and judicial system on Afikpo, as in every other part of Nigeria. The colonial government also introduced certain regulations on trade and other economic activities, including Taxes. It was also the colonial government that abolished the killing of twins and the system of slaves. The British colonial authorities also established the Afikpo Native Authority Court for the resolution of conflicts by the Afikpo people with supervision of colonial authorities.

The fourth period of Afikpo history starts from around 1955 to the present time. By this time, the Divisional headquarters were administered by, other educated Igbos from other parts of Igboland. The administration of the country was virtually in the hands of Nigerians as the struggle for political independence from Britain was almost won. A clear difference between the administration of the area under Nigerian administrators and that of colonial authorities is a remarkable interaction between the administrators and Afikpo people. Ottenberg notes:

> These administrators did not remain as aloof from the Afikpo as did the British, and they seemed to stand out less distinctively and to exhibit less power. What we find then, by the 1950s, is a rather open class system, headed by three groups, the new traditional leaders, educated Afikpo, and Nigerian administrators, which interact considerably with one another, with the remainder of the Afikpo below them, covering a wide range of wealth and status (1971: 31).

Until 1902, most of the history of Afikpo was not recorded. Afikpo history was passed down through oral accounts from one generation to the next. Ottenberg (1971) observes that there was no organized effort to teach village history. Every social gathering was an opportunity to recount historical landmarks, and during this time some inaccuracies are either challenged or ignored if it was not central to the case in question or where the motive of the narrator is not in question. Ottenberg cites three major avenues through which historical information is recounted and reviewed. These are "when a case is being tried, often to claim rightful ancestry or the ownership of property; when priests call up the ancestors during a sacrifice in a genealogical recall of the dead; and when men talk of past Afikpo heroes" (1971: 40).

This brief historical sketch illuminates the structure and background of the various traditional channels of conflict resolution. Again, an understanding of the history of Afikpo is imperative, which according to Palys (1995) is because "we must realize that the past has continuing relevance for the present because past constructions become the raw material for new constructions." How the Afikpo system of conflict resolution developed to what it is today is open to anybody's speculation.

There is archeological evidence that there were human settlements in Afikpo in the Neolithic ages, and that the original inhabitants of Afikpo were non-Igbo speaking. These groups of people were, assimilated by Igbo invaders in the 17th century. Most Igbo societies are relatively egalitarian and democratic. It is also possible to argue that the Afikpo democracy developed after a protracted conflict among the earlier settlers of the town. Ottenberg (1971) asserts that Afikpo is comprised of several ethnic groups who, over time, have completely assimilated into one homogenous group.

The Afikpo democratic system was disrupted twice in its history—first by the Amadi in the 19th century, and the British colonial authorities at the turn of the century. The Warrant Chiefs instituted by the colonial authorities became autocratic and corrupt. It is safe to conclude that democracy is deep rooted in the culture of Afikpo people as these interventions rather than destroying the system have tended to strengthen it. The historical accounts will be brought to bear later in our discussions of the Afikpo systems of conflict resolution.

THE AFIKPO ECONOMY

To appreciate the economic status and relevance of Afikpo entails the description of other political and social institutions operating at Afikpo since there are no statistics on the economic activity of Afikpo. Afikpo, besides being the administrative headquarters of Afikpo North local government, is also a zonal headquarters and the second most populous and important town in the newly created Ebonyi State. There are many Federal, State and Local Government offices in the area, including a Zonal and Divisional Police Office and High Court. Afikpo is a class B Nigerian urban area.

In 2000, there were approximately 46 primary schools with an enrollment of 17,817 pupils and a staff strength of about 819 in the local government. There are sixteen government secondary schools in Afikpo North local government, with combined total enrollment of 12,744. In addition private individuals operate more than ten secondary schools in the area. Other tertiary institutions in the area include schools of Nursing and Midwifery, a Teacher Training Institute and a Federal polytechnic. In the absence of statistics on the issue, it is nevertheless believed that the literacy rate in the area is quite high.

The majority of Afikpo, especially the elderly, are involved in subsistence farming and fishing. Afikpo has a strong farming culture, which is encouraged by the communal land ownership system that makes land available for everyone interested in farming. Again, Afikpo is favored with clement weather conducive for yam, cassava and rice production, food crops that are the staple food of most Nigerians. Because of this agricultural endowment, Afikpo is fondly referred to as the food basket of the South Eastern Nigerian area. Other food crops produced in Afikpo in commercial quantities include vegetables, peanuts, okro, and different kinds of fruits. Fishing is another occupation that attracts a sizable percentage of Afikpo indigenes. The Cross River that runs through Afikpo provides opportunities for people interested in fishing. There are also many lakes and streams in Afikpo that further boost fish production. There are many small-scale agricultural and fishing industries. Afikpo is also a major commercial center, which accounts for the existence of five commercial banks in the area.

Nigerian State Courts in Afikpo: the Customary Court[2]

There are three government courts in Afikpo: the High Court, the Magistrate Court, and the Customary Court. The High Court and Magistrate

Court are modeled after the English courts. The Magistrate Court and High Court, are presided over by one magistrate, and one judge respectively, who are trained lawyers. The Customary Court, on the other hand, is designed as an alternative system of conflict-resolution. It is meant to bridge the gap existing between the colonial imposed judicial system and the African indigenous laws. Section 4 of the Customary Court Edict states that: "Every Court shall consist of a Chairman and two other members who shall be styled Customary Court members, all of whom shall be appointed by the Judicial Service Committee." The Customary Court judges are not trained in law but, are expected to be versed in the customary laws of the area they preside.

The major difference between Customary Courts on the one hand, and Magistrate and High Courts on the other hand, as it pertains to criminal and civil causes and matters is that Customary Courts are empowered and encouraged to seek reconciliation at any stage of the trial process. In other words, the rules of evidence and other legal technicalities shall be relaxed, and the adjudication process should be open to wider range of facts. Further, the disputants legal rights are played down, with emphasis on reconciliation. Section 18 and 19 of the provided 1984 Customary Court Edict states:

> In civil causes or matters a Customary Court may promote reconciliation among the parties thereto and encourage and facilitate the amicable settlement thereof. Section 19 of the Edict states that in criminal causes where the Court has jurisdiction, a Customary Court may promote reconciliation and facilitate the settlement in an amicable way.

The Customary Courts impose a range of sanctions, including fines and compensation. Customary Courts also impose the sanctions of imprisonment. The Customary Court was established under the Imo State[3] government Edict Provisions of 1984. According to the Edict, "Customary Law, means a rule or body of customary rules regulating rights and imposing correlative duties being customary rule or body of customary rules which obtains and is fortified by established usage and which is appropriate and applicable to any particular cause, matter, dispute, issue or question."

According to the provided 1986 Amendment of the Edict, section 75, "the Jurisdiction of a customary court to try civil and criminal causes and matters under this Edict shall not affect the jurisdiction of the Magistrate's Court or the High Court to try such causes and matters."

The Customary Court Edict derives its authority from Sections 247 and 249 of the Nigerian Constitution. This section of the Constitution empowers State Governments to set up either Customary or Sharia[4] Courts according to the needs of their people. The only condition however, is that the laws applied by the Sharia and Customary Courts "are not repugnant to natural justice, equity and good conscience." Otherwise, the laws and operations of the Customary and Sharia Courts must not violate any laws of the Federal Government of Nigeria.

Informing the Customary and Sharia Courts policy is the government's interest in devolving justice making to the grass roots. The power granted to the states by the Constitution to establish either Customary or Sharia Courts according to the interest of the people constituting the state is in recognition of the diverse nature of the Nigerian people. There are more than 252 identifiable ethnic groups in Nigeria. Each of the ethnic groups have a distinct language and culture. Religion is also a major factor determining the policy. More than ninety-nine percent of the population of the northern part of Nigeria, are Moslems, and they account for more than 50 percent of the total Nigerian population. Christianity is dominant in the Southern part of Nigeria, which accounts for about 35 percent of the country's total population, while adherents to African religion makes up the balance.

Some historical information on the Customary Courts could further the understanding of its objectives. The Customary Court is a reformed version of the "Afikpo Native Authority Court," established in 1904 by the British Colonial Authorities following the colonial rule. Its legal backing derives from the 1900 Proclamation of Colonial Authorities Native Courts. It was part of the "direct administration" policy of Igboland by the colonial government, a marked departure from the "indirect rule"[5] policy applied in the Northern and Western Nigeria. Igboland was characterized as living in "ordered anarchy," by the colonial authorities since they could not identify any governmental institution. On the other hand, the institutions of Oba and Emir (Monarchy) in the Western and Northern part of Nigeria existed and wielded powerful influence over a large territory.

Afikpo, like most of the Igbo according to Uchendu (1965) had no political arrangement that could be called a federation, a confederacy or a state, similar to what the colonial authorities were used to. In most Igboland, when there is a case or matter that affects the whole village groups, representatives of the villages meet in a general assembly. Jones (1956: 5) notes that no village "could be bound by a law or decision made at a meeting in the absence of its representatives" (cited in Uchendu 1965: 45). All persons, including the villages, had equal rights and privileges. Decisions reached at these general meetings were through consensus, which was essential for order as sanctions against recalcitrant persons or groups were rarely forcefully enforced. Every adult Igbo has a voice in these meetings, despite the fact that the elders, especially the ruling age grade wielded a lot of influence.

At the village level however, what exists can be characterized as direct democracy. All adults, including men and women are represented. It is important to point out that the talks are, dominated by men. Women talk only when they are directly involved, either as witnesses, plaintiffs or defendants. The set-up is aptly summed up by Uchendu (1965: 46):

> The picture of the Igbo political community which emerges from these settings is one that is territorially small enough to make direct democracy possible at the village level as well as representative assembly at the village-group level; a government in which the principle of equality is respected; in which the use of force is minimal or absent; and in which there are leaders rather than rulers, and political cohesion is achieved by rules rather than by laws [sic] and by consensus rather than by dictation.

The political arrangement of the Igbo did not fit the criteria of a state with which British colonial authorities were familiar. The highest recognition accorded the Igbo is "ordered anarchy." Thus, dictating the imposition of direct colonial administration on Igboland, as against the "indirect rule" system on other parts of Nigeria. In this respect, Igboland was arbitrarily divided into Native Court Areas. The arrangement brought together otherwise autonomous communities. Each Native Court Area was an all purpose administrative set-up. The system was financed mostly through indirect taxation. The Native Court Area was headed by, a British district commissioner. Other officers of the administration included warrant chiefs, court clerks and court messengers.

The warrant chiefs were appointed by, the district commissioner often as representatives of his community. The criteria used in appointing the warrant chiefs were "those who impressed the District Commissioner with their courage to come forward and meet the Europeans. The traditional rulers seldom passed this test, and so were, for the most part, left out" (Nwabueze 1963: 70), cited in Uchendu (1965: 47). The warrant chiefs were given a cap of office and a warrant of authority, which was backed by the coercive force of the administration. Uchendu notes that while warrant chiefs were heads of the native courts their actual role was more as advisers to the colonial administrator. The native courts had the full paraphernalia of modern criminal justice system. Prisons were established. There was the office of the court clerk who supervised the court messengers. The court messengers were responsible for serving summonses, making arrests and maintaining order during court proceedings. The courts' judgments could be reviewed on appeal to the Colonial district commissioner.

What emerges from the foregoing is a struggle by the colonial authorities right from the beginning with understanding how to apply their concept of law and order to the Igbo peoples. The people could hardly relate with the European notion of justice. Such is the basis for cultural conflict and misunderstanding. The colonial "legal reformers" believed that the informal network of relationships that characterize traditional justice were not compatible with industrial societies. However, the Igbo people rejected the new arrangement. Colonial administration and the social and political institutions introduced affected the democratic character of the society. These were especially so with the imposition of warrant chiefs as custodians of the courts. These chiefs were blamed for inaugurating a painful era of political and social disharmony, political corruption, authoritarianism, and various forms of colonial oppression and exploitation. Shaidi, describing corruption in the Native Courts in Tanzania, notes:

> Many people think that the Native Courts, or rather those who function in them, are losing touch with the ordinary people who come to have their affairs settled by due process of law . . . A more serious criticism of these men is that they are even losing the confidence of the ordinary peasant, secured in their places by government backing and no longer subject to the former sanctions to which an African chief was liable at the hands of his people if he does not comport himself well, is losing them much measure of popular support and acceptance (1992: 9).

The visible collapse of the warrant chief system began in 1928 with the introduction of direct taxation which was exercised through the Native Court system. But things came to a head in 1929 when the property of women, were ordered to be assessed in one of the divisional headquarters. Women interpreted the assessment of their wealth as a prelude to their taxation since the same assessment had preceded the direct taxation of men in 1927. This sparked off a protest by women popularly called the "1929 Aba women riot," which left thirty-two women dead and several scores wounded. Reports of two Commissions of Inquiry into the riot led to the reform of the Native Courts between 1930–1931. Attempts were then made to integrate the native court system with indigenous political and social institutions. "Warrants were given to social units, such as villages, instead of to individuals. The villages selected court judges to represent them. The degree of flexibility allowed was such that some courts either selected presidents for each sitting or had no presidents at all" (Uchendu 1965: 48). The number of judges in the native courts was also expanded. The reformed native courts with several judges proved unwieldy, leading to further reforms.

Presently, the Customary Court or a Customary Court of Appeal according to the provided Edict as stipulated by the Constitution, shall administer:

a. the customary law prevailing in the area of jurisdiction of the Court or binding upon any of the parties, so far as it is not repugnant to natural justice, equity and good conscience or incompatible either directly or by necessary implication with any written law for the time being in force in the State;
b. the provisions of any written law which the Court may be authorized to enforce;
c. the provisions of any enactment in respect of which jurisdiction is conferred on the Court by the enactment;
d. the provisions of all bylaws or rules made or deemed to be made by a local government or statutory corporation having authority in the area of jurisdiction of the Court;
    A. provisions relating to general tax, rates or levies payable by the local community or imposed by the State Government, local government or town union.

2. A customary law shall be deemed to be binding upon a person according to Customary Court Edict of 1984, where that person:
    a. is an indigene of a place in which the customary law is in force;
    b. being in a place in which the customary law is in force, does an act in violation of the customary law;
    c. in cases of claims under a customary law of inheritance, makes a claim in respect of the property or estate of a deceased person and the deceased person was an indigene of the place in which the customary law is in force;
    d. agrees or is deemed to have agreed to be bound by the customary law.

Review of Customary Court Policy

The customary court is the Nigerian government sponsored alternative conflict resolution program. It is in response to the Nigerian populace's disenchantment with the modern criminal and civil justice system bequeathed to political

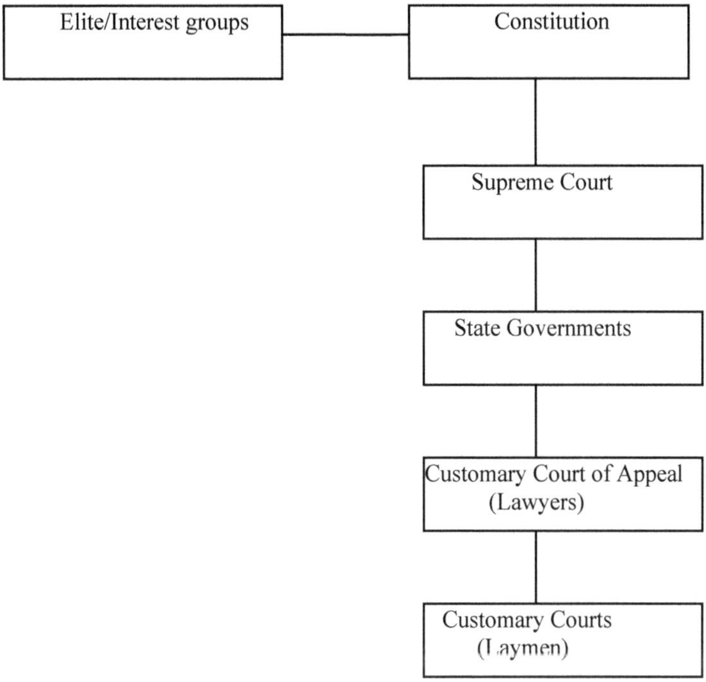

Figure 5.1. Diagram of line of authority in the customary court policy-making process.

independent Nigeria in 1960. Indictments against the Nigerian criminal justice system are that its process is lengthy, burdensome, and too expensive for Nigeria's level of economic development. Many also perceive the legal system as an alien system, which does not fully accommodate the custom, cultures and religions of Nigeria. The customary court is designed to address these conflicts, but its critics insist such policies failed in the past and will continue to fail to meet its set objectives. To appreciate the policy, an understanding of the policy and the policy-making environment is imperative.

First, the diagram above depicts the line of authority in the customary court policy-making process. Describing the line of authority in the policy making process as a top down arrangement may not be wholly correct. The 1979 Nigerian Constitution empowered the States as the diagram above shows to design policies that reflect the local customs of their people. Partly influencing the policy is the political climate of the time. The two major anti-colonial ideologies of the time were: the Negritude and Ujama[6]. Further informing the present customary court policy is the incrementalist[7] principle.

Introducing completely whole new programs may not have been feasible under the time, political and financial circumstances. It seemed practical to adopt and reform the colonial Native courts. Incrementalism reviews and revives past government policies. This approach is considered expedient since the new government lacks the money, time and knowledge to invest in designing new alternatives to existing policies. Political, time and economic constraints must have been instructive against adopting or searching for new alternatives. Dye (1978: 33) notes that "policy makers accept the legitimacy of previous policies because of the uncertainty about the consequences of completely new or different policies." Incrementalism, conscious of the complexity and difficulty in problem solving tends to adopt a cautious and step by step approach. The rational model as a policy making process can also apply here. In this case, a policy maker who is confronted with policy options bases his/her decision on a scientific approach to determine viable policy alternatives. He/she begins by identifying the objectives or problems. The alternative costs, benefits and means in solving the problem is examined. The best option is selected and implemented. Doern and Phidd (1992) recommend first identification of the problem and the objective of the policy. The alternative costs, benefits and means are thoroughly assessed. The best option is selected and chosen. The success, if any, is evaluated and changes are made to rectify errors.

Christie (1976) argues that the state has interest in maintaining its presence in all aspects of the peoples' life. The socialist government of Tanzania's sponsorship of alternative conflict resolution, according to Christie, should be understood in this respect. Here, local party officials with other villagers organize themselves for the purpose of resolving conflicts amongst the people. Stangeland (1985) in support cites the "comrade court" of the European Socialist Countries as established to handle cases that would have otherwise erupted into political conflicts. The courts act as "important safety valves in this society where strikes never happen and the labor unions are under strict state control" (p.3). In the former German Democratic Republic, for instance, according to Stangeland, the "Konfliktkommissionen" apply arbitration techniques in resolving labor disputes and other conflicts at the work place. Minor criminal cases are referred to this alternative conflict resolution board by the public prosecutor.

Giddens' (1989) critique of Durkheim's concept of the state suggests that all states have interest in maintaining control of the social and economic life of its citizenry. As such the state's involvement in all aspects of social control is in pursuit of the state's desire to exercise full control. Giddens states: "Durkheim treats modern democratic state forms too much as a simple extension of state power in general and he also underestimates how far the state apparatus can become a source of power independent of the rest of society" (1989: 18).

Further examination of state-society relations reveals that the state has more than a bureaucratic interest in setting up alternative conflict resolution institutions. In this respect, all states, including post-colonial states have similar interests in expanding government bureaucracy for the purpose of control. From this perspective, state policies have been motivated by its desire to acquire and maintain power. The resulting power relations can best be described as manipulative and exploitative. Kenneth (1977: 67) puts it thus:

> But one need only survey the record to realize that here, as elsewhere the development of the state has been that of constant aggrandizement. Necessarily, that aggrandizement has been at the expense of the two other components in political life—at the expense of society and the individuals who create society because it is their nature so to do. Of course this does not mean that the state has made no contribution to social and individual welfare.

Furthermore, in examining customary court policies, we must remember that the concept of customary law in Igboland is a very recent phenomenon. Customary laws are not coded.[8] The notion of laws as a matter of formal Bills and Acts of Parliament or Decrees and Edicts, is also novel. As such, it is imperative to address the issue from its origin. The notion of customary law came with colonialism. When Africa was integrated into the world capitalist economy through colonialism, the effect on African social and economic systems was enormous. Rwezaura (1992: 3) observes that customary law developed through the "interaction between the colonial administration and the various African political and social systems" (cited in Armstrong, et al 1993: 13). Rwezaura adds that the development and transformation of customary law during the colonial period occurred through a process in which:

> . . . custom and tradition became a means by which the local rulers and family heads bargained with the colonial state for retaining a part of their political power in their communities while individuals especially women and young people appealed to the colonial state to lighten some of their burdens, under tradition through the deployment of liberal values such as natural justice and equity (cited in Armstrong, et al 1993: 13).

Post-colonial African states operate several legal systems. The hybridization of African legal systems results from African colonial experience.

There is the customary and religious laws on the one hand, and the received laws, and the general laws, on the other hand, often based on the legal systems of the erstwhile colonial authority. The courts have the onerous duty of choosing the laws that are applicable. During the colonial times, customary laws applied to the indigenous Africans, while the received laws were applicable to the Europeans.

Customary law, according to Okere (1986: 25), "is a custom that has acquired the force of law." Okere further defines custom as the habitual practice of a group. Customary laws, Okere argues, are "essentially statements of natural rights and duties covering areas such as marriage and filiation, succession and inheritance, land ownership, acquisition and alienation; farming, crops and livestock, exchange, property and civil wrongs" (ibid.). Okere insists that Customary laws are laws because "not following them could invalidate actions, and they are customs because they sprang from long usage" (ibid.). Customary laws in Africa derive from the following sources:

CUSTOMARY LAW PROVED IN EVIDENCE

During native (customary) court proceedings, elders, warrant chiefs and other court officials were often asked to give evidence in matters concerning African customs. Regarded as experts on African customs, it is testimonies like this customary court proceedings that colonial officials, missionaries and European anthropologists drew up their lists of African customary rules. There are arguments that customary laws emanating from such sources are bound to be influenced by either the individuals giving the evidence or by those who wrote based on their observance of customary practices. An instance of this was given by Rwezaura (1992: 5):

> what the elders and other witnesses gave as evidence of customary law was a distorted and rigid version of customary law designed to express their idea of what the law should be and not what it really was . . . their versions were greatly influenced by the elders' anger and frustration at the loss of political power and challenges they were facing at the time from women and young men (cited in Armstrong et al 1993: 14).

The recorders of the court proceedings who were often Europeans tended to classify the court processes in the terminology they were familiar with. Besides, processing customary laws in colonial courts was an aversion of a sort. Customary law is process oriented, while colonial legal systems were based on rules. African legal systems' emphasis was on the process of bringing about peaceful resolutions to a conflict rather than on using rules as the basis for resolving the conflict. Armstrong et al (1993: 14), note:

> Customary dispute resolution processes de-emphasized rights and sought to achieve solutions to social disputes, which were considered just and fair. Thus in relation to customary law it was misleading and inappropriate to talk of rights and rules. However the preoccupation of Western courts with ascertaining rules of substantive customary law where, in fact, none existed resulted in the construction of rules which were often neither customary nor equitable.

CUSTOMARY LAW ARISING FROM PREVIOUSLY DECIDED CASES ON CUSTOMARY LAW

Precedence is an integral part of colonial court systems, as such previous decisions of the courts influenced subsequent cases. Armstrong et al (1993) argue that precedent cases were uncritically cited as evidence of the applicable custom in subsequent cases. It happened that such versions of customary law were accorded authoritative status and applied even to different ethnic groups who had different customary practices.

Customary Law decreed by State bodies such as Chiefs Councils and Native Authorities

These were efforts made by colonial authorities to regulate and systemize the diverse and diffuse sources and content of living (law) custom, (Armstrong et al 1993). The initiative was often from the colonial authorities through their agencies for indirect rule, such as the chiefs and other traditional leaders. The customary laws arising from these were made to serve the interests of the colonial authorities even if, they were formulated by the traditional rulers.

During the colonial period, the practice was to separate the judicial systems through the choice of law rules and the jurisdiction of courts, observe Armstrong, et al (1993). The practice changed with African states becoming politically independent, such that there is now more interaction between customary law and received and/or general law. The Constitutions of most neo-colonial African states provides for courts to apply customary laws. The customary courts must however, apply laws that "are not repugnant to natural justice, equity or good conscience." However, the nature of the justice, equity or good conscience is often not defined. Armstrong, et al (1993) note: "The most troubling aspect of this is the question, whose justice, sense of equity, morality or conscience are these to be tested against? (p.17).

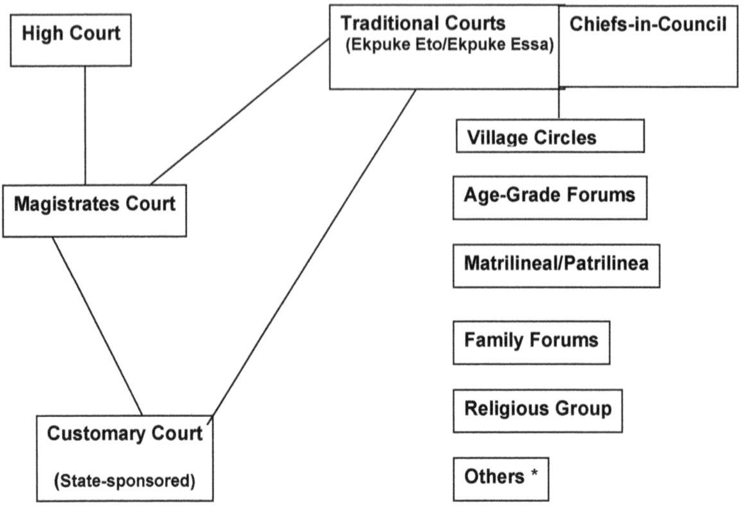

Figure 5.2. Diagram Showing State and Indigenous Institutions of Conflict Resolution in Afikpo. Includes The Elders Ad-hoc Tribunal, "Ogo" Cult, Okpota General Assembly, Oath Shrines, Diviners, the masquerades and so on.

There are two forms of customary laws applied by post-colonial African states (Armstrong et al, 1993). The lower courts are more responsive to changing patterns of the living customary law and are therefore inclined to apply it. The higher courts, on the other hand are rather slow to change, and are likely to invoke old colonial precedents, which generally deny women rights.

CONCLUSION

The planned study of the Afikpo Customary Court was abandoned because the Judges of the customary courts failed to cooperate with the study. All attempts to examine the records and interview Judges of the courts were refused. The Judges did not give any reasons for failing to cooperate with the study. The plan to interview past litigants of the courts failed too. Interviews with the few litigants we could track down was discontinued because the responses became too predictable and not helpful to this study. Litigants who won their cases approved of the courts, while litigants who lost their cases attributed their loss to corruption by the Judges. However, observing the courts in session was allowed, hence the brief remark on the structure and processes of the customary court.

The Customary Court sits at the Mgbom town hall. The court is presided over by three judges, all laymen. One of the judges is chair, and the other two judges are members of the Customary Court. All the judges are elders of Afikpo and are retired senior civil servants. They are all highly respected individuals of the community. There is a policeman standing by the door of the court during proceedings. His role is to enforce order and also to escort convicted criminals to the Afikpo prisons or to the police station for remand. Lawyers appear for litigants at the courts, ostensibly to guard against the tyranny of the judges.

Like all government establishments, the language of the court is English. The clerk of the court also translates proceedings to Igbo language if the litigants express difficulties with understanding English. During the visit to the court, the clerk of the court was from another Igbo-speaking town. He does not speak the Afikpo dialect. Some rural Afikpo people have difficulties understanding other Igbo dialects. Yet, the clerk was interpreting to the litigants, while the Judges who are from Afikpo and speak the local dialect conducted the proceedings in English.

Some litigants were unable to produce their witnesses when demanded. Apparently, some Afikpo people are weary of the length of time it takes to resolve a case in the customary court. Further, the presence of the police, and the fact that the Judges have power and authority to imprison people who do not conduct themselves properly are very intimidating. Some of the litigants found it difficult to speak up. Later my respondents confirmed that Afikpo people find the customary court processes intimidating and easily lose their power of speech. The atmosphere of the court was quite solemn, elitist, threatening, with no room for the democratic participation of litigants. Although the Judges of the customary courts are laymen, the structure, language and processes of the courts were very similar to that of the Magistrate and High Courts in the town. Based on the few cases witnessed, it seemed the Igbo justice goal of reconciliation and restoration of relationships were not important values for the court. The presence of lawyers, especially for some of the litigants who can afford it did not help matters. There is no legal aid for litigants who cannot afford a lawyer. The brief observations of the structure and processes of the courts left much to be desired, hence the study was abandoned, and all efforts concentrated at the Afikpo indigenous institutions of conflict resolution, which are examined in the next section.

Chapter Six

Indigenous Institutions of Conflict Resolution in Afikpo

"If there is light in the soul,
"There will be beauty in the person.
If there is beauty in the person,
There will be harmony in the house.
If there is harmony in the house,
There will be order in the nation.
If there is order in the nation,
There will be peace in the world"
—(Chinese Proverb)

There are many institutions in Afikpo for justice making. Some of the indigenous institutions for conflict resolution in the community evolved from the family and other primary groupings. In these institutions, justice-making is cost-free, participatory, and effective. Disputes receive immediate attention and resolution. Judgments and opinions of these institutions are respected and taken into evidence in the more formal institutions of justice-making. Mediative[1] approaches are applied since the goal is the restoration of peace and harmony in the group. At the more formal, centralized institutions of conflict resolution in Afikpo, cases also receive attention without delay. In some cases, these bodies insist that matters before them first pass through the primary groupings mediation forum. They will rather handle a case only after the primary groupings failed to resolve them, unless they are serious conflicts, violations against the land, or conflicts that are classified as abominations. Here cases are arbitrated and fines and other applicable punishments imposed. Here, as in other Afikpo life, the participatory, consensus and restorative principles in conflict resolution are followed. Some of the popular indigenous institutions of conflict resolution in Afikpo are discussed in this chapter.

THE AGE-GRADE SYSTEM

The age grade system is perhaps the most significant indigenous social and political institution in Afikpo. Most social and political activities are organized through the age grade system. The age grade is a strong medium for conflict resolution and the enforcement of compliance to social norms. The age grade[2] system is built on a cohort principle that organizes people born within approximately three-year intervals, initially at the ward level. In the larger villages, there are several wards, and the age groupings in the wards together form one big and strong age-set in the village. The village age groupings identify and relate with their counterparts in other villages to exercise roles that affect the village-group as a whole. Ottenberg (1971: 67) observes, "the age-set arrangements permeate Afikpo life. Age ranking is of considerable significance, as can be seen most clearly in the deferential behavior of members of younger sets toward those older ones, and in the rewards to the senior ones of food, drink, and money in various ceremonials." The significance and authority of the age grade system is partly a consequence of its membership. Presently, the age grade system attracts nearly total participation of all Afikpo adults. Consequently, it is very difficult, if not impossible, to perform any social and political function in Afikpo outside the age grade. Even the Afikpo political republican system is carried out through the age grade system. Most classifications and distribution of tasks and duties are through the age-grade system.

The origin of the age grade system is not known, but it is believed to be as old as the Igbo people and culture. This system is a secular institution hence it is not connected with any religious practice. Unlike other social institutions in Afikpo, the age grade has "no shrines that would connect them with past tradition, and no history of common origin" (Ottenberg 1971: 52).

The age grade system cuts across descent and class lines. As Ottenberg (1971: 52) observes, "ascribed status at Afikpo is mainly based on the principles of organization by descent and age; these two features create the groundwork of village life." Social class division and consciousness is low in Afikpo, and this is partly due to the age grade that groups together people of different socio-economic status. The only social distinction the Afikpo recognize is that based on age. It is noted that gender and wealth are important, but doubtful if wealth bestows political power, since leadership is exercised through the age groupings. This practice is quite widespread among the Igbo. Uchendu (1965: 85) notes, "In one context, the distinction between child and adult superficially overrides other status considerations in Igbo society. An Igbo child remains a child, no matter what his other status distinctions are. His senior who is less distinguished socially loses no time in reminding him of his age."

Formal age groupings begin as early as 17 to 20 years of age. This grouping is the most junior set, and their role generally consists of tidying the villages and enforcing discipline among its members, especially during social activities. According to Ottenberg (1971: 52), "there are usually between fifteen and twenty age sets in the community, each one covering a span of approximately three years." However, formal registration and recognition, especially at the village level, begins with the age grade of about thirty years of age. The age grade at this stage adopts a name through which it is registered and known. The age grades retain their names throughout the life of its members. Their roles and authority in the village and within the village-groups change with age. Depending on the size of the village, a particular age grade could number between about ten persons to a hundred persons or thereabouts.

The age-grade system has the following leadership hierarchy:

(a). the junior elders made up of men in their fifties and early sixties known as the "Ekpuke Eto" age grades

(b). the middle and senior sub-grade consists of members in their mid-sixties and above and they are known as the "Ekpuke Essa" age grade.

These last two sets make up the Council of Elders, and they are the major authority in the town and constitute the traditional government. The age-grade of persons in their fifties serve in executive roles and are responsible for the mobilization of the more junior age grades. They also assist the eldest age grade set to execute community projects. (See table below for the Afikpo men's age grades).

Female social and political activities are carried out separately from those of males. While females have a distinct organized age grade set, they are linked with their male counterparts. Their organization is limited mostly to married females, widows, and divorcees, and they cooperate with the male age grade set to execute community projects. One of the male age grades I observed has a joint meeting with their female counterparts annually on the 27th of December, when there is a need, or if they are planning a common project. The coed meeting serves to strengthen the age grade association and provides a forum for discussing issues that affect the age

Age-Grade	Afikpo Name	Approximate age of members	Basis of organization
Young Men	Ekpuke Eto Ogo or Uke Ekpe	28 – 39 years	Village
Junior Elders	Isi Elia	40 – 54 years	Village
Junior Elders	Ekpuke Eto (Ehugbo)	55 – 64 years	Village Group
Middle Elders	Ekpuke Essa	65 – 83 years	Village Group
Senior Elders	Onikara	84 – 90 years	Village Group
Retired Elders	Hori	91 years and over	Village Group

Figure 6.1. Table Specifying Afikpo Men's Age Grades.

grade. Since men tend to marry women younger than themselves, it is a rare occurrence when a man and wife belong to the same age grade. When this occurs and there is a combined meeting, everybody is treated equally and is encouraged to have open minds and contribute freely during deliberations. Meeting matters are confidential and can only be discussed with members and during meetings.

The Social Benefits of Age-grade

Members of the age grade organization derive tangible and intangible benefits from the age organization. The age grade therefore derives its legitimacy and authority from the social, economic and emotional support it provides its members. Until recently, the Afikpo economy was not money-based. As an agricultural economy, Afikpo adults depended to a large extent on the labor of the age grade members. Houses were built through cooperative efforts, and the age grade members were obliged to support one of their own. When age grade members assist a member in erecting a house or in farm work for example, the beneficiary of the age grade largesse is expected to feast the age grade afterwards. When individuals perform funeral ceremonies for their dead parents, they anticipate moral and material support from the age grade.

Another benefit the age-grades provide is loans with little or no interest to members. Age grade members can borrow money to pay hospital bills for their family members. Members can also borrow money from the age set for educational purposes, either for self or for family members. Members borrow to put themselves through professional apprenticeship, or to raise capital for business. The age grades raise money through monthly dues and special levies for communal projects. Money accrues to the age grades from their savings in banks. Some age-grades have also gone as far as investing their money in commercial projects. Other major sources of money to age grades come from the interest on money lent to members, donations from wealthy members of the age grade, or philanthropic members of the community.

Further, there is a strong sense of comradeship and connection within the age-grade members. The basis for this can be attributed to the tangible and intangible benefits that members derive from the organization. Besides, members of the same age set have grown up together and are involved in activities as part of growing up. As Ottenberg (1971: 59) points out, "with age mates a person can relax and joke and talk freely. Still, there is often minor bickering over whether a set member has fulfilled his obligations properly, and there may be much debate and talk over the matter, as is typical of many arguments at Afikpo."

The Functions of Age-grades

The age-grades collectively exercise many public roles. The age-grade is the basis of all social and political organization in the community. Prior to colonialism, the age-grades were like the reserve army of the state, to be mobilized in times of war or other emergencies. Presently, the age-grades play many policing roles for the indigenous government. They collect fines and enforce the laws of the land. They mobilize their members to construct and repair the market, schools, hospitals, community buildings, and farm and market paths. Above all, the age-grade's most important function is the control it exercises on the behavior of its membership. Any bad behavior of an age-grade member affects the reputation of the age-grade. Members who misbehave or are involved in criminal activities are heavily fined.

The age-grades effect control through reward for good behavior, and imposing sanctions for behavior falling short of expectation. For example, alcohol or drug abuse is an offense against age-grade rules. Failure to provide hospitality or support to a member of the age- grade in trouble could attract a fine or rebuke. Theft, fighting in public places, especially during age-grade meetings, is a serious offense. The use of harsh or curse words during meetings are also punishable offenses by the age grade. The age grade rules of behavior are strictly enforced, and penalties include fines and a letter of apology to the age-grade. Further, if any court of competent jurisdiction finds a member guilty of crime, the member is penalized again by the age-grade. Failure to comply with the age-grade penalty could lead to more punishments, including ridicule, ostracism and ex-communication.

A further function of the age-grades is to hold court to resolve conflicts within their membership. As Amadi (1982: 13) observes,

> among the Igbo age groups are very important. . . . These age groups are usually active in community development. However, they may react

> sharply when a member fails in moral duties. If, for instance, a member beat his parents or refused to care for them when he was in a position to do so, his age groups might penalize him quite harshly through the imposition of fines.

The punishment for elder abuse is fines. In addition, the culprit is required to engage all members of the age grade in wrestling, which ostensibly means been beaten up by your age-grade. Afterwards, the delinquent is required to buy presents of clothes, drinks and so on to appease the aggrieved parent. The offending member is also required to apologize to his/her parents and the age grade. However, the parent victim must first lay a complaint to the age grade. The age grade will constitute a tribunal to hear the case and make a determination based on the presentations by the aggrieved parent and the accused member. Witnesses are generally called to corroborate the testimonies of the parties to the conflict.

To conclude, the age-grade sets that wield authority within and beyond their age grades are that of the junior elders between the ages of 40—54 years, the junior elders within the 55—64 age bracket, and the middle elders, between the ages of 65—83 years. These three age-groupings form the major authority in the town.

The Role of the Age-grades within the Compound

Some villages in Afikpo are large, comprising more than one compound and populated by one or more patrilineages. The patrilineage is the extended family traced through the father. Some patrilineages are quite extensive, reaching up to a hundred or more persons. At the compound level, the three age-groupings play three important roles, namely, administrative, judicial and religious. Within the patrilineage groupings, the elders function separately in matters that affect only the lineage. However, they pull forces together in matters of interest to the entire compound. Here, the governmental authority resides with the elders. Other age grades may assist them in their administrative, judicial and religious duties, which create learning opportunities for younger age-grades who will eventually take up the mantle of leadership.

Within the compound, the administrative duties of the elders' grouping include sharing and allocating farm and residential lands, organizing community labor, and constructing and maintaining common houses and develop paths to markets and farms. They also organize the younger age grades to perform in ceremonies and other social activities.

The religious roles of the elders include the maintenance of the spirit shrine belonging to the lineages of the compound. The elders claim their power and authority for the exercise of religious and judicial roles derive from the spirit of the founding lineage ancestors of the compound. During festivals, birth and funeral ceremonies, the elders pray to the lineage's founding ancestors for guidance and protection. They also give a share of the food and drink presented for the ceremonies to the spirits of the founding ancestors. According to Otuu (1971:117), the principal function of the spirit shrine "is the control of the moral life of the inmates of the compound, especially the moral life of the women."

Another important role of the elders at the compound level is of a judicial nature. When there is a conflict between members of the compound, the elders arrange for the settlement of the conflict at the central meeting place of the compound. Here, every member of the compound, women, men and children assemble and contribute their opinions during the proceedings. The parties to the conflict state their cases, and are interrogated by the members present. After exhaustive debate, a decision is reached through consensus of the members present. If it is a dispute between members of different compounds, the elders of each compound gather with the litigants to settle the case.

It must be reiterated that while the elders are the major authority in the compound, they are assisted by the younger age-grades in their administrative, judicial and religious functions. Participating in these activities, the younger age-grades learn about the roles which they will play one day when it is their turn. Both at the village and village-group level, the governing authority resides with the elders. Here, their functions are mostly of an administrative, judicial and legislative nature. The role of the age grades within the village and village-groups level are as discussed in the "Traditional Courts" section later in this chapter.

THE MATRILINEAL GROUPINGS

In Afikpo, every person is a member of a matrilineal grouping. Ottenberg (1971:18) enumerated about "thirty-five matrilineal clans (ikwu), corporate, exogamic groupings, unranked with reference to one another or to other Afikpo groupings." The members of the matrilineage grouping can trace their descent to between three and seven generations. The members of a matrilineage can number between a hundred to a couple of thousands. The Matrilineage groupings, unlike that of the patrilineage, are not residential and are scattered all over the villages of Afikpo and beyond. While the matrilineal groupings are recognized, they are not represented in both the village and village-group.

The matrilineal groupings identify their membership through their common uterine ancestry. This is symbolized by the "Nja" shrine housed in the compound of one of the matrilineal elders. When the matrilineal groupings feel there is something amiss amongst their membership, such as illness, low birth rate, frequent deaths or failing harvest, they consult a diviner who directs them on how to appease their ancestors. However, the major source of power of the matrilineage groupings is the amount of land they control. As Ottenberg (1971:17) notes, "matrilineal descent plays a significant role in Afikpo, where some 85 percent of the farmland is controlled by uterine groups, as well as some stream areas and groves."

The matrilineage head is an elder male who wields a lot of power and influence deriving from his control of the grouping's farmland. As Ottenberg (1971:20) observes: "a matrilineage head must be a skillful diplomat to meet the demands of the members of his descent group for land while maintaining his authority." He is expected to judiciously allocate the matrilineage farmlands to members. This is not always the case, leading to mistrust and conflict over land allocation within the groupings.

PATRILINEAGE (UMUNNA OR UMUDI) GROUPINGS

Members of patrilineage groupings generally live in one compound or village. The Afikpo child is born and raised within his/her patrilineage. According to Ottenberg (1971:9), the "major patrilineage, *umudi* (children-husband), is a named, corporate, nonexogamous descent group claiming descent from a male ancestor, from whom it usually takes its name; its genealogical depth is approximately five to seven generations." The patrilineages vary in size from about a few members to several hundred persons, according to Ottenberg.

The leadership of the patrilineage groupings rests on its elders. In matters affecting the entire groupings, everybody is involved in decision-making. Like the rest of Afikpo, leadership is by consensus. Everybody contributes to decision-making by speaking during proceedings. What is important is the personal quality of the individual member—his speaking ability and knowledge of the issues under discussion.

Like matrilineal groupings, the patrilineage groupings also control farmlands and residential lands. Residential lands are allocated to members according to need and availability. The elders of the groupings are the custodians of the land, and it is expected that they will allocate the land judiciously to every adult member of the group.

Furthermore, the patrilineage groupings assemble to resolve conflicts within its membership. Most of the cases that are presented to the groupings are "disputes [that] occur between brothers and other male members of the minor patrilineage, and between wives and co-wives of members" (Ottenberg

1971:17). Disputes over land allocation are sources of conflict within the groupings. Cases that are not resolved within the groupings are taken to the village circles or any of the village-group traditional courts for resolution.

To conclude, it is important to note that every person in Afikpo is a member of both the patrilineal and matrilineal groupings within the society. Members of patrilineal groupings generally live in one compound or village, while that of matrilineal groupings are scattered all over the Afikpo village-groups and beyond. Both systems, explains Ottenberg (1968:5), are "corporate and property controlling with regularized internal leadership." Ottenberg, citing Goddy and Forde, observes that "fully developed double descent systems with organized matrilineal and patrilineal groupings seem to occur mainly in Africa, where they are well dispersed" (ibid.). Ottenberg argues that double descent sometimes results when a matrilineal grouping migrate and settle amongst groups with strong patrilineal arrangements. In this case, the Igbo group that has developed patrilineal arrangement migrated and settled in Afikpo inhabited by non-Igbos with a matrilineal system. Further, new political arrangements resulting from external pressure or just internal upheaval can lead to the development of double descent. Double descent can also result from internal conflicts within a group, arising from changes in productive controls and other economic changes. Again, changes in marriage rules and residence arrangements can also contribute to the development of a double descent system.

Patrilineal and matrilineal groupings play a central role in the molding of the Afikpo person's character. As Ottenberg (1971:8) notes, it is within the patrilineal and matrilineal groupings "that persons are initially socialized to many of the basic patterns of behavior which they later act out as adults. Here, attitudes towards authority, law, achievement, status and decision-making are largely developed in the early years."

It is important to point out that even though the members of the matrilineal grouping are dispersed over and beyond the villages of Afikpo, it is a stronger relationship when compared to that of the patrilineal. Matrilineal relationships are blood relationships, hence considered sacred. In Afikpo, one cannot marry or have sex with anyone within the matrilineal grouping, no matter how distant the relationship. The opposite is true for patrilineage groups. While relationships within the patrilineage groupings can also be functional, supportive, and expedient, it is frequently characterized by rivalry and bickering, though not in the magnitude or manner of that of co-wives. This phenomenon is aptly captured by Nsugbe, (1974:94), who writes:

> Or if, for instance, members of a matrilineage meeting as a group were taunted by a passer-by and jokingly accused of conspiring against their

> patrikin, the quick retort would be: 'Yes, but don't you hear the Ohaffia say that a man's worst enemy is his patrikin? . . . Sometimes the retort is the jibe 'Yes, father's penis scatters, but mother's womb gathers.'

FAMILY GROUPINGS

The polygynous family is common in Afikpo society. Every child is socialized from his/her family inculcating in him/her the values of respect, restraint, responsibility, and reciprocity. There is no other social basis for ranking among the wives or children of the extended family. Age remains the sole basis for social ranking, as is pertinent in all social and political life of Afikpo. As Ottenberg (1971:21) points out, "older boys and men have authority over younger persons and can order them to obey or carry out duties. A child soon learns that adults hold generalized authority over him, not only in his compound and family but in the village as well."

The family head is generally conferred with the authority to resolve all conflicts emanating within the family. It must be pointed out that the extended family is comprised of many men with their wives and children who live in the same large compound, where the oldest of the family is the family head. The family head is generally responsible for the allocation of land and other family assets to members of the extended family, but compliance with family rules is imperative.

The type of cases that come before family meetings include disputes over who should own what size or area of farmland for farming, or plots of land for building. The rules and conventions governing this practice are well established. Farmlands are divided unequally, with older males and widows choosing first. On the other hand, lands for building purposes are allocated according to need and means of the family member. Disputes emanating from this practice that are not resolved within the family circle may carry over to the traditional courts and beyond. Other cases that are handled within the family groupings include juvenile delinquency and domestic problems. The family groupings also function as crisis counselors, marriage and children's counselors.

Children are taught early in their lives not to take laws into their hands and to recognize all the channels of authority and conflict resolution. This is the case with boys of extended families, who as early as the age of five or six, are made to share sleeping arrangements. Here they must learn to organize themselves, make and enforce rules amongst themselves, and to report any case beyond them to the elders of the compound. As Ottenberg (1971:21) points out, "the freedom of boys to organize their own play groups, and to emulate adults, leads to age-graded groups. Boys have few formal responsibilities and they early develop the skills of taking part in and creating organized groupings, much more so than the girls, who are tied to the domestic female scene."

THE ELDERS AD-HOC TRIBUNAL

The elders of Afikpo could constitute a tribunal at anytime to hear a case. The elders of a compound, village or village-group assemble to hear a case, be it related to land, divorce or remarriage matters, or violations considered high crimes such as stealing from the sacred shrine or forest, having sex in the farms or yam barns, and so on. A litigant could call the assembly, or the elders could decide the hearing of the case. Since it is vital to avert a breakdown of law and order in the community, if the nature of a case is not suitable for the traditional courts or the courts will not sit early enough, a tribunal will convene. As Ottenberg (1971: 268) observes, "the elders' special court is not part of the regular administrative machinery of the descent groupings or the villages. It has no formal structure even in the village-group; courts are created and disappear as cases are tried and ended."

It is the nature of the case that determines where and when the elders ad-hoc courts sit. If it involves a man, an initiate of the "Ogo" cult, stealing from any of the shrines for example, the court would sit at the "Ogo" cult playground. If it is a remarriage matter, the court would sit in the village of one of the litigants, the one who initiated the case. This could be in one of the common houses in the village or an elder's house.

One advantage of the elders' special court is the immediate attention conflicts receive without waiting for the regular courts to convene. Further, it brings about the quick resolution of conflicts. Furthermore, as Ottenberg (1971: 269) opines,

> The lack of formal alignment of the judges with Afikpo groupings gives these courts an air of impartiality, though, as we have seen, this system is quite complicated. In theory, at least, it frees them from obvious commitments to social groupings. They are to act as elders, for they represent the voice of the Afikpo seniors in general.

Evidence of past judgments supports the thinking that justice, just like in the regular courts, could be miscarried. Sometimes, it is a strategy by a litigant to undermine the opponent's case, as he/she has little time to prepare his/her case and lobby influential court judges.

THE "OGO" CULT

The Ogo cult is the basis of Afikpo social, political and cultural life, especially where men play active leadership roles. Almost all social and political institutions in Afikpo derive from the Ogo institution. Ottenberg (1971) classifies the Ogo institution as a secret society. Perhaps this is so because its membership is limited to males—both indigenes and non-indigenes—and its rituals and practices are shrouded in secrecy from women and non-initiates. Every village, and sometimes wards in the case of larger villages, has an Ogo system. The Ogo institution, according to Ottenberg (1971:113), "is another world in the community, with its own special rituals, organizations, and rules of order, yet it is very much a part of Afikpo life. Some of its activities are unknown to the villagers at large, though others are public."

In pre-colonial times, initiation[3] into the Ogo cult could take as long as seven years. Presently, however, the process can last from a minimum of twenty-four hours to a maximum of four months or thereabouts. Boys from about the ages of three are, qualified to be, initiated into the cult. The educational value of initiation is now replaced with modern education and other skill and professional training, hence its shorter duration. One can say that initiation into the Ogo cult is now more or less symbolic. Young initiates are not immediately let into the Ogo cult secrets. They will acquire the knowledge with time if they show interest and participate in the activities of the cult. Nonetheless, such symbolism embodies training, improvement, and refinement of the mind, morals and taste. It is during initiation that Afikpo men are inculcated into the important values of Afikpo, such as intelligence, foresight, wisdom, leadership qualities and courage. Above all, Afikpo men must exhibit strength and manly qualities, must take an uncompromising stand against injustice and fight relentlessly to preserve life and the integrity of humanity. The initiation process is very similar to modern para-military training. Describing the initiation process, Ottenberg (1971:116) remarks:

> The basic pattern of all the initiations is the same: they stress physical strength and the ability to endure hardships. Initiates go into a sacred bush area in the village where they undergo physical ordeals and are introduced to the spirit of the society at its shrine. When they return, they are isolated from the normal life of the village for a period of time, during which they are instructed in the affairs of the society and are taught some of its secrets.

Any Afikpo male not initiated into the Ogo-cult cannot marry. If he gets a girl pregnant before going through the initiation rites, he commits a crime against the land. This behavior is also classified as an abomination for which the punishment is fines and ridicule. His family must offer sacrifices and perform certain rites to escape the wrath of the gods. A tiny part of his ear is also cut off to leave a permanent mark, and to deter others. It is the responsibility of parents to initiate their sons into the Ogo cult, and it is a responsibility every Afikpo parent takes very seriously, because non-initiates are prohibited from any adult social, cultural and political activities in Afikpo. As Ottenberg (1971:114) points out, "initiation is not only a prerequisite to serious political activity in the village but to the whole range of adult functions. It must be done before marriage, before taking any non-secret titles, and before joining an age set and grade."

In addition, most male activities in Afikpo like masquerade, dancing, wrestling, whipping, and so on are organized and displayed at the Ogo cult playground. Conflicts arising from the Ogo activities are quickly resolved within the Ogo to avoid it leaking to the outside world. Violations and conflicts are amicably resolved and fines are imposed on offenders. Participation in Ogo cult activities is very popular and voluntary, and the rules governing activities are strictly enforced. Because Ogo cult practices and processes are shrouded in secrecy, it is important to maintain this code of ethics, for there lies the major part of the Ogo cult's power. Ottenberg (1971:114), identifying the importance of secrecy to the Ogo cult, has this to say: "however true this may be, the society maintains its influence in the village and its controls over females partly because of this secrecy."

Conflicts that are heard at the Ogo cult relate to assaults, and the abuse of masquerade exhibition rules and regulations. It is widely believed that the Ogo cult is the basis of the sacredness of Afikpo peoples' traditions. Any violation against the Ogo institution itself is treated as a treasonable felony in Afikpo.

The Okpota General Assembly

The Okpota general assembly functions as the supreme court of the land. It is the court of last appeal and deal with issues bordering on the security of the community. It is at Okpota that decrees, laws of the land are enacted and changed. For example, it is at Okpota that the bride price is fixed and changed. Cases of political or constitutional significance are also addressed at the Okpota meeting place at Amaizu village. Other matters addressed at the Okpota include inter-communal or group disputes, murder cases (especially when it involves neighboring towns), and cases of corruption involving the traditional court judges. Cases tried at Okpota could originate at the traditional courts and are transferred to Okpota if they are of a very sensitive nature and deeply affect the culture of Afikpo. It is true that the elders sitting at the traditional courts are the ultimate authority in Afikpo, but at the traditional courts, there is no requirement that all the constituent village groups be represented.

At Okpota, all Afikpo adult males in principle participate in the meeting. An Afikpo male is considered an adult when he has gone through the Ogo initiation rites, which could be as early as the age of three. Women do not participate in the Okpota general assembly. Before the meeting takes place, a roll call is made to ensure that all the component villages of Afikpo are represented, otherwise the meeting will not hold, as no village not represented at the meeting will be bound by any decisions made at the assembly. At Okpota general assembly, participants sit in sections reserved for their age-grade—there is a sitting place for the senior, middle and junior subgrades during the assembly. There is also a place for visitors and litigants. Anyone present may contribute to the proceedings. Cases are presented and thoroughly debated before a decision is reached. Again, the consensus principle prevails. If the general assembly fails to reach a consensus on the matter, the case is usually postponed. If it is a matter involving two or more parties, the litigants are asked to leave after presenting their case and their cross-examination. Their absence is to allow participants at the assembly free hand in deliberation. As Ottenberg (1971:276–7) points out,

> General agreement is usually necessary before a matter is settled. Again, the verbal quality of the Afikpo is evident: there is much talk and argument, and debate is likely to be lively and skillful. When a decision is reached, those who were asked to leave can return, and the elders' spokesman, frequently the oldest man present, gives the decision. If he does not wish to do so, he may ask another to spell it out, or let the elders select a person, sometimes the spokesman of the middle subgrade.

At Okpota general assembly no oaths are administered. However, there is a strong belief that the Okpota ground is a sacred place, and there are repercussions if one tells a lie during deposition in the assembly. Aside from Okpota, another Afikpo general assembly takes place at Amangbala village Ogo playground. Here other issues of political and cultural nature are addressed. If women are involved in the matter and are to participate in the deliberations, only a section of the meeting place, not the entire meeting ground is used. As in all meetings in Afikpo the consensus, egalitarian and democratic principles apply. Further, the third place where Afikpo general assembly takes place is at the Ogo playground at Amachi village. Only ceremonial activities, like the crowning of the Afikpo traditional chief takes place here.

OATH SHRINES[4]

Oath swearing is very central to the resolution of conflicts, and as such oath shrines are major institutions of conflict resolution in Afikpo, considering the Afikpo society lacks any scientific methods of ascertaining facts. In cases where the truth or falsity of the matter is difficult to prove, oath swearing becomes the only alternative if the case is to be resolved. Oath swearing and divination is used to identify the wrong doer and to determine guilt. It works both ways. The accused uses oath swearing to demonstrate his/her innocence, while the accuser uses it to corroborate his/her position. The notion is that the supernatural will acquit the innocent and convict the guilty. If a litigant who swears an oath gets sick and dies within the year, she/he is presumed guilty and that permanently resolves the case. The litigant is absolved of all guilt if she/he does not die after a year of swearing an oath. Either way, the case is finally resolved after the oath swearing. Ottenberg (1971: 254) declares that:

> Swearing an oath is one method of resolving a case when disagreement seems to hinge on the words of one of the litigants, often over whether he took a certain action or not. The judges usually determine whether an oath should be taken, although litigants often suggest it themselves. Clearly, the threat of swearing is often used by groups or litigants to direct the course of a case.

Ottenberg identifies three of the most important cases where oath swearing is used. These are "(1) when a person is accused of theft and denies it; (2) cases of adultery, where the woman usually swears; and (3) matters concerning the illegal use of magic or poison." Men also swear oaths in adultery cases. However, a man's involvement in adultery is only an issue when he and the woman involved are from the same village.

For the purposes of oath swearing, there are six main oath shrines in Afikpo located at Amachi, Amaizu, Amankwo, Enohia, Ugwuegu elu and Ozizza villages, and they are controlled by a major patrilineage who also appoints the shrine priest from within the lineage. Some of the shrines are more popular for some cases than others. However, which shrine to use for the oath is determined by the elders/judges presiding over a case, informed by their personal experience or knowledge. Proximity to the litigants is also an important factor. The complainant or defendant can also suggest a shrine, but this will have to be negotiated and consensus on the matter reached. In the case of a woman accused of adultery, however, the shrine is sometimes brought to her village by the priests, otherwise, all swearing is done at the shrine ground.

People swearing oaths, must be supported by the family, especially from the matrilineal lineage. The family members of the litigant are in attendance to verify that the wordings of the oath are appropriate and accurately convey what the case is about. Fears that the priests could be bribed to manipulate the wordings to say something else other than what is being contested is widespread. As such, the wording of the oath is agreed upon in advance before the actual swearing takes place. As Ottenberg (1971:206) describes, "the swearer stands before the shrine, repeating what he has agreed to claim. The priest then takes a palm frond, dips it into the shrine pot, waves it about the swearer's head, and touches it to the person's tongue. This seals the oath."

However, oath swearing as a method of establishing one's innocence is problematic in many respects. An individual one has a dispute with could falsely accuse the other of wrongdoing or another offense. The only way one can extricate him/herself from the stigma of crime is to swear an oath of innocence before the shrine. Refusal to swear to the oath is automatically interpreted as guilt of the crime alleged. This then leaves a permanent stigma for an individual, with serious repercussions made worse by the close knit living arrangement in the community. Sometimes, "relatives or age mates of a potential oath taker may acknowledge the person's guilt and pay the fine to prevent him from risking his life, especially if it does not seem to be a major matter," notes Ottenberg (1971: 255).

Notwithstanding the frequent use of oaths in Afikpo judicial processes, oath taking is a very serious undertaking. Few families would allow their own to swear to an oath until extensive conferences and probings have occurred, and they are assured of their relation's innocence, bearing in mind the strong belief that any guilty person who swears an oath will die within one year. Further, one that swears an oath is not expected to leave town for a period of one year. The reason is that people would suspect the individual of having procured a charm to neutralize the effects of the oath. As a precaution, the individual is forbidden to consult fetish doctors or consult a diviner. The individual is also not allowed to perform sacrifices for him/her self or use certain medications. Yet allegations that people who swore the oath already possess amulets as antidotes to the workings of the shrine are not uncommon. Nevertheless, elderly people as litigants are not supposed to swear to an oath for the fear that they may die of old age related illnesses and that might be attributed to guilt of the crime. Although, younger relations could swear on behalf of their old parents or relations, few would be willing to take such risks for there is always a chance that the individual is guilty.

If an individual who swears an oath does not die after one year, he/she is deemed innocent. He/she and family, friends and other well-wishers celebrate all over the village and the central market. Further, if a pregnant woman swears an oath and safely delivers her baby, she is deemed innocent of the charge. If an individual prompted the oath swearing through his/her accusations, he/she is expected to ring a bell throughout the village and the central marketplace, renouncing his/her allegations.

When parties to a case are related in any way in Afikpo, however, oath swearing is not permitted. In instances where oath swearing would have been administered, the litigants are made to prepare food each, mix them up and eat them together. This act of food sharing symbolizes a communion, which according to the cultural beliefs signify permanent settlement of the case, and agreement that no party to the conflict can plan any evil against the other without suffering unpleasant consequences.

Oath swearing in Africa has other uses besides that of settling disputes. Oaths are used to either build or strengthen relationships. For example, when two or more people are entering into business partnerships, they could take oaths of truthfulness, honor and association. People involved in oath taking are morally and mystically bound by the conditions of the oath. Violation of the spirit and conditions of the oath are said to bring misfortunes and even death to oath takers. Mbiti (1970: 212) describes other positive uses of oath swearing in Africa, and states:

> Formal oaths are used as another method of establishing and maintaining good human relationships. There are oaths, which bind people mystically together, the best known being the one which creates what is rather loosely referred to as 'blood-brotherhood.' By means of this oath, two people who are not immediately related, go through a ritual which often involves exchanging small amounts of their blood by drinking or rubbing it into each other's body. After that they look upon each other as real 'blood' brothers or sisters, and will behave in that capacity towards each other for the rest of their lives. Their families are also involved in this 'brotherly' contract, so that for example, their children would not intermarry.

DIVINERS

Diviners play very important roles in conflict resolution in Afikpo. Diviners are believed to have supernatural powers to see what the ordinary person does not. As Parrinder (1970:119) notes, "divination or augury, foretelling the future by magical acts, is very popular in Africa. Geomancy, divining by figures on the earth, is found throughout the continent. . . . Divination is not only a means of discovering things to come, but is also used to uncover past secrets, and to smell out witches and sorcerers."

There are many diviners in Afikpo, and hardly any village is without one. They are consulted when culprits are not known. They are also useful in the identification of offenders when there are many suspects involved. They are very popular in the resolution of theft and sorcery cases. People accused of wrongdoing may suggest going to a diviner to prove their innocence. Consulting diviners to establish one's innocence is cheaper, faster and less risky than that of oath swearing. Diviners' roles are of a multipurpose nature in Afikpo. Some are more popular in one aspect of their occupation than others. They are fact finders, soothsayers, religious specialists, and herbalists. Describing diviners, Ottenberg (1971:207) states,

> they represent the major source of explanations for "troubles" of all kinds, recommending sacrifices and preparing medicines and magical substances to use as cures. They prescribe remedies for virtually all physical and mental illnesses, for the lack of children, for financial troubles, for persons who have numerous accidents, and for crop failures, and they are asked to determine the causes of death or the reasons why absent persons do not return home. They may help persons carry out sacrifices or rituals that they themselves have prescribed, if no priest is involved.

Diviners have high social and economic status and enjoy considerable respect in Afikpo, especially if they are good at their occupation. Diviners are sometimes held in awe and few would like to get into a dispute with them. Prior to the advent of modern medicine, they were, together with herbalists the few 'doctors' around, and popular ones got wealthy from their practice. However, diviners are consultants in all aspects of life in Afikpo. They are consulted at the onset of the farming season for advice on how to ensure a good crop yield. People planning a business trip consult diviners to ascertain if their trip will be fruitful. They are also asked to prepare amulets to fortify an individual against misfortunes such as accidents and loss of valuables through theft, and so on.

Another important role of diviners in Afikpo is their identification of ancestors that have reincarnated into the children of their clients. They perform sacrifices to ward off evil spirits on land, especially lands that are under dispute. They also prepare love potions for people, popular amongst co-wives and young suitors.

Nevertheless diviners' opinions as to the guilt of an individual in theft matters are hardly accepted as gospel truths, unless the offender confesses or his/her guilty conscience gives him/her away. Sometimes several diviners can be consulted with contradictory outcomes. Although, this makes it very problematic in the resolution of a case, their revelations remain important and can be entered into evidence during trials in any of the judicial tribunals of Afikpo. Further, diviners play major roles in promoting the moral values of the community. Diviners are agents of resocialization, "particularly in giving reasons why people have died, be a considerable factor in expressing and upholding the moral code of the community, since death often comes as a result of an offense against this code" (Green 1964, as reproduced in Ogbaa 1999:145).

THE TRADITIONAL COURTS

In Afikpo, cases not resolved at the aforementioned indigenous institutions of conflict resolution are taken to the traditional courts. There are two traditional courts situated at the central market square. One of the courts is administered by the junior sub-grade made up of men in their fifties and early sixties known as the (Ekpuke Eto age-grade). The second court is managed by the middle and senior sub-grade consisting of members in their mid-sixties and above and they are known as (the Ekpuke Essa age-grade). These age-grades constitute the Council of Elders, and they are the ultimate authority in Afikpo who oversee the traditional government.

The two courts sit simultaneously every four days,[5]every eke day, which is the main market day when Afikpo people do their major buying and selling. My respondents could not confirm whether the traditional courts were located at the central market by design or coincidence. The courts may have been located there for ease of meeting and dissemination of its decisions and for constitutional symbolism. However, Ottenberg (1996) suggests that the location of the market and traditional courts are neutral grounds, as such no village or group of people of Afikpo could lay claim to the land. In any event, major decisions of the courts are announced in the market. Further, judges of the courts are directed to announce decisions that are of public interest to their respective villages. Since the courts hold at the market days, decisions easily circulate round the market, which the people pass on to their villages. Attendance to the courts by the constituting age-grades is not compulsory. However, money realized from litigants and other ceremonial performers for each day of business is distributed to members present. Members who were not present in court do not partake in the sharing of the money realized during the day's business.

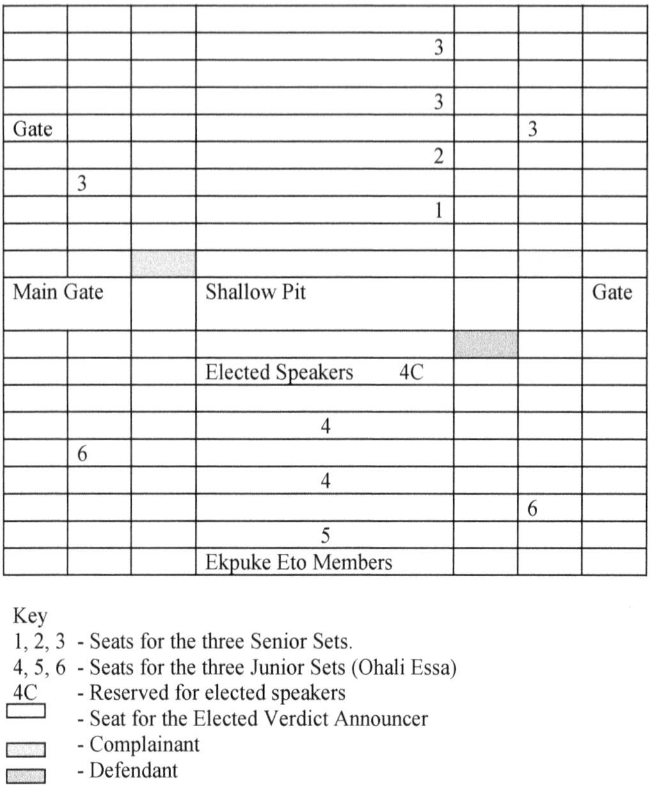

Figure 6.2. Diagram of Sitting Arrangements in the Essas' Court (source: Otuu 1977)

The Ekpuke Essa (Traditional Court)

Some understandings of the operating methods of one of the courts, the court operated by the middle and senior sub-grade will suffice for our purpose. The court's duties are twofold—one is legislative, and the other is judicial. Let us first examine the sitting arrangements of the court.

Sitting positions in the court are not arbitrary but follow certain hierarchical order. As indicated earlier, the Essa age-grade is comprised of six age-sets. Otuu (1977) points out that at the court members sit according to their ages, with the first three age sets known as the upper (isi Essa) sitting together in seats numbers one to three similar to the sitting arrangements at the Ekpuke Eto court. The age deference principle governs every Afikpo life, and is also applicable at the court. However, age only determines functions and to some extent authority, but what is more important at the courts' is one's speaking ability and knowledge of the custom and tradition of the land. Seats numbers four to six are occupied by the three junior sets (Ohali Essa). The court also has four elected members who are functionaries of the court. The elected members generally come from the third and fourth age sets—in other words, they are drawn from the last set of the upper Essa and the first set of the junior age set. The four elected judges occupy the front seat close to the litigants. The basis for election, are one's speaking ability, wisdom, intelligence and knowledge of the customs and tradition of the land. One of the elected members of the court is the secretary who keeps records of the courts' transactions. As Otuu (1977: 126), describes,

> The selected members are powerful speakers who take leading part in deciding cases and making laws. These are, selected by the general body, on the day the Essa's take up office. Those selected are men who have distinguished themselves as orators, who have a vast knowledge of local history and men who can draw from their rich store of proverbs to give weight and conviction to their argument.

Another elected position of the court is the court announcer. The court announcer generally comes from the upper Essa sub-grade. The court verdict announcer's seat is in the front row and close to the litigants. The court verdict announcer's position is also a very important position in the court, and one that requires high speaking skills and intelligence, a good combination of wit and humor, and ability to interpret the speeches and nuances of other speakers.

Legislative functions

The Ekpuke Essa traditional court is the only branch of the Afikpo indigenous government authorized to enact laws and decrees. However, this legislative function is also exercised by the Afikpo general assembly meeting at the Okpota. The court passes laws governing marriage, especially fixing bride-prices and marriage and re-marriage procedures. Other laws enacted by the court include that governing the farming cycle—especially the planting and harvesting of yams, the chief crop of the people. The court also determines the wage rate on hired farm labor. It is important to note that the court regulates only farm labor wages and not that of any other economic or social activity. However, they have been known to determine the prices of some staple foods, and also make laws prohibiting the sale of certain food commodities outside the town. The laws are generally intended to stabilize the price of labor or to reduce the cost of some foodstuffs to reduce inflation in the town.

The Ekpuke Essa court also passes laws designating the dates of the various festivals observed in the town. In December 1997, during the field trip for this research, the court passed a law banning the showing of pornographic movies in the town. Recently, the court passed a decree limiting the operations of the Union of Road and Transport Workers and Owners of Afikpo. The Union had vehemently protested this decision on the grounds that their activities were outside the administration of the traditional government, since the Union was legitimately registered with the Nigerian government. The court insisted that the control of some of the activities of the Union fell within their jurisdiction since the actions of the Union affects the life of the Afikpo people. The Union had increased the tariff on the haulage of foodstuffs into and out of Afikpo. This policy of the Union led to the increase of the cost of staple foods in Afikpo. The court claimed the decision of the Motor Workers Union raised inflation in the town and was likely to lead to the breakdown of law and order in the town.

The court has also been known to pass a decree restricting the places where Afikpo women could go to buy and sell foodstuffs. Such laws are passed when the court believes the lives of the women traders are in danger, either due to known cases of women actually killed doing business in such places, or the threat of danger due to known hostilities between Afikpo and the towns in question. Sometimes, the laws barring Afikpo women from trading in certain places are ostensibly to regulate the chastity of Afikpo women due to information or rumors that the women traders were also partly prostituting in the trade posts.

The Ekpuke Essa's law making function, like their arbitration roles, is governed by the consensus principle. Extensive debates follow the introduction of any proposed law until a consensus is reached on the issue. When a decision is reached on the issue, a member of the junior grade is invited to go to the central market and announce the decision of the court. Other members of the court are also directed to announce to their respective villages the decisions of the court.

Judicial Functions and Procedure

Most of the cases handled by the Ekpuke Essa traditional court include sorcery, witchcraft, bride wealth cases, divorce, and remarriage matters. Others are land, debt affairs, inheritance matters, theft, assaults, the failure of persons to perform communal labor and debt recovery. The court also handles cases relating to the violation of the traditional custom.

The procedure for bringing cases to the court is simple. A complainant walks into the court through the main entrance and drops a token amount of money into the shallow pit, indicating he has a case. An elder then asks him what the matter is about. The complainant presents his case without going into details since the defendant may not be present in court at the time. The court then fixes a hearing date during the next sitting or so and asks a member from the village of the defendant to inform him or her that there is court order for him or her to appear before the court at a given date.

On the day fixed for the hearing of the case, the defendant enters and drops some money into the shallow pit to indicate his or her willingness for the case to be heard by the court. Thereafter, one of the oldest members of the court judges stands up and gives a formal greeting, announces the presence of the litigants and directs the court proceedings to begin. The trial will commence, unless a member raises an objection.[6] Following the rule of the court, the complainant presents his or her case, without any interruption. After that, the defendant is asked to respond to the allegations of the complainant. The litigants after presenting their cases are asked to call witnesses. After hearing from both litigants and their witnesses, the litigants and their witnesses are cross-examined. Leading the cross-examination are the four elected members of the Essa age-grade. The litigants are asked to step out of court after presenting their cases, and when the judges believe they have sufficient facts to deliberate upon. The litigants and their witnesses are asked to leave the courts so as not to influence the deliberations of the court. Subsequently, according to Otuu (1977: 128),

> The views of the disputants and their witnesses are rigorously examined. Debate on the issue continues and any Essa member present is free to air his views. This is the occasion for the elders to display their forensic eloquence and knowledge of the tradition and custom of the land. The matter is discussed until a consensus is arrived at. When a majority gives the approval sound—"Iyaa" or "Ehee," then it is taken that a solution has been reached.

When an agreement is reached on the matter, the litigants are invited back to the court. The court announcer will then pronounce judgment, first by reviewing the views of members and the basis for the decision. The presentation of the judgment is carefully worded such that no one is alienated. Litigants show their satisfaction for the judgment by donating a token sum to the court. The amount donated before and after judgment is not fixed and is left to litigants to give what they please. However, a litigant must put down some money—initially to indicate acceptance by the court to arbitrate on the matter, and after judgment, to acknowledge the court's judgment. Nonetheless, judgment on cases may be postponed to a later time if an agreement is not reached on the matter. In such cases more evidence or witness may be required.

When a litigant belongs to the same age-grade as the judges, his title of Essa is dropped and he is called by his names. He must also put down some money like other litigants before the case is heard. Women[7] litigants do not enter the court house, but must address the court from the court's entrance. Members of the public are free to listen in during proceedings but must do so from outside the courthouse. Only members of the judges' age-grade can sit down in the courthouse. All litigants must stand during court proceedings except women litigants who must address the courts sitting down. However, they sit outside the courthouse.

THE EKPUKE ETO (TRADITIONAL COURT)

The second traditional court is conducted by the Ekpuke Eto age-grade—the junior sub-grade made up of men in their fifties and early sixties. Like the traditional court administered by the Ekpuke Essa, it holds once every four days, on Eke day between the hours of 1100 and 1400. The court is modeled after that of the senior court and shares the same management structure. The Ekpuke Eto's court function is also two-fold, that of executing the decisions of its court and that of the senior court. Fines imposed by the senior court are, collected by the junior court. The court also arrests or summons offenders to either its court or that of the senior court. The major role of the court is the maintenance of law and order both in the central market, during social and political activities within the villages and the village-group.

Another function of the court is the arbitration of cases brought before the court by litigants. The type of cases handled by the court include landlord/tenant conflicts; fighting in the central market; petty theft; fraud and pyramid scheme offenses; other business related conflicts and the failure of people to perform communal labor. The court is also enlisted by the Afikpo Community Bank to recover its debts.

In the traditional courts, both victim/s and the offender/s actively participate in the defining of harm and the resolution of the conflict. The judges of the courts, sometimes numbering more than a hundred persons, adequately represent the community in the process. The guiding principle in the traditional courts is the vindication of the victim, and holding of the offender accountable to both the victim and the community. Further, attempts are made to reconcile the victim with the offender. The harm and confidence of the community affected by the victimization is also restored. Furthermore, according to Gluckman (as cited in Elechi 1996:345), the traditional courts all operate on the same principles as all modern judicial institutions in Nigeria. This is the "regulation of established and the creation of new relationships, the protection and maintenance of certain norms of behavior, the readjustment of disturbed social relationships, and the punishing of offenders against certain rules."

The jurisprudence of the traditional justice system has in common with other legal systems many basic doctrines, points out Gluckman, such as "right and duty and injury; the concept of the reasonable man; the distinction between statute and custom, and between statute and equity or justice; responsibility, negligence, and guilt; ownership and trespass; etc." (as cited in Elechi 1991:52)

The Chief-in-Council

The Chief-in-Council is another important institution in Afikpo for conflict resolution. Its role in conflict resolution is steadily declining however. In the 1980s, the Chief-in-Council played a more active and extensive role in the resolution of conflict. Perhaps, this is because the government sponsored customary court was suspended at the time. The institution of Chief (Eze) is not indigenous to Afikpo. Leadership in Afikpo is exercised through the council of elders and representatives of the age-grades. The Chief has no traditional role. The Office of the Chief is completely symbolic and like one of my respondents put it, "the Chief does not rule, he reigns."

The Chieftaincy institution was created by the central government of Nigeria to enhance the role of traditional rulers in the community. On July 19th, 1976, the Afikpo community in compliance created the Chieftaincy institution (Eze). "Omaka-Ejali" is the traditional name of the Afikpo Chieftaincy institution, and the Eze represents Afikpo community in the National Council of Traditional Leaders. The Chief (Eze)'s selection is the prerogative of the Afikpo Traditional Council of Elders. However, the selection must be endorsed by majority of the representatives of all the Afikpo age-grades. The Chief must be at least 65 years of age, and must belong to either the middle or senior age-grades. To be selected for the office of Chief (Eze), the elder must be known to be humble, of high moral standards, impartial and have a keen interest in the community's customs and traditions. The office of the Chief rotates among the five components residential areas of Afikpo. A new Chief is appointed on the death of the incumbent. It is important to note that following a recent policy by the Ebonyi State government, that five traditional rulers have been approved for Afikpo and each represents one of the five village groups that make up Afikpo, namely *Ohaisu, Itim, Ugwuegu, Nkpogoro and Ozizza.* It is important to observe that other traditional conflict resolution institutions of Afikpo are not affected by the establishment of traditional rulers for the five village groups of Afikpo.

For the purposes of conflict resolution, the Chief constitutes a council comprising the Chief and five members of the Council of Elders representing the five component village groups of Afikpo. This supports the claim that the Chief (Eze) of Afikpo does not rule but reigns. He is a symbol of authority, but actual decisions are, made by the Chief in Council. In conflict resolution matters and other decisions that affect the Afikpo people, two members of the Afikpo Town Welfare Association are incorporated into the Chief-in-Council.[8]The Chief is the only one who draws a salary from the State government. Other members of the council see their services as extension of their age-grade functions. Most of the cases mediated or arbitrated by the Chief-in-Council are either appealed from other courts in Afikpo or delegated by State institutions such as the government courts, the police or local government. Few cases originate from the Chief-in-Council. However, some Afikpo elites may seek the intervention of the Chiefs in their conflicts since the Chiefs wield strong moral authority.

The Chieftaincy institution as earlier pointed out is not indigenous to Afikpo. As such, few Afikpo people perceive the office as agent of conflict resolution. The Magistrate and Judge of the Magistrate and High Court respectively used to delegate some cases that border on Afikpo custom to his office. Other elders of Afikpo were integrated into the office to give this role a customary authority. In recent times, few cases are delegated to the office of the Chief. In the eighties when cases were devolved to the Chief, the Government sponsored customary court was not in operation. It is noted that the Afikpo indigenous courts were always there, but the Government was more comfortable dealing with institutions that have organizational structure similar to that of the government. The Chief-in-Council met this criteria, it has a hierarchical structure, and is able to record its proceedings. However, it must be noted that with regards to conflict resolution, all the members of the Chief-in-Council have equal power and say. However, the Chief is the government's representative in the community in customary affairs. The government arguably prefers an institution with a head that they can hold responsible. Another significance of the Chief (Eze) institution is that it is a formal link between indigenous institutions and state institutions.

The Masquerades

No one takes cases to masquerades for resolution, neither are masquerades a regular institution for the resolution of conflicts in Afikpo. Nevertheless, the role of masquerades in conflict resolution in Afikpo is significant and deserves brief mention here. Masquerades are a regular feature of Afikpo culture. There is hardly any cultural ceremony or activity originating from the "Ogo" Cult without a masquerade. As earlier stated, "Ogo" is a man's institution, hence, only men display masquerades. However, since the primary function of masquerades is entertainment, men, women and non-indigenes attend when masquerades perform. Although women do not participate in the exhibition of masquerades, satire is employed by women to accomplish analogous objectives.

There are three masquerades in Afikpo, who in addition to their primary function of entertainment and recreation are also involved in social control. There are "Oteru," "Okpa" and "Okumkpo." Masquerade displays like most cultural activities in Afikpo take place during the dry season—between the months of September and March. As a farming community, most farming work, including harvest take place during the rainy season. The dry season is a time when economic activities are slow and the people turn their attention to other matters. Ottenberg (1972:101–2) describes some of the activities of the Afikpo when they are not involved in their farm work. He states:

> This half of the year is one which the highly achievement-oriented Ibo of Afikpo turn their attention to realigning social relationships. It is the period when men take important titles by joining special title societies, thus raising their status and sometimes their power and influence. And it is the time when the elders have the opportunity to judge cases and disputes, especially in land matters. It is thus a period of productivity in social relationships. In the other half of the year attention focuses on gaining material wealth and subsistence through farming and fishing.

All masquerades in Afikpo wear masks and costumes. The men wearing the masks are not to be identified publicly especially by women and non-initiates into the 'Ogo' cult. Comments or information presented by masquerades are privileged. No information presented during the masquerade performance can be identified with any individual or groups of individuals' dead or living. As such all the actors are immune from prosecution or sanction of any kind. It is generally believed in Afikpo that it is the spirits who reincarnate in masquerade form. As Ottenberg (1972:102) points out,

> "[But] the crucial act of placing a mask on the face of a secret-society member changes his status from "mortal" to "spirit," and thus allows him to behave in certain ways with respect both to other players and to unmasked members of the audience . . . Masks in Afikpo help

> to create an illusion of distance between player and audience—people who are otherwise in close social terms.

To unmask a masquerade in Afikpo is a treasonable felony and one of the worst crimes one can commit in the community.

The "Oteru" and "Okpa" masquerades when they are not entertaining are employed in the enforcement of rules. When there is an intractable quarrel or fight in the village, the masquerades will intervene with the threat of force and disperse those involved and other spectators. Generally, the sight of the masquerades is enough to send everybody scampering to safety. Further, when an individual is convicted of treasonable felony, and fails to pay a fine and perform the required expiation rites, it is the masquerades that carry out the looting of the individual's property. They also have the power to demolish the houses of the lawbreakers and their paternal relations.

The "Okumkpo" masquerade's role in social control is of a different kind. The "Okumkpo" masquerade organize and perform drama for the community pleasure. Ottenberg (1972:107) observes that an "Okumkpo" "play may involve over a hundred actors, singers, and musicians, all masked and costumed." The masks accord the "Okumkpo" masquerades a certain level of anonymity essential for the important role they play in the community. One major function of the "Okumkpo" according to Ottenberg (1972:112) is that the "plays establishes them as effective devices for airing tensions in the village and for getting comments across that are otherwise difficult to articulate." In addition, the "Okumkpo" masquerade display reverses roles and youths instead of the elders direct the course of affairs in the community. That is, masquerades are, organized by younger men below the ages of 45. Some older men can participate, but the majority of the actors are not generally part of the ruling age-grade. Elders of the community, however, provide support. What is important is that the acting and the initiative to perform is taken by men outside the ruling age-grade. That the "Okumkpo" theater performed by younger men is a kind of role reversal, is aptly described by Ottenberg (1972:113):

> The spiritual forces of the Afikpo community are normally under the guidance of senior men who control and direct sacrifices and other religious rituals, in which young men play supportive roles, supplying materials to be used in sacrifice and food for the feasts that accompany some religious activities. But in the Okumkpo plays younger men, as masked spirit dancers (*nma*), are the spirits and control and direct affairs. The elders, as ordinary members of the audience, sit passively,

> having only the secular role of reacting to the players. This is another aspect of the reversal of the leadership roles of elders and younger men that occurs through the masked plays.

The "Okumkpo" acts and songs are loaded with moral rectitude. The "Okumkpo" through their songs and acts express disappointment and sorrow over behaviors by prominent community members, elders and leaders that deviate from Afikpo norms and that are unethical. The acts and songs decry the greedy, selfish and foolish tendencies of some elders. For example, elders who may have abused their power of authority in some ways, or may have exploited some situations in a clever manner, or a man or family or lineage who exploit their in-laws during dowry negotiations are targets of the Okumkpo drama. The plays are also intended to criticize men or groups that invest their time and money in endless conflicts. Criticisms are humorously directed against the ruling elders for decisions they may have made that they consider inappropriate or that are self-serving. Afikpo women as a group are also ridiculed in the plays for behaviors that deviate from their traditional gender roles.

The "Okumkpo" plays also deal with serious crimes that are difficult to prosecute. In 1993, an indigene of the community in his 40s disappeared without trace. Suspicions were rife that the victim's brother who is a wealthy businessman in the town may have killed him for ritual purposes. There was no way this case could be proved. Yet suspicions were strong that the accused was responsible, especially since the accused's antecedents are less than desirable. The case could not be formally tried in the traditional courts or taken to governmental courts without any evidence. Besides, the powerful but shrewd businessman suspected of this heinous crime is also the victim's brother. It was not clear if the suspect was made to swear to an oath. Generally, oaths are not administered in cases between blood relations. It was a very shocking but complicated case. Yet the "Okumkpo" drama managed to present the case in a humorous manner. However, the significance of the messages, especially the moral contents of the acts and songs are never lost on anyone. Ottenberg (1972:113) points out that the "Okumkpa" plays "stress normal and expected behavior by ridiculing deviancy; a wide range of deviant acts may be dramatized. The emphasis is on maintaining traditional roles, traditional forms of sex polarity, and traditional leadership."

Based on the foregoing, the "Okumkpo" is an important agent of social control and resocialization in Afikpo. Some of its functions border on investigative journalistic role which is particularly useful in dealing with issues of complicated and delicate nature. Some cases are not amenable to regular court processes, yet need to be addressed somewhat in the interest of village peace and harmony. Abuse of power by the elders in the administrative and judicial functions is a good example. The masquerade performance is a trial in the court of public opinion within a humorous setting. It is akin to the American late night talk-show TV program, except that in the case of the masquerades display those whose behaviors are being ridiculed are almost always part of the audience. The Jay Leno late night talk-show program handling of the Lewinsky-Clinton sex scandal is a good example. As Ottenberg (1972:115) points out,

> . . . [a] major function of Okumkpo plays centers around the use of the theatrical situation to air anxieties and aggressive feelings that the young men hold concerning the elders. Here again the Afikpo see as a manifest function the fact that the plays and songs ridicule the elders who do not behave as elders should, who are greedy, foolish, bribe takers, and so on.

This section examined the major indigenous institutions and processes of conflict resolution in Afikpo. Some of the institutions as observed are extensions of primary groupings. These institutions are less formal and are more flexible in their response to crime and victimization. Others are more formal and are likely to pass definitive judgments. However, the objective of all judicial processes is the restoration of peace and harmony in the community. We shall in the next section examine the responses of the Afikpo indigenous system of conflict resolution to specific norm violations. Further, frequent criticisms against culturally based justice system are that it is patriarchal and thus oppressive to women and other minorities in the community. We shall therefore inquire into the position and perception of Afikpo women and other minorities (including non-indigenes in Afikpo) as regards the system.

Chapter Seven
Afikpo Women and the Traditional Justice System

All knowledge that is about human society, and not about the natural world, is historical knowledge, and therefore rests upon judgment and interpretation. That is not to say that facts and data are nonexistent, but that facts and data get their importance from what is made of them in interpretation (Said, 1981:154–56 as cited in Kirby and McKenna, 1989:23).

INTRODUCTION

Social control in society is effected through formal and informal mechanisms. Formal social control methods are coercion-oriented, as in the functions of criminal justice officials. Men tend to be more controlled through formal mechanisms, since they dominate the public sphere. On the other hand, informal mechanisms of social control tend to be persuasion-oriented, and relate to the controls exercised by the institutions of marriage, family, and peer groups. It is generally believed that women are more controlled through informal mechanisms since they prevail in the private sphere. Morris (1987:17), however, considers such characterizations an overstatement, noting "men and women are both controlled by such mechanisms as the family, marriage, work and concepts of "masculinity" and "femininity." Regardless, Morris (1987) agrees that social control mechanisms can operate differently on men and women. To understand the status of Afikpo women under the community's traditional justice system, an examination of the institutions of marriage and family, as well as the laws and customs of the people, is important. The marriage systems and the African extended family not only reflect both the social and economic conditions of the societies, but also have implications for the status and rights of the women. In addition, customary laws have been known to oppress women. Recent experiences of Canadian Aboriginal women with customary laws, according to Nahanee, confirm "customary sanctioning of sexual offenders in particular has been ineffective in curbing sexual violence against women, children. Besides, certain customary cultural values of kindness, reconciliation and family cohesiveness may in fact prevent Aboriginal women from officially reporting violence in the home" (Jackson 1994:17).

This chapter begins by reviewing the literature on African institutions of marriage, family, and other cultural practices as they relate to women. Further, these institutions and cultural practices are examined to understand how gender plays out in the process. The chapter concludes with the examination of the perspectives and experiences of Afikpo women with the community's system of social control, both formal and informal.

MARRIAGE

In contemporary Afikpo, marriage is a voluntary union between a man and a woman or women, and their extended families. Marriage is a partnership for life for participants. As in other African societies, marriage systems are, for all intents and purposes, different from the Western concept of marriage. As defined in *Hyde v Hyde* within Western society, marriage is the "voluntary union for life of one man and one woman to the exclusion of all others" (cited in Wilson 1986: 6). Consequently, marriages in Africa serve other purposes beyond the interests of the parties to the marriage. These purposes include the "continuation of the lineage group through natural reproduction, the provision of domestic labor by the wife, and as means by which wider political and economic alliances were established between the families of the wife and that of her husband" (Armstrong et al 1993: 5). The interests of the wider family or community are not safeguarded at the expense of the couple. The interests of the man and his wife, or wives in the case of polygynous marriages, were protected within that of the extended family or community.

In Afikpo, polygynous marriage is the ideal. Men strive to enhance their corporate and social standing with many wives and children. This marriage system has its origin in precolonial Afikpo. Then, the economy depended on subsistence agriculture, and fishing, both of which are labor intensive. Therefore, the more wives and children in the family, the more wealth, prosperity and status for the man. Secondly, families seek to immortalize their names through the succeeding generations. Since infant mortality was high, the more children a man had, the more chances of the continuity of his family and lineage. As Mbiti (1970: 142) remarks:

> The philosophical or theological attitude towards marriage and procreation is that these are an aid towards the partial recapture or attainment of the lost immortality, the more wives a man has the more children he is likely to have, and the more children the stronger the power of 'immortality' in that family. He who has descendants has the strongest possible manifestation of 'immortality,' he is 'reborn' in the multitude of his descendants, and there are many who 'remember' him after he has died physically and entered his 'personal immortality.' Such a man has the attitude that 'the more *we are*, the bigger *I am*.' Children are the glory of marriage, and the more there are of them the greater the glory. (emphasis in original).

In contemporary Afikpo, marriages may be contracted either through Customary law, or Ordinance law, also known as the Marriage Act. Marriages can also be instituted through the Church. Marriages undertaken under any of the systems are duly recognized as valid in Nigeria. However, it is not uncommon for couples who are married through the Ordinance law or the Church to have first completed the customary marital processes. As a matter of fact, most Churches are reluctant to formalize marriages until the customary marriage rites are fulfilled. Similarly, most parents or families will withhold their blessing to the marriage until the customary marriage rites are fulfilled. Hence, the Church sometimes demands evidence of blessing of both couples' parents before they are married under the Church.

Only marriages contracted under Customary law, however, allow for polygynous arrangements. It is an offense for a man who married under the Ordinance Act or the Church to marry more than a wife. As stipulated under Section 48 of the Marriage Act (chapter 115) Vol. 4 laws of the Federation of Nigeria, "Whoever, having contracted marriage under this Ordinance or any modification of such marriage contracts a marriage in accordance with native law or custom shall be liable to imprisonment for five years" (cited in Wilson 1986: 10).

Further, section 47 of the Ordinance states that

> . . . whoever contracts a marriage under the provision of this Ordinance, or any modification or re-enactment thereof, being at the time married in accordance with native law or custom to any person other

> than the person with whom such marriage is contracted, shall be liable to imprisonment for five years (ibid.).

Other Systems of Marriage

Monogamous and polygynous marriages are the most popular forms of marriage. However, there are other kinds of marriages instituted by the African people geared towards accommodating everyone in different circumstances. Every adult, male or female, in Africa is expected to be married, at least once in his or her lifetime. To die without having a child is considered a waste, and the individual is treated as a pariah. People who die without any offspring are not accorded any full burial, and are thrown away into the evil forest. This practice is very rare now and obtains in the most remote villages of Afikpo. However, the individual who dies young and without an offspring is not given a full burial and is not mourned publicly. They cannot become ancestors, and nobody will pour libation to them. Further, the individual is considered as having not contributed to the survival and continuity of the group who depend on the succeeding generation for their survival. As pointed out earlier, the institution of marriage in Africa has social, religious and economic dimensions. As Mbiti (1970:133) points out,

> Marriage is a drama in which everyone becomes an actor or actress and not just a spectator. Therefore, marriage is a duty, a requirement from the corporate society, and a rhythm of life in which everyone must participate. Otherwise, he who does not participate in it is a curse to the community, he is a rebel and a law-breaker, he is not only abnormal but 'under-human.' Failure to get married under normal circumstances means that the person concerned has rejected society and society rejects him in return.

In furtherance to this marriage objective, certain marriage types emerged to cater to everyone in all circumstances. One example of this is the *levirate* marriage system, where the death of the husband does not mean the end of the marriage. A male member of the deceased man's family is appointed to step in and provide the functions of a husband for the widow and as a father for the children. However, it must be borne in mind that, children begat under the arrangement belong to the dead man from whose estate they shall inherit. This arrangement obtains when the man dies before the marriage is blessed with children, or where it is believed the woman is still very young and is capable of having more children. Marriage in Africa is a process, which runs its full course with the birth and growth of children.

Mbiti (1970: 133) puts it succinctly: "marriage and procreation in African communities are a unity: without procreation marriage is incomplete."

Another form of marriage in some Igbo societies is known as *widow inheritance*. This form is similar to the levirate marriage system. In this type of marriage, the widow marries a man from the deceased husband's family. It is noted that the widow is free to choose from any of the dead husband's relatives and she is not inherited like property as the name suggests.

Another kind of marriage system is known as the *sororate* marriage whereby a man is given another woman from the wife's family as a substitute after her death. This occurs in very exceptional cases especially where the relationship between the two families are more than cordial. Sororate marriage can also be employed to save a marriage due to the failure of the wife to bear children.

Some African societies also practice a kind of marriage known as the *ghost* marriage. Here, parents of an unmarried man who dies marry a woman in his name to procreate and continue the lineage. Another form of marriage that is common in Igbo society is where a woman marries another woman for her husband. This happens where the woman, often a wealthy one, is unable to bear a male child or child at all. She then marries another woman by paying the bride-wealth, and her husband mates with this woman to procreate. The woman and the children from this relationship belong to the household of the wife who married the woman.

FAMILY

The generality of African families is extended. The African extended family consists of the husband, his wife or wives, their children and other relatives who live in the same household or compound, often that of the man's. Sometimes the extended family can also include the parents of the spouses who live with the family. Even where the elderly parents of the spouses do not live with the extended family, they can, in time of old age or terminal illness, move in with the family. Further, the adult married children of the spouses who live separately from the family are considered members of the extended family. They have certain rights as well as responsibilities which derive from their membership of the extended family. For example, in times of divorce or other crisis, married children of the spouses can return with their children and live either temporarily or permanently with the extended family. However, there are other African societies that are matrilineal, where the man moves into the household of his wife and resides with them. Armstrong et al (1993) describe the Bemba people of Zambia that practice the matrilocal residence system.

These are by no means the only family patterns found in Africa. In urban areas of Africa, there are quite a few couples cohabiting without formal marriages. The couples live with their children and other members of the extended family. There are also families of single parents, widows and widowers. There are still others where one of the spouses is working outside the town where they reside. However, what is common in all African families is that members of the extended family are not excluded, notwithstanding their temporary absence. The extended family structure has both social and economic implications. As mentioned earlier, precolonial African economies depended mostly on human capital, hence the greater the number of wives, children and relatives, the better. Again, since the aged could not do farm work, their survival depended on the younger members of the family who carried on after their retirement. The extended family system therefore gave base to the economy and social relations as Rwezaura (1985:57) delineates:

> In many African societies the household constitutes a centre for production, distribution and consumption. The strong kinship ties which pervade social relations provide an effective framework for the organization and management of the household economy. Kinship relations are hardly distinguishable from property relations and, indeed, the former serve as a device for obscuring the latter (cited in Armstrong et al 1993:7).

Owing to the social and economic interests, and the political affiliations which marriages and families provide in Africa, parents and other relations have more than a passing interest in whom their relations marry. Wilson (1986:7–8) characterizes marriages in traditional Igbo society as an institution where economic and social interests prevailed over love and emotional concerns. She states that "love and consent played a minor role, if they played any role at all, in strict Igbo custom where parental or extended family influences were paramount in the choice of partner." Wilson observes that one reason why love and emotional ties were of secondary consideration in African marriages could be attributed to the prevailing economic conditions where human capital was vital. Procreation, therefore, was an important consideration for marriages and survival. Further, the pragmatics of social and economic relationships between the families overrode that of the emotional ties between the couples. Besides, marriages tended to be polygynous, thereby mitigating the emotional tie between the man and the woman.

Divorce

Divorce is rare in many Igbo and other African societies (Wilson (1986) and Mbiti (1970). However, in traditional Afikpo, divorce[1] is both common and easy. If my survey of my village is representative of Afikpo, over seventy percent of Afikpo women are likely to marry two or more husbands in their lifetime. The marriage could be dissolved at anytime after the bride-price is paid, or after the couple has lived together for some time. Cruelty, especially on the part of the man, is a major basis for divorce. Other grounds for divorce in Afikpo include adultery, especially on the part of the woman, desertion, and other misconduct such as theft, and where the wife is accused of practicing witchcraft. The man's impotence or the wife's inability to bear children, are common grounds for divorce. A woman's inability to live in harmony with her co-wives can also jeopardize the marriage. Other provided explanation for the high divorce rate in the community is that men frequently married much younger women, and as was often the case, the husbands died when their wives are still young. Widows who are still at a childbearing age are generally encouraged by their family members to remarry.

In Afikpo, divorce occurs the moment the woman picks up her belongings and walks out of her husband's house. A divorce is also said to occur if the man picks up the possessions of his wife and throws them out of the house. However, there is no divorce if the wife refuses to move out of her husband's household. Generally, any male from the patrilineage can put back the woman's belongings, thereby revoking the divorce. If the man throws the woman's things out and no man from the extended family intervenes, it is an indication that the whole family is fed up with the woman and is willing to let her go.

However, if the woman ignores her husband's actions and refuses to move out of the husband's household, the marriage is assumed to not be terminated. The women of the patrilineage and community can also effect a divorce by ejecting the wife of a family member out of the family home. This happens where the divorced woman is a known thief, practices witchcraft, and, or is involved in conduct unbecoming of an Afikpo wife. After divorce, the husband can demand the return of the dowry he paid for the marriage. However, in most cases, the dowry is returned only after the woman remarries and the new husband repays the dowry.

Mbiti (1970) provides an explanation for the high divorce rate in some African societies. Marriage in African societies, he explains, is a process. In some societies, according to Mbiti, the marriage is complete after the first child is born. For some, the marriage is completed the moment the bride-wealth is fully paid. For others, the marriage is complete only after the wife is past the childbearing stage. Since marriages are for procreation, barren women and women who have passed the child-bearing stage have difficulties remarrying. Some of them may move back to their maiden home and settle. As Mbiti (1970:145) notes, "since, on the whole, African girls marry before the age of twenty-five, the process of their marriage is complete by the time they pass childbearing period and it is rare for divorce to take place after that age."

The following section examines some of the feminist theories and other African traditional institutions and practices to understand how gender plays out in the African judicial processes. Traditional institutions of marriage, family, and other African cultural practices are said to victimize women. In 1995, the Fourth World Conference on Women in Beijing identified some African cultural practices as instruments of women's victimization. It states that "women fall victim to traditional practices that violate their human rights. The persistence of the problem has much to do with the fact that most of these physically and psychologically harmful customs are deeply rooted in the tradition and culture of society" (UN, 1999).

FEMINIST THEORIES

Most societies are patriarchal, hence women are neglected and dominated by men. Consequently, women have struggled to free themselves from the domination of men. These struggles predate feminism. Boyd and Sheehy (1989), as cited in Burtch (1992:68), note that women's resistance to the oppression of men is "not strictly a twentieth century phenomenon. Women's groups have been lobbying for legislative and judicial reform since the late nineteenth century."

Feminism follows the Marxian philosophy of challenging liberalism's conception of law as just and impartial, and attributes gender inequality to structural factors. Further, gender is imposed, learned and internalized, through socialization. Gender governs every aspect of personal and social life. Feminist theorists insist that sex and gender are not synonymous terms. Sex describes the biological and physiological differences between men and women. On the other hand, gender refers to the culturally and historically developed patterns of behavior and relationships between males and females. Gender prescriptions, account for the unequal relationship between males and females. Feminist theory "is a woman-centered description and explanation of human experience and the social world," notes Mona J.E. Danner in (Maclean & Milovanovic (eds.) 1991:51). Further, Danner states that "feminist theory is activist and seeks social change to end the neglect and subordination of women. The goals of feminist studies are to describe, to understand, to explain, and to change" (ibid.). Feminist theories are concerned with the socio-economic marginalization and political oppression of women in society. These theories articulate strategies for social change and women's empowerment.

Feminist theories are not a homogenous perspective. Danner (1991), citing Jagger (1983), identified four varieties of feminist theory, namely, liberal, radical, Marxist, and socialist feminism. Tong (1989), according to Danner (1991), further identifies psychoanalytic, existentialist, and postmodern feminism. Traditional, or conservative feminism, is yet another perspective of feminism. Despite the diversity of approaches concerning the understanding and strategies for social change, as it relates to the oppression of women, feminism is an "overarching and paradigmatic way of seeing and overcoming the subjugation of women" (Menzies and Chunn 1991:67). To differentiate feminism from other theoretical perspectives, Kathleen Daly and Meda Chesney-Lind (1988:504) list five main elements of feminist thought:

- "Gender is not a natural fact but a complex social, historical, and cultural product; it is related to, but not simply derived from, biological sex difference and reproductive capacities.
- Gender and gender relations order social life and social institutions in fundamental ways.
- Gender relations and constructs of masculinity and femininity are not symmetrical but are based on an organizing principle of men's superiority to and social and political-economic dominance over women.
- Systems of knowledge reflect men's views of the natural and social world; the production of knowledge is gendered.
- Women should be at the center of intellectual inquiry, not peripheral, invisible, or appendages to men."

Daly and Chesney-Lind (1988), in their articulation of the various feminist perspectives, observe that a liberal feminist perspective was one of the earliest feminist theories. Liberal feminists focus on gender discrimination and identify different socialization processes that are responsible for men's social dominance and women's oppression. Women are socialized to be passive in society, thereby constraining their full participation in social, economic and political activities. Liberal feminists' specifically denounce the private/public dichotomy, which restricts women's activities to the private sphere. Further, it accuses the Criminal Justice System of paternalism and chivalry. Liberal feminists advocate the removal of all obstacles that limit women's participation in the public sphere, such as education, labor market and political activity. It seeks equal rights, opportunities and treatment for women. However, it is noted that working class women who are in the public sphere are doubly burdened.

Marxist feminists, on the other hand, blame capitalism for women's subordinate position in society. They argue that class relations override gender relations. Capitalist economy is class-based and hierarchical. Capitalism justifies private ownership of property and its inheritance by men. The capitalist economy is based on profit-making and unequal distribution of property and power, which marginalizes and exploits women. Women are reduced to a secondary and surplus labor force, which leads to their dependence on men, or on welfare when there is no man in the family. Women's behavior is criminalized, following capitalist moral imperatives. Marxist feminists argue that gender equality will be achieved through the socialist democratization of society, which will allow for the full integration of women into the economy. Therefore, marriage and sexual relations that derive from private ownership of property should be abolished. Further, with the overthrow of the capitalist class, women's and working class peoples' economic and political empowerment will be guaranteed.

Radical feminists contend that patriarchy is to blame for women's socio-economic and political marginalization in society. Men's desire to control women's sexuality and reproductive potentials is the root of women's oppression in society. Men's biological need to dominate women is responsible for the socialization process inculcating in boys and men the attitude that they are superior to girls and women and therefore have the right to subjugate women. Radical feminists advocate the elimination of private/public dichotomy in gender roles. They also push for legal reforms and the introduction of laws that are gender sensitive. However, radical feminists disagree with liberal feminists' contention that women's liberation will increase female criminality. Women's liberation will rather reduce female criminality and even has the potential of reducing male violence against women.

Socialist feminism is a combination of radical and Marxist principles. Unlike Marxist feminism, however, class and gender relations are the fundamental basis of women's domination in society. Class conflict is identified as the major cause of crime in society. Lower class men commit crimes in their attempt to resist oppression. Women's criminality, on the other hand, results from their accommodation. Marxist feminism argues that a capitalist, patriarchal system marginalizes women to control their sexuality. This explains why men are more involved in street crimes and why women are more likely to commit property and status crimes. Salamon and Robinson (1987:30), citing Jaggar (1983:9), argue that "socialist feminism provides the most appropriate interpretation of what it is for a theory to be impartial, objective, comprehensive, verifiable and useful . . . [S]ocialist feminism is the most adequate of the feminist theories formulated to date." To eliminate men's dominance and women's oppression in society, patriarchal and capitalist class relations must be transformed, according to socialist feminism.

On the other hand, *traditional* (or conservative) feminists deny the existence of gender inequality. What other feminist theories perceive as male domination in society derives from biological sex differences. Men and women's social behavior in society reflects biological sex differences rather than socialization. Greater testosterone production in males account for, their strength and innate aggression and dominance. Women, on the other hand, have natural nurturing and care-giving capabilities. Traditional feminism is, seen by some as a critique of other feminist perspectives.

There are some women of color who have a different perspective on male dominance and women's oppression in society. What is absent from these perspectives is the notion of race and racial inequities which affect women of color.

BLACK FEMINISM

Women of color critique western feminists' notion of the 'generic woman.' For Spelman (1988), mainstream feminists have tended to portray women as a homogenous group, thereby perpetuating "the privileged position and domination of white middle-class feminists" (as cited in Handler (1992:25). Spelman insists that sex, gender and identity be separated, for it is a fallacy to analyze gender in isolation from identity. Spelman notes that "identity is constructed by race, ethnicity, class, community, nation; it is both multiple and unstable" (ibid.). Further, Rice (1990) observes that mainstream feminism acknowledges that femininity and sexuality are social constructs, yet fails to appreciate the "different socialization patterns" and different cultural experiences of black women (in Ahluwalia 1991:59). Mainstream feminists, according to Rice, have falsely assumed the universality of gender differences. For example, prison research in Britain until recently focused exclusively on white female offenders. Such research fails to compare the sentencing patterns of black and white women. As a result, the peculiar problems of black women in prison, like isolation and discrimination, are generally overlooked.

Ahluwalia (1991:59) argues that black feminists are skeptical about "malestream" feminists equation of masculinity with violence.[2] Singling men out as oppressors "denies the privilege that white women have over black men and also neglects to implicate white women in perpetuating racism and using violence against black people." Apparently, violence and power are synonymous, and since black men tend to be socially, economically and politically marginalized with regards to both white men and women, it is wrong to assume black men are also in a position to oppress others.

Furthermore, mainstream feminists indict sexism as responsible for women's oppression and marginalization in society, while racist stereotypes are overlooked. Rice (1990:62 as cited in Ahluwalia 1991:59) contends that "in assuming a universal dimension of men's power, this approach has ignored the fact that race significantly affects black women's experiences in the home, in the labor market, of crime and in the criminal justice system." Ahluwalia observes that while many white women have negotiated their way through a white male-dominated labor market, it was the lot of black women to provide the domestic labor. Hence, she insists black women dismiss "feminism as a racist and bourgeois project" (ibid.). Feminism, she points out, does not give due consideration to issues that affect black women. She cites the case of Susan Edwards (1990:1148) who rightly observes that "when black people are the subject, the law is extremely oppressive." At the same time, Edwards supports white feminists demand for "more intensive policing, stricter laws, more control of men's power and regulation of men's violence" (ibid.) The consequences of this is the over policing of black communities, especially the police harassment of young black men. Black women suffer more as a result, for when they report domestic violence, police use the opportunity to conduct immigration or housing checks.

African-American women argue that their position both as women and members of a minority group puts them in a more unique and precarious situation. Further, their lower social economic class position only makes matters worse. Lewis (1977:343) describes the African-American woman as facing "double jeopardy" deriving from their race and sex. African-American women suffer discrimination on account of their race and sex. Lewis states that

> because African-American women have membership in two subordinate groups, African-American and women, they lack access to authority and resources in society and are in structural opposition with the dominant racial/ethnic group (Euro-American) and the dominant sexual group (male) (as cited in Barbee and Little (1993:183).

Collins (1990) argues that African-American women still suffer from the same slavery ideology once used to control them. These externally imposed images are the "mammy, the faithful, obedient domestic servant, the matriarch, the welfare mother and the Jezebel. The prevailing images of mammy, matriarch, welfare mother and Jezebel provide the ideological justification for racial oppression, gender subordination and economic exploitation." These negative images of the African-American woman combine with their disadvantaged position as members of a racial minority and sex to undermine their health. Racism, sexism and classism are blamed for the high rate of hypertension, lupus, diabetes, maternal mortality, cervical cancer and other illnesses afflicting African-American women. Further, experiences from post-colonial societies support the thinking that oppressed men tend to be more abusive people. Fanon (1968), in the "pedagogy of the oppressed," discusses how colonization can have such a deleterious effect on the colonized, and how the colonized can quickly turn to the oppression of others. In this respect, Christensen (1988: 191) points out that "no other woman has suffered physical and mental abuse, degradation, and exploitation on North American shores comparable to that experienced by the Black female," cited in Barbee and Little (1993:182).

AFRICAN FEMINIST PERSPECTIVES

African women's position in their society further underscores the point that there is no "universal woman" and that the political, economic and cultural context is important in understanding the conditions of women. While women in other societies bemoan their social, economic and political marginalization, contemporary African women suffer a different kind of oppression. For example, while the African-American woman is wont to characterize her situation as sometimes "double-jeopardy" and at other times "multiple-jeopardy," the African woman claims her burden is comparable to an individual with six mountains on her back. As Ogundipe-Leslie (1993:107) puts it,

> . . . the African woman has six mountains on her back: one is oppression from outside (colonialism and neo-colonialism?); the second is from traditional structures, feudal, slave-based, communal, etc.; the third is her backwardness (neo-colonialism?); the fourth is man; the fifth is her color, her race; and the sixth is herself.

Oppression from outside: Foreign Intrusions

Slavery, colonialism and neo-colonialism significantly affected African economic systems and human relations. Slavery, according to Ogundipe-Leslie (1993), not only brought about changes in the "production processes and the relations of production," but also further undermined the position of women in society. Slavery also affected inter-ethnic relations and introduced a regime of terror which constrained women's social and economic activities. Further, colonialism tied Africa's economy to the international capitalist system. One effect of Africa's integration into the capitalist economy was the shift in emphasis from food crops to cash crops required by the colonial economy. As a result, African economies became dependent on foreign economy, and this resulted in social upheaval, with women mostly at the receiving end. Colonialism imposed an alien culture, educational, political, economic and religious system on Africa, with serious consequences on the peoples' development and well-being. Worse still is the status of inferiority on the African people and their loss of their productive capacities. Chambliss (1979:18) points out that the transformation of African economies from a self-sufficient and independent one, to an economy that depended on that of the colonial authorities was achieved through coercion. When coercion failed to compel Africans to seek wage labor, the colonial authorities introduced Poll tax and other laws that made it mandatory for all adults to seek wage labor from the Colonial authorities. As Girovord and Lees (1924:186) describe,

> We consider that taxation is the only possible method of compelling the native to leave his Reserve for the purpose of seeking work . . . it is on this (taxation) that the supply of labor and the price of labor depends. To raise the rate of wages would not increase but would diminish the supply of labor. A rise in the rate of wages would enable the hut or poll tax of a family, sub-tribe to be earned by fewer external workers (cited in Chambliss 1979:18).

The introduction of wage labor on African society by the Colonial authorities affected the peoples' attitude and gender relations. Compounding the situation further was the shift in emphasis from "food crop" to "cash crop." Women's marginalisation in the production process increased. The economic changes affected both the political and religious systems of the people, especially the cultural attitudes towards women. Most affected was women's agricultural activity and autonomy. As Ogundipe-Leslie (1993:108) explains,

> Both men and women, with the intrusion of the West, were pushed into dependent economies resulting in the pauperization and the "proletarianization" of the whole continent. Whole societies became geared to the upholding of foreign metropolitan economies of the colonizing powers. Women in the labor process became the "proletariat" of the proletariats, becoming more subordinated in the new socioeconomic schemes, and often losing their old and meaningful roles within the older production process.

Colonialism is also denounced for either introducing new patriarchal structures or reinforcing existing ones. These patriarchal values came through two of the major colonial religions—Christianity and Islam. Women, as a result, became more marginalized in public affairs. Women were excluded from all social and political activity, since the new religions became the basis of political, social and cultural leadership.

A major argument against colonialism is that it imposed alien cultural, educational and judio-political systems on African societies. African peoples' ways of knowing were undermined, their self-reliance and productivity lost. African peoples must now rely on their colonial masters for all ideas and practices required for societal development. African peoples' dependence on their colonial masters for political and economic development is partly responsible for the inferiority complex, which African peoples suffer from. As Fanon (1968) points out, a colonized mind is a terrible thing, and worse still, is a worse oppressor of other people under him or her. In support, Ogundipe-Leslie (1993:109) claims that

> Within this cultural universe of Third World dependency, the woman is the dependent of the dependent, being pulled along in the whirligig of neo-colonial meaningless behavior. Like her male counterparts, she imitates everything European and despises her traditional culture and race while she fails to understand her own true needs.

AFRICAN TRADITIONAL SYSTEMS

Many traditional African systems are said to both marginalize and oppress African women. Traditional African marriages and family institutions and other cultural practices are identified as oppressive to women. Polygyny, female genital mutilation, son preference, dowry-related violence and early marriages are some of the cultural practices that violate women's rights. The UN (1995:4) notes that "women fall victim to traditional practices that violate their human rights. The persistence of the problem has much to do with the fact that most of these physically and psychologically harmful customs are deeply rooted in the tradition and culture of society."

POLYGYNY

Polygyny is the system whereby a man can marry more than one wife. This practice is waning due to Christian and other modern values such as social, political, and economic power. Ironically, it is more widespread amongst the upper class and under class in contemporary Africa. Polygyny arguably is not popular among the middle class. Armstrong et al (1993:25) explain the phenomenon thus,

> Today, although many people enter into potentially polygynous customary marriages, few marriages are in fact polygynous. As long as marriage is based on the norm of a *dependent* woman and a 'breadwinner' man, rates of polygyny will inevitably be low, as it will be difficult for a wage-earning man to support more than one woman (italics in original).

Arguments against the institution of polygyny are legion. Many believe the socio-economic system that gave base to polygyny no longer exists. In precapitalist Africa, men and their wives lived together and worked the field. The marriage institution and the rights of the man and the wives were clearly defined. Today, men tend to be involved in paid wages in urban areas, while either one or all the wives live in the rural areas fending for themselves. Polygyny of this nature tends to be abusive to the woman, especially the older wife who is likely to be the one staying back in the villages, while the younger wife lives in the urban area with the husband. Many argue that it was not possible for one man to distribute his affections equally amongst his wives. Here, the man tends to neglect the older wives, and the wife heavy with child or nursing a baby. The neglected wives suffer both emotionally and psychologically, especially if they entered into the marriage expecting emotional support from their husbands. It is understood here that some women may enter into a polygynous arrangements for economic and social security.

There are other arguments against the institution of polygyny and how the practice violates women's rights. For example, men have the option to marry more than one wife, while women do not have that privilege of multiple spouses. Further, polygyny is said to encourage competition amongst co-wives, as they pander for the man's love and attention. My experience with polygyny is that conflict amongst co-wives can be endemic. Competition rather than solidarity tends to define their relationships. In traditional settings, to reduce conflict amongst co-wives, the senior wives were generally consulted and involved in the search for a second wife. And the senior wives' position and leadership in the family was always secured. This cannot be said to be the case today.

There are suggestions that no woman is forced into a polygynous relationship, that women are free to opt out of it. There are questions whether polygyny is an informed choice for some women. For example, some are not properly informed about the relationship and so enter into it only to regret their decision. Others are forced by economic and social security, since there may not exist employment opportunities for such a woman. And even to take up farming, only married women are recognized as adults in most African societies and so qualify for land allocation.

Polygyny does hold some benefits to some women. Arguably, more women are economically marginalised in Africa and will not survive on their own. Polygynous marriages become an option where their social and economic needs may be protected. As Armstrong et al (1993:27) explain

> As long as women have less access to economic resources, they will want the protection of marriage, sometimes at any cost. Polygyny will allow more women to marry, and therefore theoretically be supported by a man. Polygyny in this way accords with the customary concept of marriage, which emphasizes economic and social considerations more than the western ideals of love and companionship.

Polygyny is also said to work against divorce. Here, the pressure on barren women to bear children is reduced since, the man's need for more children are met by other wives. Marriages that would have broken down in a monogamous relationship may survive in a polygynous one, thereby providing social and economic security to the women.

Dowry

The dowry—money or property paid by a man for the right or privilege to marry a woman—is a very established and widespread practice in Africa. The rationale for this practice is shrouded in mystery and cultural practice. One explanation from my informants is that it is a symbolic practice to determine the maturity and ability of the man to cope with the responsibility of marriage and to cater for a family. Other justifications for the dowry institution, as provided by Cotran (1987:36), are that

> in the nature of a bond uniting the two families that it is a mark of the man's respect for his wife; that it is merely a symbol to seal the marriage contract; that because of the liability to repayment on divorce it acts as a deterrent to misconduct on the part of the wife; and that it is the price for the children from the marriage (cited in Armstrong et al 1993:28–29).

In Afikpo, for example, the amount of dowry payment is a token of UK#10.00 or its equivalent, and later fixed at Nigerian #600.00. In other Igbo societies, it can be quite expensive and impossible for salaried people to afford. This has prompted the government to fix the bride-price at a rate commensurate with socio-economic reality. This has rarely worked in practice, as prosecution of violation is difficult, if not impossible. Where the law and the culture are in conflict, the cultural practice tends to prevail. Wilson (1986:10–11) illustrates

> Under the Igbo customary system, bride-price was a symbolic gesture, but today the symbolism has been replaced with naked greed. . . . In spite of the Government edict limiting bride price to sixty naira (#60.00), would be bridegrooms are still made to pay two thousand naira (#2,000.00) or more.

Arguments against the dowry institution claim that it oppresses women in marriage. Further, the system portrays women as exchangeable commodity. There are also suggestions that the dowry institution reflects an oppressive regime against women, which obtained in other patriarchal systems, and which have been done away with. Opponents of the African dowry institution, for example,

> point out that there is nothing peculiarly African about the institution since it exists in India and can also be traced back to ancient Europe and the Hebrews (Ncube 1987:204). Others have argued that the practice turns women into exchangeable objects (Mpofu 1983:27) and thereby contributes to their subordination in marriage where, in the circumstances they cannot claim equality with their husbands (Armstrong et al (1993:29).

Armstrong et al (1993) believe that the dowry institution in Africa has both merits and demerits. Dowry payment created certain rights and obligations in marriage not only between the spouses but by other family members. Dowries guaranteed the woman in marriage certain rights, and as such, the husband could not on his whims and caprices divorce his wife without the extensive involvement of other family members. However, Armstrong et al (1993) stated a demerit is that the dowry payment, since it is the man paying, accords greater rights and claims to the man than the wife. Through dowry payment, the children are seen to belong to the man rather than the woman in patrilineal societies. Further, the dowry payment transfers the guardianship to the husband from the woman's father. The dowry institution is said to compel a woman to remain married to her husband for fear of being asked to repay the bride-price in the event of a divorce. As such, the woman is obliged to remain with her husband against her wish. As Armstrong et al (1993:29–30) point out,

> She is bound to her husband and his family for a number of reasons. Firstly, if the payment of bridewealth is the price of acquiring her procreative capacity, she becomes obliged to produce children for her husband. Secondly, since the payment of the bridewealth was and is dreaded in the event of divorce, a wife would be hesitant to leave her husband for fear of being castigated by her family for bringing dishonor to them.

FEMALE CIRCUMCISION

Female circumcision is another very controversial cultural practice in Africa. Female circumcision "includes a range of practices involving the complete or partial removal or alteration of the external genitalia for non-medical reasons and appears in widely varied cultural contexts in African and other populations" according to Shell-Duncan & Hernlund (2000:3). They observe that circumcision can be performed at infancy, before puberty, and at puberty. Some are carried out at the time the girl is contracting marriage, during the seventh month of her first pregnancy or after the birth of the first child. Some circumcisions are done during initiation rites. Apena (1996:7) describes female circumcision as a "cultural ritual whose nature varies among the different groups which practice it. As an essential part of cultural values, it affects the integrity and survival of communities." It relates to issues of womanhood, family system and religious beliefs. Further, female circumcision is also a lesson on female education and health care. Lightfoot-Klein (1989), as cited in Apena (1996:7), says that twenty-eight out of fifty-three countries in Africa practice female circumcision.

Most Western commentators characterize the practice as 'genital mutilation,' and condemn it in absolute terms on the grounds that the practice abuses children and is a tool of women's oppression. Western discourses often portray African women as ignorant and powerless victims of an oppressive culture. Female circumcision is perceived in the West as barbaric, savage and primitive, done to diminish the sexuality of African women. Some Western governments' condemnation of the female circumcision has led to the criminalization of the act. Many African women have also successfully sought political asylum in western countries on the grounds that they will be circumcised when they return to their homelands in Africa.

Some African women commentators, notably Iweriebor (1996), Matias (1996), and Apena (1996), take exception to the Western position. For them, what Western commentators describe as 'female genital mutilation' is actually better known as 'genital surgery,' and it has its origin in Ancient Egypt where it has been practiced since 5,000 B.C. Genital surgery is also referred to as "pharonic custom" to delineate its origin. They accuse Western commentators of evaluating African cultural practices through Western cultural perspectives. Further, the whole analysis is done without situating the act in its cultural context hence the whole issue is misrepresented and distorted.

Iweriebor argues that the motives for genital surgery are many and vary from society to society. It is also important to bear in mind that genital surgery is performed on both men and women, hence it is wrong to characterize the practice as an instrument of female oppression. Other cultural bases for genital surgery are as stated here:

> For some cultures it is a component of a rite of passage to socially acceptable adulthood. For others it is a nuptial necessity. For yet others, it is a mark of courage, particularly where it is carried out on older people. For some it is a reproductive aid, increasing fertility. For others, it enhances sexuality (1996:2).

Female circumcision is further seen as a rite of passage which some have compared to baptism and confirmation practice in the Western world. Female circumcision marks a girl's attainment of adulthood and whose sexual invasion will not be tolerated. Matias (1996:5) notes that "the three most difficult and joyous times in a woman's life are at her circumcision, marriage and on the birth of her first child."

Other issues to consider in the female circumcision controversy, according to Apena (1996), are that it is not a gender issue since men also go through circumcision. So if the practice violates peoples' rights, it is certainly not that of the girl or woman but that of a "violation within a group." As such, the young girls and women who undergo circumcision have no rights that are separate from that of their communities. Further, African culture does not bestow the same rights to both the youth and elders, and it is from this perspective that the issue of female circumcision would be better understood. According to Apena (1996:7), "While Western societies are youth driven and oriented, the African society emphasizes the significance of elders, who embody the collective wisdom of the people and guard tradition and custom. The rights of the youth, like the rights of others, are integrated into the rights of the community."

DISCUSSION

In line with the approach of this study, this chapter emphasized the process of conflict resolution. Specifically, it looked at the Afikpo indigenous institutions of conflict resolution. Consequently, it was difficult to ascertain whether litigants' gender affected the outcome of a case. Notwithstanding, litigants in the Afikpo indigenous institutions of conflict resolution are supported by their families and well-wishers. Some major decisions such as oath swearing may not be made unless family members of a litigant are present. All participants in the justice process are equal and actively participate. With regards to women for example, their disadvantaged position may be presumed from the system's structure and processes. There is no reason to believe women lack confidence in the Afikpo traditional courts. Some of the cases reproduced in this study were, sponsored by women. The plaintiff in the paternity dispute reproduced in the next chapter for example, is a woman. She filed the case on behalf of her son who was working in another town and could not afford to be present during the proceedings. However, the perspectives of women at this juncture will be in order.

The following is an excerpt of my interviews with two Afikpo women. The opinions expressed by these women are believed to reflect the views of two categories of women—the educated urban Afikpo woman and the uneducated rural Afikpo woman. The first interviewee is a community organizer in her late sixties. She is a farmer and part time petty trader. She is a typical rural Afikpo woman. She is an elder, and plays active role in the community's conflict resolution processes.

Question: How do Afikpo women resolve their conflicts?

Elder: If there is a dispute, the complainant, if a woman, will approach a woman of the village of the ekpuke eto age grade. Women hold court in the villages to resolve conflict amongst themselves. I play an active role in dispute resolution in the village. Women can also take cases directly to any of the institutions of conflict resolution just like men. However, cases of adultery or sorcery and any other case against the earth goddess must be taken to the village groupings presided over by the men of the community. Wherever a case is heard—the process is the same—all cases are heard in the open with every community member participating.

Question: At the village-group courts, and the village conflict resolution forum, women are not actively involved in the dispute resolution processes—do you think the interests of women are affected as a result?

Elder: I do not believe women's case suffer because they are not part of the decision- making body at the village and village-group courts. Every case is determined according to the custom of Afikpo. Every case is tried in the open with family members of litigants present. However, they have been instances when decisions that were inimical to the well-being

> of women were made. In such cases appeals were made and the cases reversed. Sometimes, such appeals fail because of the stubbornness of the men. But where we feel strongly that our case deserves better attention, we do not relent in pursuing what we consider to be a just outcome.
>
> One of the cases that I remember very well in my village happened a long time ago—it was the case of a widow whose husband's family refused farmland. The court had decided in favor of the late husband's family. The village women group employed every customary method to persuade the men to rescind their decision without success. The village women embarked on a protest according to Afikpo custom. The women marched through the village playground naked. When this usually effective customary method of protest failed, the women of the village decided to divorce their men enmasse. The women of the village took with them only their children that were breast-feeding at the time. The men responded very quickly—revoked the decision on the matter and sent high -powered emissaries to plead with the women to return. The men fulfilled other demands made by the women including certain expiation rites before the women returned.

There are several instances when Afikpo women refused to abide by rules which they find offensive and discriminatory against the women of the community. Last year the village women refused to swear to the oath of chastity decreed by the village men. The basis for the women's refusal was that only rural women were directed to participate in the oath swearing. For some time now, Afikpo men have failed to persuade women Christian elites to swear to this oath. We met and decided that unless every Afikpo woman is made to participate in the oath swearing, our members will not cooperate with the men. Since after that confrontation, the men have not raised the issue of oath taking again. As far as we are concerned oath taking by women to establish their chastity is a dead issue in our village. We have noticed other villages have copied our strategy.

Satire is another effective method employed by women to express their displeasure with certain cultural practices. Women use the names of some men who oppress their wives and children derogatorily in songs. Certain cultural practices that discriminate against women are also challenged through songs. Some of our recorded songs remain very popular like you know. The songs lament the prevalent attitude in the community where women are blamed for not having male children as if the woman is God. One of the songs also decries the cultural practice of penalizing women for adultery. In many cases men are not even questioned for adultery.

The following is excerpt of the second interview with an urban-based Afikpo woman in her forties. She is also a University lecturer.

> **Question:** Do you think the litigant's gender affects the outcome of the case in the Afikpo traditional courts?
>
> **Answer:** I believe the status of the litigants are important and can influence the direction of justice. I will argue that status is more important than gender. The court processes are politicized. Some of the traditional courts' judges are greedy and corrupt. The educated Afikpo woman in particular is greatly disadvantaged. All her behaviors are suspect. People are quick to label her a liberated woman and attach motives to all her behaviors and utterances. On the contrary—the rural Afikpo woman is better organized, economically independent and have established customary lines of resistance against the oppression and control of the men.

Based on the interviews with the women respondents, it is difficult to conclude women litigants lose out in the Afikpo traditional institutions of conflict resolution, on account of their gender. It is reiterated, however, that all the major institutions of conflict resolution in Afikpo are, operated by men. Women are involved only as litigants, witnesses, and observers. At the village-group courts, for example, women even as litigants present their cases from outside the courts and not from inside as men. The initial salutation to the courts is, done by men on the women litigants' behalf. Incidentally, only a small minority of the women I spoke to saw this policy as disadvantageous to women. Women present their cases with more efforts since to be heard they need to raise their voices. Some women saw this practice as useful to women since they can present their cases outside the gaze of the judges. Those who have problems speaking in public find the arrangement to their advantage. Some might interpret the arrangement as sending a message that women participants in the system are less than equal to the men participants. Explanations provided by my interview respondents for this practice is that women tend to be emotional and argumentative and are therefore likely to disrupt the proceedings if they were sitting inside the courthouse. This is quite interesting considering that the culture encourages extensive arguments and discussion on an issue before a decision is made. Other provided explanations are that it is an attempt to avoid contamination by women who are unclean. Women are assumed to be unclean during menstruation and if they gave birth to twins unless they perform the necessary expiation rites. It is important to note that men who do not belong to the age-grades that administer the traditional courts are also not allowed to sit down during litigation. If a judge of the court is a litigant in a case, he is treated like any other litigant. He stands all through the proceedings and his title of "Esaa" or "Eto" is dropped. He is addressed by his names.

It is noted that women have analogous institutions where they resolve conflicts amongst themselves. Similar to men, women age-grades and village groupings are involved in the resolution of conflict. However, women are not represented in other major institutions of conflict resolution where more far-reaching decisions are made. Women non-participation in the justice process is not a prima-facie case against the system. The Afikpo women are highly organized and have established and effective means of pursuing their cases or resisting the domination of men. This dual sex based institutional arrangement is not unique to Afikpo. Nzegwu (1995) describes precolonial Onitsha—Igbo social and political organization as polarized along gender lines. This gender based separate political and social institutions does not indicate antagonistic relationship between men and women, according to Nzegwu. The community valued a harmonious gender relationship as essential for the progress and stability of the community. Describing the Onitsha-Igbo system, Nzegwu notes that:

> Under this dual-symmetrical structure, women had their own Governing Councils—*Ikporo-Onitsha, nd'inyom*—to address their specific concerns and needs as women. The councils protected women's social and economic interests, and guided the community's development. This dual-symmetrical structure accorded immense political profile to women both in communities with constitutional monarchies (on the western side and some parts of the eastern banks of the River Niger—Onitsha, Ogbaru, and Oguta), and in the non-centralized democracies of the eastern hinterland (1995:445–6).

Nonetheless, a preliminary examination of the cases that women are involved in the village-group courts is an indictment of broader social forces. Some of the cases I witnessed concerned women defendants accused of procuring love charms intended to give them an edge over their co-wives or their husband's mistresses in the man's affection. Some were also accused of employing witchcraft or sorcery against their co-wives to stultify the co-wives childbearing abilities. That women are more involved in these cases is a testimony on how the institutions of marriage and family bear upon women in the community. It must be observed however, that few of the cases involve men who are accused of employing the services of medicine men to win the love of a woman. While the traditional courts may provide a forum for women to bring to the public their marital problems, few do bring cases of physical and sexual abuse to the central courts. Most abuse cases are handled informally in the families. Spousal abuse is a major ground for marriage break up as few families will allow their daughters to remain in abusive relationships. During divorce proceedings or other marital problems, issues of physical and sexual abuse may be raised and discussed at the traditional courts. Women age-grade or village-group meetings do discuss issues of women abuse and neglect. They also take up such cases with men as the case earlier discussed where the women of Amachara village in the mid-seventies decided as a group to boycott the beds of their husbands to protest their neglect by the men.

Unlike elder abuse, the physical and sexual abuse of women in the community does not attract public sanctions. While there is rapid and established community response to elder abuse in Afikpo, this is hardly the case for women physical and sexual abuse. Elder abuse in the community attracts stiff punishment and stigma in the community. Women abuse is also considered a shameful act but there is hardly any formal reproach as such. Men who physically abuse their wives are, usually censured by their families, friends and age-mates. It is not clear if there is any standard cultural or conventional punishment as such. Nevertheless, abuse is a major base for divorce. Few families will allow their own remain in an abusive relationship. It is difficult for physical abuse to be concealed in the community. Houses are so close together that it is not possible for physical abuse to escape the ever-prying eyes of neighbors. In addition, most of the cases of adultery in the traditional courts involve women. This practice implicates gender bias against women. Men are tried for adultery only in instances where the man accused of adultery comes from the same village as the husband of the woman.

The average Afikpo woman is economically independent. They do most of the peasant farming, although men are custodians of the lineage farmlands. Men and women as individuals also own lands as the decided case below indicates. Lineage lands are available to anyone interested in farming. The lineages own most of the land and make land available to lineage members, both men and women. However, men are more involved in the cultivation of yam, which is the cash crop. Most Afikpo men are subsistence farmers. The high status of yam crop in Igboland is of more symbolic value than its wealth generating worth. Women can also cultivate yam, but rarely do. When women are involved in yam cultivation it is not in large scale as that of men. Unlike other crops, yam cultivation is labor intensive and involves intricate processes. Other farm products where women farmers are dominant, such as cassava, coco-yam, okro, vegetables, groundnuts and so on are readily sold by women both at the local and distant markets. Certain crafts such as pot making, ropes, and cloth dyeing are areas where Afikpo women excel. They are also highly profitable ventures. The local market activities are, also dominated by women. Women make a lot of money through farming and trading, and exercise full control over their resources. One positive aspect of polygamy is that women tend to have high social and economic autonomy.

P. Ottenberg (1959) and Amadiume (1995)'s viewpoints contrast with the above position. Amadiume (1995:24) citing Ottenberg (1959), argues that "not even in the face of colonialism and the subsequent growth of petty commodity trade, did this sexual imbalance change for Afikpo women, who remained immobile, unorganized, and under the firm control of their men-folk." Amadiume also claims that since Afikpo women are not incorporated into the lineages of their husbands, that the women's statuses in their husbands' housholds are usually ambiguous. Furthermore, that since most of the lands are controlled by the matrilineal lineage, women's usefulness to their husbands depended on the amount of land they can provide to their husbands. This position hardly describes the Afikpo woman today. There is also no indication that this describes the lot of Afikpo women in the 1950s when this research was carried out. Afikpo women arguably dominate the subsistence economy. Women just like men have unfettered access to matrilineal lands. (The reproduced case below decided by the traditional courts supports this position).

Most farmlands in Afikpo are owned by the matrilineages. Women are the spiritual leaders of the matrilineages. They are the custodians of the matrilineage shrines as the decided case below confirms. Women are likely to depend on their matrilineage for their farmlands, rather than on their husbands. However, husbands may benefit from their wives' lineage lands. One should have thought this arrangement would accord the woman more bargaining power in the marriage. The woman's dominant position in the control of farmlands, the most important factor of production in agrarian communities accords her certain degree of economic independence and autonomy from her husband. The dominance of the women in petty trade has further boosted women's economic power. One is tempted to argue that the high divorce rate in Afikpo has a lot to do with this economic independence and autonomy enjoyed by Afikpo women. As earlier indicated, over 75% of marriages in traditional Afikpo are likely to end in separation or divorce. It is not uncommon to find a woman in Afikpo who married over four husbands in her lifetime. The high divorce rate in Afikpo could also occur because family members do not hesitate to intervene in the marriages of a family member if they have reason to believe either their daughter or son is having a bad deal in his or her marriage. As Amadiume (1995:82) rightly observes, in "Igbo culture, it is her brothers that a woman expects to fight for her and protect her, *not her husband* (emphasis in original). African families look after their own and this protection does not cease after the daughter is married away for example. One other reason for the high divorce rate, is that divorce does not attract stigma in Afikpo.

The gender balance that obtains in Afikpo seems rather consistent with matriarchal societies. Kashagama (in an e-mail exchange of May 29, 2001) describes the Pre-Islamic Tuaregs as matriarchal. The Tuaregs according to him live between present day Algeria and Niger, and they trace their origins to Queen Tin Hinan. According to him, it is the men that wear veils, and the women wear a head-dress in Tuareg custom. Kashagama (2001) states:

> Although the generally unveiled Tuareg women lost some of their power after their conversion to Islam in the 11th Century, they still retain more economic and social power than most of their present urban counterparts. They live in a completely matrilineal society. Tuareg women regard themselves as men's equals, marry at will, speak in council and serve as heads of encampments. Wives go where they please, hold property, teach and govern the home. Tuareg women in this distinctly classed society, have their mother's rank and regard maternal uncles as next of kin. Matriarchs preside over some tribes and the men who head others are chosen by women.

In Afikpo, men and women take turns to name their children. The first son by custom is named after the father of the man, and the second son takes after the father of the woman. Same goes for naming the daughters, with the first faughter taking after the name of her father's dad, hence *Nnenna,* and the second daughter named after the mother of her mother, thus, *Nnenne.* The third son takes after his father's name as in *Ogbonnia or Junior.* Likewise, the third daughter is named after her mother as in *Ogbonnie.* The belief in reincarnation further reinforces this culture, as it is strongly understood that it takes two people to create a human-being—one from both the mother and father's lineage. The following case illustrates some of the issues raised in the discussion above. It also supports the argument that one's gender does not affect one's right to inherit the lineage's farmland. Further, restoration and reconciliation as the goals of justice making are emphasized. The case further brings to the fore the relationship between the State courts and Afikpo indigenous courts. The case originally started as a criminal case in the Afikpo Chief Magistrate Court. The defendants were, accused by the Commissioner of Police of tampering with Nigerian government survey plans. Though a criminal offense, the court decided that establishing the ownership of the land in dispute is essential to understanding why the defendants in the case committed the offense. The case was referred to the Afikpo Chief and his Cabinet to determine the true owner of the piece of land in dispute, and also to reconcile the warring parties.

Figure 7.1. Case Note (Land Matters)

ARBITRATION BY EZE O TUU OYIM 1 AND HIS CABINET – DECISION GIVEN ON WEDNESDAY (AHO) 9TH JAN. 1985 - ARBITRATION IN COURT CHARGE NO. MAF/267C/84

COMMISSIONER OF POLICE

VS

i. AZU OKPANI (M) 60 YEARS

ii. OKPANI EGWU (M) 32 YEARS

iii. DARLINGTON IBE (M) 37 YEARS

A. This matter was initially commenced as a criminal case in the Chief Magistrate's Court, Afikpo, where the 4, defendants were charged with (quote charge…), vide Charge No. MAF/267C/84. His Worship the Chief Magistrate, Afikpo, later referred the case to the Omaka Ejali of Afikpo and his Cabinet for arbitration, in order first of all, to ascertain and determine the ownership of the piece of land in dispute.

B. During the three days sittings the Arbitrators took evidences from the two sides of the parties in the dispute as follows:

Mgbor Onwu Oko (F)	Plaintiff
Orum Mgbor (F) Otu Ekoh (M) Oko Agbi Raphael Oko Alu	Witnesses for Plaintiff
Azu Okpani Okpani Egwu Darlington Ibe	Defendants
Essa Ibe Ogbuh Essa Uhere Oko Essa Esseh Azu Egwu Udeh	Witnesses for the Defendants

The parties were warned that only those witnesses who must be out of sight and out of hearing that would give evidence before the Arbitrators.

In her evidence, Mgbo Onwu Oko, as the main spokesman for the plaintifss, told the Arbitrators that the piece or parcel of land in dispute was her bona fide property. She proceeded to narrate how this piece of land came to belong to her. And the story was that her grandmother by name Ola Isu was the wife of one Isu Iduma of Ugwuegu Elu and that the eldest daughter to the marriage was one Ogeri Ola Isu (F).

Isu Iduma performed the Omume Title and during the ceremony, Ogeri Ola Isu, as his first daughter, danced the traditional dance called 'Aja' for him. Hence he (Isu Iduma) bequeathed this piece of land called Ebor Ihie to her. Isu Iduma was of the Ibe Ogbagi extended (Ikwu) family while his wife Ola Isu belonged to Ibe Otiama extended (Ikwu) family. At the death of Isu Iduma, his wife Ola Isu got remarried at Ngodo and was blessed with a child by name Chi Idam.

This means then that Ogeri Ola Isu and Chi Idam were both Ola Isu's daughters. Ogeri Ola Isu got married to one Nwafor of Ezi Ekuma of Ugwuegu-Elu and got a child by name Alu Aja. And Chi Idam herself was married to one Onwukwe Mgbor Oko of Ugwuegu and got a child by name Mgbo Onwu Oko – the 1st plaintiff in this case. For the defendants, Azu Okpani was the spokesman. He had not much to say. He told the arbitrators that this particular piece of land called Ebor Ihie formally belonged to Egwu Ihite of ibe Oriete extended (Ikwu) family. He averred that this piece of land was a gift to his (Egwu Ihite's) son Ezeali Chi for making 400 yam mounds in one day. That is Iko Nnu, in Ehugbo dialect.

This man, Azu Okapni also told the arbitrators that Alu Aja, that is the plaintiff's senior brother now deceased, showed this piece of land to him.

C. The detailed proceedings of the case at the period of arbitration are contained in the official records book of the Omaka-Ejali-in-Council and is available on demand.
D. Following is the SUMMARY of the FINDINGS:

   1. The arbitrators were convinced beyond reasonable doubt that Mgbo Onwu Oko (plaintiff) and the three respondents Azu Okpani (M); Okpani Egwu (M) and Darlington Ibe (M) are of the same extended kindred group (Ikwu) – Ibe Otiama.
   2. It was established that even though both are under the same umbrella of Ibe Otiama kindred, each has her own 'breast' lineage.

   It is pertinent to note here that according to Ehugbo customs and traditions some landed property may be inherited in succession by the eldest surviving person (male or female) of the same (Ikwu) kindred group. There are also some landed property that may be exclusive of others and inherited by ONLY the eldest surviving member of the immediate descendants of the deceased. Such a group in the kindred group (Ikwu) are known and called "Nhileho" otherwise known as people who sucked from one female breast. As a result, in Ehugbo the (Ikwu kindred group is referred to as resembling the meat guinea fowl which is set in layers (Akpalakpa) so to speak. So that while all form the flesh meat of the bird, each layer is easily identifiable. (emphasis added).

> Consequently in Ehugbo, the saying that OURS is OURS and mine is mine applies very conveniently in the (Ikwu) kindred group context. It is therefore a common practice in Ehugbo that people of the same maternal lineage do not equally own ALL landed property referred to as belonging to the Ikwu.

3. Evidences were adduced by both parties to show that even though Mgbo Onwu and Ogeri Ude are of the same Ibe Otiama kindred, each one claims to be keeping the Adudo Ukwu. For the avoidance of doubt, in Ehugbo there is ALWAYS ONLY ONE Adudo Ukwu in ANY Ikwu of immediate descendants.

(Adudo Ukwu) is a portable juju shrine that symbolizes the root of maternal breast relatives. It is usually kept by the eldest woman of that lineage. In a particular Eke Day during the Ehugbo Dry Season festivals, every married woman of the same maternal lineage, prepares a nice foofoo dish which she carries to the custodian of their Adudo Ukwu. This is done once every year and serves as a roll call and symbol of identifying maternal relations. At the death of the custodian the next eldest female member of the lineage transfers the juju (usually in a small oblong wooden base basket (abo) to her own home. This practice still persists today save that those women who are Christians or Moslems no longer take part in the exercise. However, they still know and recognize such a woman as the eldest in the line and a root of the lineage).

4. It was discovered that whereas Ogeri Ude (respondent) inherited their adudo ukwu in place of Chi Efor of Ukpa who went to Church about five years ao, Mgbor Onwu inherited hers from Ogeri Ola Isu long before the Nigerian Civil War. Mgbor Onwu is older than Ogeri Ude in all respects.
5. At one time the Ibe Ogbaghi family attempted to reclaim the land and lost, when Onwukwe took oath on behalf of the plaintiffs and survived it. Azu Okpani averred that this dispute once went before the Ibe Otiama elders and it was decided that the defendants should apologise to the plaintiff Mgbo Onwu by buying for her yams and fish. At another time the dispute went to the Essa of Ugwuegu who also decided in favour of the plaintiff and asks the defendants to apologise to her.
6. The arbitrators find it difficult to believe that if both the plaintiff and the respondents wanted them to accept, they could have been ordered by two independent bodies and at different times to apologise to the person who sold their jointly owned parcel of land.
7. Ogeri Ude is the eldest woman keeping adudo ukwu in the Respondents side while Mgbo Onwu is the oldest and keeping that of the

plaintiff. Thus just is clear that though both are of the Ibe Otiama kindred they have different breast relations. Both agreed on this.

8. From all the pieces of evidence collected it is proved beyond doubt and infact is agreed to by both sides in the dispute that the Otiama extended (Ikwu) family was not the original owners of the land. The plaintiffs claim that the land belonged to Isu Iduma of Ibe Ogbagi while the defendants claim that it belonged to Egwu Ihite of Ibe Oriete who bequeathed it to Ezeali Chi of Ibe Otiama.

   Thus it is proved that the land is not, according to Ehugbo custom, an 'Eburu Ebu' of Ibe Otiama family meaning that the Otiama family was not the original founders. It belongs exclusively to Ogeri Ola Isu's house, the eldest of whom now living is Mgbo Onwu Oko the plaintiff. Alu Aja her senior brother having died.

E. DECISION

In order to promote reconciliation between the two parties who are of the same Ibe Otiama family kindred (Ikwu) the arbitrators have leaned heavily on the customs and traditions of Ehugbo. They therefore have decided as follows:

1. Since Mgbo Onwu (Plaintiff) and Azu Okpani (Defendant) belong to the same Ibe Otiama family kindred, no attempt should be made by any side to further disrupt the peaceful co-existence of the family (emphasis added).
2. Though both parties are of Ikwu Ibe Otiama it is clear from the existence of two Adudo Ukwu that Mgbo Onwu's section of the lineage is different from that of Azu Okpani. This customary provision therefore confers on each side a measure of autonomy in inheritance of landed property without prejudice to those landed property exclusive to the entire matrilineal lineage.
3. The fact that even the Ibe Otiama male elders decided at one time that Azu Okpani and group should apologise to Mgbor Onwu who sold the piece of land is indicative that she had the customary right to do so. The apology was only meant to sustain the family relation, otherwise nothing prevented the Ikwu to rebuke Mgbo Onwu if she overstepped her bounds.
4. Both sides are agreed on the fact that a piece of land given for 'Aja' dance belongs exclusively to the recipient and in this case to Ogeri Ola Isu and her descendants. The two sides are also agreed that Isu Iduma was of Ibe Ogbagi family and that he performed Omume Title and bequeathed this piece of land to his daughter Ogeri Ola Isu the grandmother of Mgbo Onwu Oko the 1st plaintiff.
5. The Arbitrators are agreed unanimously that the piece of land in dispute, according to Ehugbo traditions and customs, belongs to Mgbo Onwu Oko and her immediate brothers and sisters from the same

womb. And that she has the exclusive right to give out any portion of the land to anybody. And that having given a portion to her grandson, Oko Agbi, the latter (Oko Agbi) has the right to sell such portion, so bequeathed to him to anybody else.

6. We therefore find for Mgbo Onwu Oko and hereby award the land to her and her immediate breast relations.

SIGNED AND SEALED UNDER OUR HANDS THIS NINETH DAY OF JANUARY NINETEEN HUNDRED AND EIGHTY FIVE IN THE YEAR OF OUR LORD.

EZE OTUU OYIM 1	-The Omaka-Ejali of Ehugbo (Afikpo)
Essa Omezue N.M. Agada	- (Nkpogoro) Cabinet Leader
Essa Alu Ezeali	- (Ugwuegu) Cabinet member
Essa D. O. Egwu	- (Ohaisu) Cabinet Member
Essa N. Enwo (Snr.)	- (Itim) Cabinet Member
Essa Azu Alum	- (Ozizza) Cabinet Member
Essa Nkama Okpani	- Special Member

Nze L. E. Oko – National President Afikpo Town Welfare Association (ATWA)

Mr. G. A. Agwo – General Secretary ATWA (both Ex officio members).

Essa Emerson A. Uchay – Palace Secretary

NOTE: On the decision day, 9th January 1985 all parties concerned were present and represented as follows:

Plaintiffs	-	Mgbo Onwu
	F.	Orum Mgbo
	G.	Out Ekoh
	H.	R. O. Alu
Defendants	-	Azu Okpani
	I.	Okpani Egwu
	J.	Darlington Ibe

Azu Okpani refused to accept the ruling. Darlington said he would like to further find out his relationship with Mgbo Oko. Raphael O. Alu on behalf of the Plaintiffs accepted the verdict as handed down by the arbitrators.

Signed
K. A. Uchay
(Palace Secretary)

In conclusion, it is important to note that in Afikpo men dominate the major traditional institutions of dispute resolution, like in most patriarchal societies. Many cultural practices underscore the subservient position of women in society. During many cultural ceremonies, women's freedom of movement, are sometimes affected. Women are penalized in the courts for violating these cultural practices. Women's sexual freedom and chastity especially in marriage remain open for public control. While there is no evidence to suggest that gender affects the outcome of cases at the traditional courts, gender bias is implicated by the nature of the cases that come before the courts. Further, cases are determined according to the customs and traditions of the land. It is noted however, that the Afikpo women as a group have a heightened sense of gender and class-consciousness. They have organized and successively resisted certain cultural practices they find oppressive. A good example of this is their recent refusal to swear to the customary oath of chastity. They have also refused to abide by the decisions of the men to dictate towns where they could travel for trade. They rightly interpreted such policies as attempts by the men to control their movements and economic activities. Their militancy and activism are not limited to the local authority. They have also successfully challenged the policies and appointments of the state government. In 1997 the Afikpo women organized to protest the retention of the principal of one of the secondary schools in the town that was oppressing and exploiting students. The state government responded by transferring the principal to another school in another town.

Women have used satire to great effect for both psychological and social benefit to address their social standing. Cultural practices that discriminate against women are song about to draw the community's attention to them. Authoritarian and irresponsible men are used in songs. Women have also used the state agencies of social control to their advantage. The welfare offices in the town have been effective in enforcing alimony and child support payments. These are areas where the traditional institutions of social control have been found to be ineffective. To further highlight the position of gender in the conflict resolution processes of the community, the next chapter examines the responses of the institutions of social control to violations of norms and other offenses.

Chapter Eight

Responding to Breach of Custom/ Regulations and Other Offenses

This chapter examines some of the common breaches of customs, regulations and other offenses handled by the Afikpo indigenous institutions of conflict resolution. To further the understanding of the prohibited acts, a review of the sanctions of other African societies is undertaken. The chapter also examines offender-victim relationships in the Afikpo indigenous institutions of conflict resolution. Through this we come to appreciate the people's processes of law making and social control, their definition of crime and deviance and their concept of justice. The specific processes and institutions involved in the resolution of conflict are analyzed in another section.

Flexibility and dynamism are important aspects of the Afikpo conflict resolution system. The system allows for the democratic participation of victims, offenders, their families and the entire community. Further, litigants are free to choose from any of the several institutions of conflict resolution that best meets their needs. Litigants can move their cases from one institution to the other, and back to the court where they started until they are satisfied with the judgment. Litigants seek out courts where they believe their cases will receive a sympathetic hearing. Afikpo traditional adjudication processes are, aptly described by Ottenberg (1971: 274). He writes:

> There are alternate procedures that can be employed at the outset, and alternate secondary and tertiary avenues to justice. One can first go to an elders' court and then to the Native Authority Court, to an oath shrine, or to the Aro oracle.[1] One can start a case with the middle Afikpo subgrade and then move to any of the others. One can also begin with the Native Court, and if not satisfied there, go to more traditional means of settlement by one technique or another. *The legal*

> *system has an open, nonhierarchical quality that serves individual enterprise and achievement needs.* This pattern is consistent with what we have already observed about other facets of Afikpo social structure, behavior, and authority. [emphasis added].

An additional characteristic of the Afikpo system of conflict resolution is that some conflict resolution institutions apply mediative principles, while others combine mediative and adjudicative principles. Litigants are at liberty to choose which system best meets their needs and interests. However, the parties to the conflict may have to negotiate and agree on the court to take their case to. The family and lineage groupings are less formal and apply more mediative principles. On the other hand, the traditional courts are formal institutions and tend to apply more adjudicative principles.

Almost all facets of life in Afikpo are regulated.[2] Some serious offenses like murder and theft attract stiff sanctions, while minor deviations are restrained through symbolic means like "superstitious" beliefs. For example, according to one of my respondents, to control obscenity and uncleanness, there is a "superstitious" belief that exists in the community. The belief claims if one urinates along the foot-paths, and a passersby steps on it, the waist of the culprit's mother will be broken. In the same vein, fish in streams and lakes close to the villages are forbidden to be eaten ostensibly because they belong to the gods. The real reason for this belief, I was told by my informants was for sanitary purposes. The people draw water and do their washing from these lakes and streams. The fish scavenge on the dirt, aiding in the water's purification. Deviations such as those listed above are often violations without direct victims which, if unchecked, can jeopardize the well-being of members of the community. Some behaviors that are difficult to control are ascribed to an offense against the gods who can perpetrate vengeance on offenders. This means of social control is known to be quite effective, according to my respondents. Further, other minor violations like rudeness and disrespect to one's parents are controlled through the culprit's peer groups like the age-grade. The age-grades, as previously noted, have standard sanctions against elder abuse. Satire is another common and strong mechanism of social control in Afikpo. Satire is applied in cases where it is difficult to prove a case against an accused despite strong suspicions. Murder through sorcery is a good example. Appeals are then put to God to avenge wrong.

Boys who are not initiated into the "Ogo" cult and young unmarried girls are not legally responsible, and cannot be tried for crimes. Boys and girls do not participate in communal labour, nor do they contribute to communal development levies. Adulthood for Afikpo men begins after one is initiated into the "Ogo" culture, and maturity for women starts after marriage. Only at these ages can they identify with any of the age-grades. For men, initiation into the "Ogo" culture symbolizes "training, improvement and refinement of the mind, morals and taste."

MURDER

As in all societies, the crime of murder is a very serious offense in Afikpo. There is a distinction between murder and manslaughter in the community. Depending on the nature of the crime, murder cases are mediated between the victim and offender's family. The victim's family and the offender's family meet under the normative framework of the community. If they reach an agreement on the amount for compensation, the offender compensates the victim's family. The offender's family also bears the cost of the funeral. Should the parties fail to reach an agreement, the general Afikpo assembly holding at the "Okpota" convenes and mediates. If the general assembly fails to reach a consensus or a decision acceptable to the victim's family, they may recommend the offender leave town and settle outside the community, a measure akin to banishment.

If the murder was committed in the course of robbery, it is a crime against the Afikpo people and the general assembly meeting at "Okpota" hears the case. Prior to the advent of the Nigerian state, the offender was tried, and if convicted, was executed by being buried alive. An iroko tree was planted to mark the grave to symbolize the evil deed and act as a deterrent.

Presently, only state courts handle murder and other serious violent crimes. Murderers are handed over to the state. Should a known murderer escape the long hand of the law through a legal technicality, the community persuades the family of the offender to advise him/her to leave town to eschew a breakdown of the social order.

The killing of a kinsman, however, is seen as more than a crime, it is an abomination. According to my informants, what the people seek is cleansing and expiation rather than punishment. Amadi (1982:58) notes that "in many tribes the killing of a kinsman, the antithesis of caring for him, was not only a crime but also an abomination. After the murderer had been executed his family would have to perform sacrifices and rites to remove the stain of evil and to ward off the anger of the gods."

Further, Amadi (1982) observes that in most African societies, the family of the murder victim and the offender's family met to negotiate appropriate compensation. The process was always under the watchful eye of the entire community. The community elders supervised the bargaining to ensure that compensation was not excessive but within the cultural rules and norms of the people. In some societies, the murderer was even forced to commit suicide. In others, the murderer's son, wife or other relation was executed in his place if he escaped. In still others, the murderer is made to die the same way that his victim did. There are cases in other African societies where the murderer was required to replace the victim with another person. As Amadi (1982: 15–16) reports,

> The Kwale (Igbo) required a girl as replacement and twenty bags of cowries as compensation. The Kakkakari tribe required the murderer to substitute either two girls or a girl and a boy. The Gamawa required fourteen slaves as recompense. In some tribes, like the Gade, the Arago, the Burra and Ikwerre, bargaining was possible, and the death penalty could be commuted to a heavy fine, usually involving replacement by a slave or free-born. In tribes like the Ikwo (Igbo) the murderer was simply handed over to the family of the deceased, which was free to do whatever it liked with him.

These examples illustrate how the sanction against murder varied from one society to the other in Africa. For example, in Orlu (Igbo), the murderer was executed by hanging if apprehended immediately after the crime was committed. But if he escaped and returned after three years, he was a free person. Some societies like the "Kadara treated murderers fairly lightly. They isolated them for a month or so, and that was the end of the affair" (Amadi 1982: 16). Still, for some African societies the punishment for murder depended on whether the offender was a stranger or an indigene. In the societies where bargaining between the victim's family and that of the offender was the norm, the outcome might be different when a stranger was involved. If the offender is a stranger and is apprehended, chances are that he/she will be killed. But if he escapes arrest, the communities of the offender and that of the victim can enter into arbitration where compensation to the victim's family will suffice.

Suicide was considered an abomination. Victims of suicide were not accorded proper burial. Their corpses were thrown into the evil forest. In Afikpo, a suicide victim is buried where the suicide took place. Most suicides are by hanging, either from the roof of the house, or a tree branch in the forest. In such suicide cases, a grave is dug under the tree where the victim hung him/herself, and the rope is cut off for the deceased to slump into the hole. Since suicide is an abomination in the community, efforts are made not to touch the body of the suicide victim. Unlike the customary practice in Afikpo, where mature[3] dead men and women are buried in their homes, suicide victims are never buried in their homes. The explanation given by my informants for burying deceased adults in their homes is that they later become ancestors to whom libation and sacrifices are offered, and so they need to be within the household reach.

Cases of suicide in Afikpo are rather low. Many of my informants could not recall any incident of suicide. Some of my informants attributed the low rate of suicide to the strong family support, and also the support of friends, age-grades, the lineages and the community. The issue was raised whether suicide cases might be concealed, or not discovered, since the traditional system lacks the technology and know-how to conduct an autopsy. The thinking was that it is possible one can take poison and die from it without people knowing, but that such an act is unlikely since people can tell when one is distressed due to the close-knit nature of the living arrangements. Further, since suicide is an abomination, no one would want to incur the wrath of the gods by concealing suicide.

Aside from the strong and extensive support that victims of crime and other misfortunes receive from their primary groupings, another reason given for the low suicide rate in the community is that hardly any behavior is so dishonorable that suicide is a preferred alternative. The Afikpo persons' sense of shame and honor is rather complex. The Afikpo culture is rather permissive, such that every behavior is considered relatively normal. The culture emphasizes contentment and satisfaction with one's position. One is rarely singled out for ridicule. If they are, it has limited duration. Almost every cultural violation has established ways of redeeming one's freedom and honor. As such, suicide, like murder, is seen as an overreaction.

SORCERY AND MAGIC

Beliefs in magic, sorcery and witchcraft seem to pervade most societies. Sorcery and magic are sometimes not easy to distinguish in Africa. Magic can have medicinal values and be used for protective purposes. It can also be used to harm other people. African thought, points out Parrinder (1973:113), rarely distinguishes between the "material and spiritual . . . hence the distinction of magic and medicine is difficult to make, and the two words can both be used, provided that their wide connotation is borne in mind." Magic, notes Parrinder (1973), is another form of religion since the African magician does not perceive his work as simply mechanical but also spiritual. The magician's power to do magic derives from spiritual forces, "even if lower in the hierarchy of forces than are the gods, [hence], . . . magic commands, religion implores" (ibid.). In a like manner, the sorcerer is distinguished from the witch. In some societies, the sorcerer and the witch are known by the same names. Both, are however, regarded with apprehension. To differentiate the two, the sorcerer is referred to as "day-witch" and the witch as "night-witch." Parrinder (1973: 117) points out that the "day-witch or sorcerer, is a conscious and deliberate evildoer; this is in contrast to the witch who works during sleep at night." The sorcerer's vocation is geared towards harming perceived enemies and is hired by clients for that purpose.

The crimes of sorcery, murder, incest and bestiality have always been viewed very seriously and attracted the harshest punishment. In Afikpo, however, belief in witchcraft and sorcery is not so deep and strong.[4] Still, people are frequently accused of practicing witchcraft and sorcery. Sorcery amongst co-wives is believed common at Afikpo due to persistent rivalry and jealousy. One explanation given for this is that the African is highly religious hence every misfortune is either blamed on the gods or an enemy. Any accident, sudden death or illness whose cause was not known was blamed on witches. Still-births, abortion, delayed pregnancy and prolonged labor are often blamed on witchcraft. Witches and wizards were thought to have supernatural powers that could wreak havoc at will. For that reason, they are greatly feared. Amadi (1982: 22) explains,

> Witches were believed to have the power of metamorphosis; that is, it was thought that they could change at will into non-human creatures like bats, leopards, mosquitoes, crocodiles. While in these guises, they could harm their neighbors. One method of killing that was widely attributed to witches was vampirism or blood-sucking. At night, using their mysterious powers, they were said to pass through closed doors to get to their sleeping victims, whose blood they drank. The victims became progressively weaker and might eventually die unless the aid of an experienced medicine man was sought. Sometimes witches left marks on the bodies of their victims.

Interestingly, most of the murder or attempted murder cases that come before the Afikpo traditional courts are witchcraft related. As I stated earlier, the Afikpo traditional courts have no jurisdiction over murder and other serious crimes. Only state courts have the authority to try murder and other violent crimes. However, even though the belief in witchcraft is very strong in Nigeria, state courts do not recognize the crime of witchcraft. Since most murder or attempted murder cases are witchcraft related, victims of witchcraft seek redress in traditional courts where the crime is recognized. However, the crime of witchcraft is not easy to prove hence, the courts resort to oath swearing and divination to establish the truth. Here, both the victim and the alleged offender are made to swear an oath—the former to prove his/her case, the latter to prove his/her innocence.

Oath swearing is ordered in Afikpo but only when the victim is still living. If the victim dies before the oath swearing, the alleged sorcerer is tried by ordeal. The alleged offender is ordered to drink some of the water used to wash the corpse of the victim. The belief is that if you are guilty and drink this water, you will die. Most accused sorcerers often drink the water washed off the deceased's body to prove their innocence. During my field trip in December 1997, a woman who later died of cancer blamed her illness on a fellow teacher neighbor with whom she had had some serious misunderstanding. The alleged witch was made to drink the water used in washing the corpse of the cancer victim. This was the only way she could prove her innocence.

Theft

Theft is, prohibited by the Afikpo people. The community's harshest punishment of fine and ridicule is meted out to thieves. Theft is a crime that brings stigma not only to the offender but to his/her family for generations. It is enough for the thief to return the goods to the victim. The victim of theft is not awarded further compensation beyond what he or she lost. This is also the case in other Igbo communities. As Amadi (1982:16) notes, "for the people of Alanso, Okposi, Afikpo and parts of Owerri it was enough for a thief to return the stolen goods."

In addition, the culprit is fined by his/her age-grade for bringing dishonor to the grouping. Some Afikpo villages can also penalize the thief for a behavior unbecoming of a villager. If a thief tries evading arrest, there is a chance those involved in the pursuit will beat him/her up. Corporal punishment is, however, not part of the penalty for theft, unless the thief is a minor.

Theft cases are heard at the village common playground. At the apprehension of a thief, the entire village meets as a tribunal to examine the case. If the theft is from any of the village shrines or sacred places, and the culprit is a man, the case is heard at the village "Ogo" playground with a men-only tribunal. The trial follows all traditional judicial processes. The determination of the facts in a case requires that all parties to the case be heard. Eyewitness testimony is generally preferred to testimony based on hearsay. Evidence obtained through threats or by duress is generally disqualified. The onus rests on the accused to prove his or her innocence.

Interestingly, in Afikpo, not every act of obtaining someone else's possessions without the owner's consent that constitutes theft. Food or other commodities taken for sustenance is acceptable provided the person taking it does not intend it for sale. Describing other Nigerian ethnic groups with similar behavioral ethics, Amadi (1982:16) writes:

> Among the Nupe stealing food was not punishable if the offender consumed what he stole on the spot. The Jarawa tribe pardoned an offender if he pleaded hunger as a reason for stealing. In Ikwerre and parts of Igbo it was quite normal for one person to take a few nuts from another's bunch of palm fruits heaped by the wayside. The quantity of nuts taken was not expected to exceed what could normally be consumed by an individual or, in the case of a woman, what was needed to yield enough oil for a pot of soup.

Punishments for theft in Africa varied from one ethnic group to another. In the Igara community, for example, the thief was expected to compensate the victim with twice the value of the goods stolen, (Amadi, 1982). In Jawara, the thief was to compensate the victim with five times the worth of the original commodity stolen. Others like Oratta forced the thief to return the goods to the owner. In addition to this, the thief was made to pay a fine and endure public disgrace. The public spectacle included the thief being forced to climb a palm tree ostensibly to the benefit of the entire community. The Ohaffia and Ibibio people painted the face of the culprit black, and paraded him through the community. Sometimes, the thief was forced to dance to a song sang by children and women of the village.

In pre-colonial Afikpo, a repeat dangerous offender was either executed or expelled from the community. People who stole yams at the farms and yam barns had one of their hands cut off. Presently, violent offenders are handed over to the Police. Some repeat, but not dangerous, offenders were disfigured somewhat. The Bolewa people were known to hack one hand off the repeat offender. The Ilesha people, on the other hand, cut off one ear of the thief, while the Ekoi chop off the fingers of the recidivist thief. Some thieves who pose problems to the community were sold into slavery. According to Amadi (1982:17), "the people of Arago, Bassa, Awka, Ndoki, Western Ijaw, Ibibio, Igbira, to name but a few, routinely sold off thieves into slavery." For some communities, the punishment meted out to a thief depends on where the theft took place. The Aro (Igbo) would execute an offender who stole in the market place, instead of the customary penalty of fine for theft. One explanation given for this discrepancy is that the market holds great value for the Aros, for whom trading is the most common vocation.

ADULTERY

Both men and women can be charged and found guilty of adultery in Afikpo. However, a man is only convicted of adultery if he had sex with a married woman from his own village. On the other hand, a married woman is guilty of adultery if she sleeps with another man. Curiously, the definition of the crime of adultery is quite broad in Afikpo. If a married woman accepts a present from a man who previously made a pass at her, she is guilty of adultery. If a man walks across her when she is sitting down or lying down, she is guilty of adultery. If the woman reveals she dreamt of another man besides her husband in a sexual manner she will be tried for adultery. If a man reveals he had sexual intercourse in his dream with a married woman from his village, he will be charged and almost certain to be convicted of adultery. The logic is that the revelation of the dream might be a ploy to seduce either the woman or man. It is widely believed in Afikpo that men are frequently trying to enlarge their families by taking on other wives, as such they "court" married women and sometimes get caught by the husbands of these women. A woman is guilty of adultery if she marries two men from the same village. If her husband dies or divorces her, she must remarry from another village outside that of her husband's. The rape[5] of a married woman is treated as adultery in the community.

Adultery in Afikpo is considered a serious offense because of the potential of such behavior to lead to a breakdown of the social order. Hence, adultery is considered a crime against the land, rather than against the woman's husband as is the case in other places. However, adultery rarely leads to the break-up of marriages in Afikpo. During the Nigerian Civil War (1967 to 1970), a considerable number of young Afikpo married women left their husbands to stay with soldiers. Soldiers were the only group of people with resources and so were attractive to some women. At the end of the war, some women returned to their husbands. They were however required to pay fines to be used to perform necessary expiation rites.

The punishment for adultery in Afikpo is that a big goat be provided to the male elders of the village where the woman is married. There is a common joke by Afikpo women that a woman has committed adultery out of necessity, yet she is asked to pay a fine of a goat. Amadi (1982) observes that among many ethnic groups in Nigeria, a fine is the most popular punishment for adultery. However, according to him, in the Chamba and Nasarawa communities, adultery was not considered an offense. In some communities adultery was a private matter between the husband of the woman and her male accomplice. Examples of such cases are the "Obowo (Igbo) [who] considered it quite sufficient for the adulterer to settle the matter with the aggrieved husband over a keg of palmwine. Among the Ekuri (Ekoi) and Ishielu (Igbo) the aggrieved husband was expected to even the score by seducing a woman from the adulterer's family," notes Amadi (1982:18). This task can also be delegated, for the aggrieved man could pass the responsibility to a member of his family to seduce a woman from the kindred of the man who committed adultery with his wife.

Amadi (1982) also speaks of other Igbo clans like Abaja, Otanzu and Isu, where adultery has no public penal consequences. Here the aggrieved man was required to regain his honor by challenging the man who committed adultery with his wife to a fight. In the Burra society, the man convicted of adultery was required to give the aggrieved husband twelve gowns. In some Igbo clans, the fine was a small amount of money accompanied by goat and drink feasts for the community elders. Amadi (1982:18) describes adultery, which attracted a cash fine among some Igbo clans:

> . . . in addition, the offender was expected to feast the elders and judges on food and soup made from goat meat, four plantains and four bottles of gin. In the Yakoro clan of the Boki tribe the aggrieved husband had the right to seize the adulterer's yams and to burn down his house. Among the Keaka clan (Ekoi tribe) the fine was heavy—a slave or twenty-five pieces of fine cloth. The Ibibio (Ikot Ekpene) would demand twenty goats and five chickens.

In some Nigerian ethnic groups, the value of the fine varied according to the status of the woman involved in the adulterous affair. Amongst the Bakundu community, the penalty for adultery was one goat and one pound, but increased to four goats, two pounds and ten shillings if the woman was the wife of the chief. In some places like the Kanuri, the Gwari, and the Kamuku, the offender was also flogged in addition to the fine. Amongst the Koro people, the penalty for adultery was 100 lashes, which could be redeemed at the rate of 500 cowries per lash. The status and wealth of the offender had implications on the outcome of the case, suggesting a two-tier justice system.

Nevertheless, some ethnic groups in Nigerian view adultery quite seriously. The Igara and the Batta, for example, sold people guilty of adultery into slavery. Among the Igara, a suspect would be subjected to a trial by "ordeal if he denied the accusation. He was made to drink a potion brewed from the poisonous saaswood plant. If he died, he was guilty. If he survived, he then had the right to sell the woman who had accused him or her husband into slavery," (Amadi 1982:18–19). However, capital punishment was the outcome if a man engages in an adulterous affair with a chief's wife in the Yoruba and Edo ethnic groups. Among the Koro people, the aggrieved husband was empowered to poison the man who had an adulterous affair with his wife. The same power was accorded the aggrieved husband to kill the adulterer if that was possible. If possible, the relatives of the murdered adulterer would pay some compensation to the aggrieved man before they can have access to the corpse of their relative for burial. However, the adulterous man could redeem his life by paying a compensation of seven goats and one dog in the Mumuye community.

RAPE

Rape as a crime in Afikpo is seldomly acknowledged unless a rape occasions violence. Rape is treated as adultery when a married woman is involved. If an unmarried girl is raped, the offender is sometimes forced to marry her. The logic behind this practice is because the victim of rape is inflicted with a debilitating stigma, no responsible person will marry the girl victim of rape. The harshest punishment of ridicule is reserved for offenders, who rape minors. In some cases the rapist pays compensation to the parents of the victim. The rapist will also be held responsible for the medical bills of the victim and any child born of the rape. The situation is, aptly described by Amadi (1982:19):

> Rape was more clearly recognized when it involved a young unmarried girl or virgin. The standard punishment was for the offender to pay damages to the parents. Such damages would be at least equal to the bride price that parents would have received from a more patient suitor. Some tribes, such as the Kanuri and the Igara, would thereafter force the offender to marry the girl. In addition, the Igara father would force the rapist to work on his farm much longer than an ordinary son-in-law would normally have been expected to do.

The entire village constitutes a tribunal to hear rape cases. The tribunal sits at the village common playground. It is important, however, to state that few victims of rape are prepared to bring up the case for hearing. None of my respondents could recall being present during a rape trial. It was not ascertained if victims of rape were more comfortable taking their cases to the state courts, either.

INCEST

Incest is, more than a serious crime in Afikpo, it is an abomination.[6] My informants spoke of cleansing and expiation rather than punishment as the redress for incest. Few in the town could recall any incident of incest in the community. The most common type of incest in the community is exogamy, where members of the same matrilineal lineage unknowingly get involved either as husband and wife, or just lovers. Where that is discovered, it is considered an abomination, and the remedy is the dissolution of the marriage. Cleansing and expiation exercises are then carried out. However, there was a case of incest in 1988 that came before one of the village-group traditional courts. It was between a mother and her son. It was the first time such a case was heard in the traditional courts. The elders were bewildered, and without precedent did not know how to address the matter. At the end, they decided on a fine to procure materials to perform the cleansing ceremony. The woman and her son were also exposed and ridiculed, which is the harshest known punishment applicable to any breach.

Ridicule entails using the culprit's name derogatorily by villagers in song. Rattray (1929:372) cited "ridicule as the strongest of the sanctions operating in Ashanti to enforce the observance of the traditional community." The same phenomenon is applicable in Afikpo, a manifestation of the community's close-knit social structure. Fines, exposition and ridicule, arguably the harshest punishment in the community, are reserved for incest, rape, and other sexual offenses. Where such offenses occasion violence, or are recidivist cases, they are referred to the state courts in the town. Otherwise, it is the victim that decides the medium of redress. Although the traditional courts wield considerable power and influence, the authority of the Nigerian State is not in question. In support, Amadi (1982:20), citing Elias, notes:

> It seems that the Criminal Code supersedes the customary law in point of penalty, though not of substantive law. The customary law of crime is still valid, even when it recognizes offenses unknown to the Code. Also, customary rules of procedure and evidence . . . may differ from those of English law; they are however still valid as long as they are not repugnant to natural justice, equity and good conscience.

My findings also support the belief that Nigerian state courts officials' attitude and treatment of sexual offenses are consistent with traditional beliefs and practices. Sexual offenses receive the full weight of the law but only when the perpetrator is a stranger, and the victim a minor. My informants illustrated this point with a known case of four teenagers who were involved in the gang rape of a sixteen year old girl. Despite the seriousness of the crime, the case was settled out of court. Explanations given for the manner this case was handled, was the concern of the after effect of convicting and imprisoning the boys, who were also first offenders. Many victims of sexual offenses generally feel doubly victimized by this manner of handling sexual offenses, hence the reluctance in reporting sexual victimizations. It is important to point out that Nigerian state courts tend to apply imprisonment as a last resort, and only when the offender is considered a danger to the community. This is because punishment undermines the goal of justice in Africa, which is primarily the restoration of social equilibrium. As Adeyemi (1990: 53) points out, Africans " . . . cannot appreciate a treatment like imprisonment, which, if it benefits at all, is benefiting only the government, in total disregard of the victim and the African need to maintain social equilibrium" (as cited in Stern 1999: 239).

Nonetheless, incest is a behavior that is universally prohibited. Societies view incest seriously and consequently reserve the harshest punishment for incest. Clifford (1974: 124) observes: "if there is a natural law then incest is an example of a natural crime. Margaret Mead has shown that the incest rule forbidden sex relationships between son and mother, father and daughter, brother and sister is a constancy in all cultures."

Incest is said to have health, social and psychological repercussions. Amadi (1982:27) further argues that the prohibition of incest has biological basis. To illustrate the social and psychological implications of incest, he states,

> " . . . it is argued that there are strong psychological reasons why incest is universally abhorred. If a man married his daughter, for instance, his son would also be his grandson, his wife would also be his mother-in-law and his other children would also be his brothers-and sisters-in-law. The resulting confusion would be enough to cause the disintegration of any family.

PATERNITY DISPUTE

Children are very highly valued in Afikpo. When paternity is disputed, many Afikpo families and lineages will go to any length to claim a child they believe is theirs. Cases relating to paternity claims are common due to the number of children born out of wedlock, and the very high divorce rate in the community. As such, a considerable number of the cases that are heard in the traditional courts pertain to paternity claims. For a society whose level of technological development is rudimentary, determining who the biological father of the child is problematic. Nonetheless, the community has standard policies on the matter. For an unmarried woman, it is the man she says who fathered her child that is recognized, unless there is overwhelming evidence to the contrary. For a married woman, it is the legally recognized husband—that is the man who paid the dowry who has legitimate claim to the child.

Reproduced below is a decided case that illustrates these principles discussed above. The report is reproduced without any editing to show the level of reasoning and language of the traditional court judges, and the principles and procedures employed.

Fig. 8.1. Case Note (Paternity Dispute)

"IN CONFORMITY WITH THE TRADITIONAL RIGHTS REPOSED ON THE EKPUKE-ESSA ELDERS OF AFIKPO TO MEDIATE IN CUSTOMARY MARRIAGE DISPUTES BROUGHT BEFORE THEM IN FULL COUNCIL FOR SETTLEMENT, THE EKPUKE ESSA ELDERS ON 4TH NOVEMBER 1975 DECIDED AS HEREUNDER:

1) COMPLAINANT:	Madam Ugo Azu of Ezi Okoro Ugwuoke Amuro.
2) PARTIES IN DISPUTE:	Madam Ugo Azu for and as pleading on behalf of her son Awoke Oko of Ezi Okoro Ugwuoke Amuro Afikpo. AND Ekuma Oko of Ezi Uzu Ihuogo Ugwuegu.
3) CAUSE OF COMPLAINT:	Customary ownership and custody of the child Oko Ekuma delivered by Udu Oko on 28th September, 1975.
4) MEDIATORS:	The Traditional Ekpuke-Essa Elders of Afikpo in full Council as customarily constituted.
5) MEDIATION ACCEPTANCE:	Both parties agree that the Ekpuke-Essa Elders of Afikpo should arbitrate on the customary custody of the child in dispute.
6) STATEMENT OF FACTS:	Madam Ugo Azu speaking on behalf of her son Awoke Oko resident at Nkalagu stated that Udu Oko was responsible for putting the said Udu Oko in a family way. That while yet in the state of pregnancy Udu Oko retreated from continued marriage with her son Awoke Oko and rejoined the former husband Ekuma Oko. That on the delivery of the child the customary "Okokoruko" gifts of fish with yams were carried to Udu Oko in establishment of Awoke Oko's natural paternity of the infant child delivered on 28/9/75. But the said Udu Oko refused to accept the gifts hence the complaint to the Ekpuke-Essa Council.

Ekuma Oko on his part stated that he proposed marriage engagement with Udu Oko right from her tender age. After 4 years wooing, the said Udu Oko was bethroted in marriage to him at her age of puberty. That the Ekuma Oko completely paid in full the customary bride price to the parents of Udu Oko before the said Udu Oko was lead to him in marriage.

That by the marriage they had first had a female issue before this second male issue now in dispute. That due to matrimonial bickerings between the wife and himself, Awoke Oko had to seduce the said Udu Oko with whom they both eloped to Nkalagu to be engaged in marriage. Before the elopement the said wife Udu Oko was already in an early state of pregnancy. When it became known that Udu Oko was keeping with Awoke Oko at Nkalagu, Otu Eni was as an emissary sent by Ekuma Oko to entreat for her re-union with him. Udu Oko acceded to the entreaty and had to desert her paramour Awoke Oko to join her legal husband Ekuma Oko with whom she lived till the child was born and is still living till date.

Awoke Oko never paid even a mite by way of dowry, refund and whatever illicit affairs he might have had with Udu Oko cannot grant him the customary right of custody and possession of the child.

FINDINGS: Awoke Oko who seduced Udu Oko away from her matrimonial home to be engaged by him cannot by custom be regarded as the legal husband of Udu Oko until such a time he should have refunded the bride price paid to her parents by Ekuma Oko. The separation of Udu Oko with her legal husband was only for brief period when they again had to rejoin in wedlock. Ude Ucha the mother of Udu Oko confirms in evidence that Ekuma Oko was the natural father of the disputed child Oko Ekuma.

DECISION: Ekuma Oko is by custom the legitimate father of the disputed child, and is by this arbitration granted the custody and paternity of the said Oko Ekuma.

SIGNED:

1. Ezeogo Ukor Ugo	2. Ndukwe Azu	3. Inya Aja
4. Okulim Nwachi	5. Aja Obiahu	6. Aluu Ekuma

7. E. A. Uchay (Member/Secretary-the Traditional Council of Elders-Afikpo)." (as cited in Elechi 1991:38-9).

INHERITANCE

Inheritance matters are a major basis for conflict in Afikpo. Inheritance in Afikpo is either through the matrilineal or patrilineal lineage. As earlier noted, every person is a member of both the patrilineal and the matrilineal groupings within the society. Both systems are property controlling, with an established hierarchy. Members of the patrilineal group generally reside in one compound or village, while the matrilineal groupings are scattered all over the town and beyond.

When mediative efforts at both the family and lineage level fail, the cases are brought to the village-group traditional courts. Commodities for inheritance in Afikpo are of two main types, moveable and immovable. Immovable properties include land, houses and fruit-trees. Common moveable commodities include livestock, clothes and jewelries, household furnishings and kitchen utensils.

Among the patrilineal groupings, conflict arises over who should inherit the father's dwelling house or farmland. In principle, a man's house is, inherited by his first son. He enjoys this right only after he has completed his father's burial rites. Other male sons of the deceased must also partake in the inheritance. If the man dies without a son, other members of his patrilineage, including his brother, his brother's son, his half-brother or his half-brother's son, or any other male member of the patrilineage, can inherit the building or the land upon which the house formally stood. As Nsugbe (1974:87) points out, "rights to patrilineal building land, therefore, are patrilineally inherited in Ohaffia as in patrilineal Ibo groups."

On the other hand, moveable commodities and matrilineal farmlands are inherited through the matrilineal lineage. This point needs further clarification. In practice what the matrilineal lineage does is preside over the distribution of the wealth of the deceased to his family members. Their involvement is also symbolic in that they demand assurance that their relation died a natural death, and also to assure the bereaved that they have their support. It is to be emphasized that the matrilineage not only, partake in the sharing of the deceased's wealth, they are also responsible for the deceased's debts and seeing to the well being of the deceased's dependants.[7] The process and practice are clearly and accurately described by Ottenberg (1965: 49) and is reproduced below. He notes that

> . . . the moveable household goods or personal effects of the deceased, including boxes, guns, cloth, and yams (the only crop traditionally grown by men), are divided among the 'houses' a short time after the burial. This is usually supervised by the matrilineage-head of the deceased, a person who generally lives outside the dead man's compound, and often outside his village as well, and thus is not

> usually a fellow patrikinsman. The head may live at some distance and may appoint a younger matrilineal relative who lives closer to the compound to carry out the duty. The value of the property to be divided is not great, and it is not considered a very exacting task to be the divider, though there is a strong feeling in Afikpo that the division should be done according to customary rules. This is based on the same ranking of 'houses' used in the division of the shillings at the burial ceremony. The 'house' of the eldest son gets the largest share, the next 'house' with the next eldest son, the second share, and son . . ."

As already noted, about eighty five percent of the farmland in Afikpo belongs to the matrilineal groupings, and does not belong to any individual, hence not subject to inheritance. However, an individual in Afikpo can buy a piece of land which he lays direct claim to. As such, an Afikpo person is entitled to three kinds of land rights, namely, patrilineal, matrilineal, and personal or private rights. If the land is not built upon, his children have no rights over the property. Even if the land is built upon, provided it is not where he ordinarily resides with members of his family, his children do not automatically inherit it unless he left a will—written or oral. Describing another matrilineal system in Ohaffia, another Igbo people, Nsugbe (1974:89) observes:

> Lands purchased or otherwise acquired by an individual are private lands. At the owner's death, provided the lands are not built on, such lands will be inherited by the appropriate member of the deceased's matrilineage, usually a sister's son, or in the absence of one by the clos est male or female member of the man's matrilineage.

Afikpo customary law differs significantly with the Nigerian state laws mostly in inheritance matters. Nigerian courts, like their Western prototype, recognize father-son inheritance, while the Afikpo customary laws do not, except in residential dwellings. Reproduced below is a decided case in the Afikpo Traditional Courts that best illustrates the principles discussed above and the socio-economic basis for the principles. It also highlights the pattern of Nigerian state and Afikpo indigenous institutions' relationship. Cases could originate from the indigenous institutions of conflict resolution and proceed to the state courts and vice versa. Sometimes, state court officials are reluctant to pass judgments on some cases that seem delicate and complicated, mindful of the social consequences in the community.

Fig. 8.2. Case Note (Inheritance Matter)

"INHERITANCE OF A COMMERCIAL BUILDING IN EHUGBO (AFIKPO)

On the 1st day of May, 1980, the Secretary of the Afikpo Local Government Area endorsed a letter (Ref. No. AFLG/430/Vol.111/23) to Eze-ogo Otuu Oyim 1, the Omaka-Ejali of Ehugbo (Afikpo) requesting him to go into a case of disputed ownership of commercial building in the Eke Market area involving Ugwube Oko and Oyo Chukwu. (The case had earlier been tried and disposed of by the Ehugbo Traditional Council of Elders at the Eke Market but one of the affected parties - Ugwube Oko - petitioned the Local Government Area Secretary to intervene. The L.G.A. Chief Executive then referred the case to the Omaka Ejali for amicable settlement).

In compliance with the provisions of the Imo State Chieftaincy Institution, and in carrying out one of his duties as the Traditional Head of Afikpo (Ehugbo) Autonomous Community regarding the maintenance of peace and good government in this area, the Omaka-Ejali, Eze-Ogo Otuu Oyim 1., summoned his Cabinet to look into the case of disputed ownership of the said commercial house located in the Eke Market area, Afikpo.

In consonance with the provisions of the Ehugbo (Afikpo) Eze/Chieftaincy Constitution of 1976 (Part 11 (eleven) Sub-sections 1 & 2, all the five Cabinet members representing the five village groups of Ehugbo were invited to sit over the issue. The Chairman and the Secretary respectively, of Afikpo Town Welfare Association (ATWA) were also invited in keeping with the provision of the section just quoted above. Thus the Omaka-Ejali-in-Council comprised nine persons - the Omaka-Ejali himself, his Secretary, the five representatives, one from each of the five village groups in Ehugbo, the Chairman and the Secretary of ATWA.

During the four days (May 25 and 29; June 6 & 9, respectively) of sitting not less than six of the nine members were present on each day. Evidences were taken from twelve persons including the Petitioner, the Respondents and their witnesses.

The detailed proceedings are recorded in the Omaka_Ejali's Official records' book. Following is the SUMMARY OF THE FINDINGS:

After considering the nature of the work of an average Ehugbo fisherman and the close relationship between Chukwu Ogbu Ebulu (deceased) and Ugwube Oko (surviving nephew), the Cabinet found that Ugwube Oko did faithfully serve his uncle Chukwu as a journey man and later became his partner in the fishing and other money-earning ventures.

2. From the evidences of Uhiom Ude (Oyo's chief witness), Uro Obasi (Ugwube's chief witness) Ngwama (elder sister and mother-substitute to Chukwu Ogbu-ebulu and Ugwube Oko), it became clear that Ugwube and Chukwu had no known disagreement and generally worked as one in all their undertakings.

3. Everybody who testified before the Omaka-Ejali in Council upheld the statement that during the settlement of the outstanding land rent in 1976, the two sides in the dispute agreed they were ONE AND INSEPARABLE. Disagreement crept in (as testified by Idam - the eldest son of Chukwu Ogbu-ebulu) from the moment Ugwube, their "father" (by Ehugbo custom) began to reconstruct part of the war damaged commercial house to accommodate his relative, Eke Otu Eke (widow). It is obvious the dispute arose from the misunderstanding of intentions.

4. Uhiom Ude (an esaa and a close friend and kindred man of Chukwu) was equivocal in most of his statements and made deliberate attempts to mislead both Chukwu's children and the Omaka-Ejali-in-Council. He is not to be relied on as a witness in this case.

5. Uro Obasi (of esaa age grade) was Ngwama's husband and Chukwu's guardian who trained him, initiated him in Ogo Ehugbo, performed his first titles, married his first wife for him and therefore was always on the know of the domestic associations and cooperation of the two 'brothers' who had no intentions of drawing lines in the possession of anything that was consistent with natural and traditional laws of the land. His evidence has been taken as a true story of the two 'brothers'.

6. Ngwama Chukwu, Chukwu Ogbu-ebulu's elder sister and mother-substitute to both Chukwu and Ugwube, testified that she was the treasurer for them and kept for them the sum of 700 pounds (1,400 naira) contributed in the ratio of 4:3 by Chukwu and Ugwube respectively for the commercial house project. No one present could disprove that she was by the death bed of Chukwu and had his last wish regarding the said house. The evidences of Uro Obasi and later Uhiom Ude, corroborate her statement that the final burial rite of Chukwu has not been performed by his children as required by Ehugbo custom and tradition.

7. By Ehugbo way of life with respect to the association of parents and children, husbands and wives, it is very unlikely that by February 1966 when Chukwu died, his late wife (Oyo's mother who died in 1974) could have been led into the secret of monetary transactions between the two 'brothers' so as to have passed on the knowledge to her children.

8. Chukwu's children (Idam, Ogbo Chukwu and Oyo) all agreed completely that their mothers and neighbors, including Uhiom Ude, had told them that Uro Obasi was their father's guardian who gave him a start in life. Thus by implication they accepted that he (Uro Obasi) should have a reliable inner knowledge of their father's property.

9. Agha Uchay, an elderly matrilineal relative of Chukwu Ogbu-ebulu, and who was privy to the acquisition of the site for the said commercial building and the building program; and who after the death of Chukwu Ogbu-ebulu introduced the anxious land-lords to the petitioner, Ugwube Oko, corroborates the statements that Chukwu and Ugwube worked very closely and in fact undertook the commercial building as a joint venture.

10. The fact that the Petitioner when introduced to the land-lord at once connected and brought in the deceased uncle's children (Oyo and his brothers) is evident that he, the Petitioner, had not the slightest intention of ousting them, the Respondents.

BASED ON THE FOREGOING STATEMENTS

The Omaka-Ejali-in-Council BELIEVES THAT:

a) Uro Obasi was the de facto father of Chukwu Ogbu-ebulu and know the family associations better than any outsider.

b) Ngwama Chukwu, Chukwu's elder sister and mother-substitute to Chukwu and Ugwube was their treasurer at a stage during the building project.

c) Ngwama was beside Chukwu on his sick bed until he died at Amaizu in February, 1966 and therefore knew more and better about his last moment on earth. And so accepts her evidence to the effect that Chukwu at his death bed cautioned that the commercial building be owned jointly by his children and his nephew, Ugwube Oko.

DISBELIEVES

Most of the evidence of the respondents and their witnesses because they were at variance and conflicting.

The Omaka-Ejali-in-Council took special note of a provision in Ehugbo customs and traditions which stipulates that any child or children who has/have not duly concluded the burial rites of his/their father does/do not normally inherit his/their father's property. (This custom under reference places the inheritance of a deceased male person's assets and liabilities on his immediate matrilineal relatives save where the deceased, while alive, conferred personally in the accepted form of ORAL WILL (ICHO-EKPE) the ownership of any property on his child or children or any other person or persons. Otherwise, it is the prerogative of the deceased's matrilineal relatives to inherit his assets and liabilities PROVIDED that such assets do not include his personal living house usually located in the Village.

JUDGEMENT

After carefully considering the customs and traditions of Ehugbo in relation to inheritance along side the evidences given by both sides in the dispute;

And with due respect to the death wish (by oral will (icho-ekpe) of Chukwu Ogbu-ebulu;

The OMAKA-EJALI-IN-COUNCIL therefore unanimously RULED that:

Chukwu Ogbu-ebulu's children and Ugwube Oko should jointly own the commercial house on a fifty-fifty basis, that is, five rooms for each party.

Signed and sealed under our hands this day, Monday (Nkwo) June 9, 1980 in the year of our Lord;

EZE-OGO OTUU OYIM 1

THE OMAKA-EJALI OF AFIKPO (EHUGBO)

ESAA NNACHI ENWO (SNR.)............................REPRESENTING ITIM

ESAA (DEACON) J. O. MBREY ..........................REPRESENTING OHA-ISU

ESAA AZU ALUM..REPRESENTING OZIZZA

ESAA PHILIP A. EZEALI ....................................REPRESENTING UGWUEGU

MR. GABRIEL A. AGWO
CO-OPTED MEMBER AND
WELFARE ASSOCIATION

NOTE:

The recordings were done by Mr. G. Agwo in place of the Secretary to the Omaka-Ejali, Mr. E. A. Uchay, who from the very beginning of the proceedings, was named as a witness to the two sides in the dispute.

(as cited in Elechi 1991:43-6).

State agencies of social control apparently are coming to the realization that their adjudication of some cases brought before them by the Afikpo fails to do justice. In fact, their judgments sometimes make matters worse. For issues of law and justice to have meaning and be relevant, they must be historically, socially and culturally sensitive. It has already been noted that state laws are product-oriented and rule-based, while customary laws are process-oriented. Rather than base the outcome of a case solely on the law, customary laws focus more on the processes of achieving peaceful resolutions of disputes. For justice to have meaning, it must involve all parties to a case, rather than for one or two parties. This balance is understandable considering the kind of conflicts that come before the customary courts, which in most cases are between blood relations, and therefore require acceptable and lasting reconciliation. With the parties to the conflict and the entire community actively involved in the search for acceptable solutions, the chances of everyone accepting the outcome is increased. This is more so since the processes of justice making is devoid of the symbols of power. All my respondents were in agreement that villagers in state courts seem lost and intimidated. Further, the processes of customary conflict resolution are speedy and inexpensive and in accordance with the adage "justice delayed is justice denied."

DEFAMATION OF CHARACTER

Cases alleging defamation of character are common and they are heard either in the village circle or in any of the traditional courts. Villagers prize their reputation highly and will go to any length to defend their honor. As in all judicial proceedings in Afikpo, the complainant presents his or her case, and then the defendant is asked to respond to the allegations. Most of the time, the defendant is unable to prove his allegation that the complainant was either guilty of theft or adultery, or any other dishonorable behavior. If the defendant stands by his or her allegation, both parties to the conflict may be asked to swear to an oath. Generally, at this point the defendant may withdraw his or her allegation. If the defendant withdraws his or her allegation, he or she will be required to ring a bell round the entire village recounting his or her allegation that the complainant was involved either in adultery, theft or sorcery. If the case was decided at the village-group traditional courts, the defendant will ring the bell round the central market announcing that he or she lied against the complainant.

LOBBYING (IPA OGU)

Lobbying the judges of the traditional courts is a recognized practice in the Afikpo indigenous system of conflict resolution. Litigants are free and even encouraged to approach known key speakers and orators of the traditional courts before their cases come up for hearing at the courts. It is within the cultural practice for litigants to present gifts to the court judges to persuade them to assist in presenting and pursuing their cases. Prior to the advent of money, litigants would work in the farm of the leading speakers of the courts. Practices such as meeting some of the judges in advance are known to help a litigant's case and if done within acceptable customary practices is not regarded as corruption.

One advantage of approaching the judges at home before their sitting is that litigants can seek advice on the effective way to present their cases. Further, the litigant is opportuned to present his/her case in a conducive and relaxed environment. However, if one has a bad case, there is no amount of oratory by the judges that might persuade other judges to view the case favorably. The judges are aware that they are supposed to play a neutral role and must not be seen to show open interest and support for a particular litigant. If that happens, that might alienate other judges and weaken their client's case. Further, it must be realized that the litigants may have approached the same judges. Above all, judges realize they are first of all the judges of the court, and not the proxy of litigants, and that showing open interest and support to a litigant's case may damage their reputation and even undermine their client's case.

It is not improbable that a well-connected, wealthy and influential litigant can identify and approach many powerful speakers of the courts and be able to sway a case one way or the other. In the end, decisions reached at the courts will depend on the evidences presented. It is argued however, that the outcomes of cases are not so predictable and may not certainly depend on how many judges consulted in advance. Outside the two village group courts, anybody present can contribute to the debate. What may decide a case one way or the other may depend greatly on how any speaker is able to articulate the issues in conflict to the satisfaction of most people present in the assembly. The applause from the gathering will leave no one in doubt where the people stand on the matter. Even at the village group courts that allow comments only from the about hundred or so judges present, the summation of the issues must convince the overwhelming majority present. It is generally understood that powerful and decisive comments sometimes come from unsuspecting quarters.

OFFENDERS AND THE AFIKPO TRADITIONAL JUSTICE SYSTEM

Afikpo, like other societies have their conduct norms, about what is good—therefore accepted, and what is bad, and prohibited. Some of the behaviors are considered serious and inimical to the well-being of the community. Such behaviors are likely to attract formal community sanctions. In dealing with the people who violate the rules of living, a distinction is made between "moral evil" and "natural evil." "Moral evil pertains to what man does against his fellow man" (Mbiti 1970: 213). The customs, laws, regulations and taboos governing behavior in society are also violated when a community member's rights are violated. Thieves, sorcerers and those involved in other offenses embody moral evil. Their behaviors harm others and undermine good relationships. Nature can also wreak havoc on people. Evils such as accidents, terminal illnesses and other misfortunes are blamed on natural forces. However, it is also believed that bad people can be purveyors of natural evil.

Further, African people believe that no individual is innately bad. However, as Mbiti (1970:213) points out, "a person is not inherently 'good' or 'evil,' but he acts in ways which are 'good' when they conform to the customs and regulations of his community, or 'bad' (evil) when they do not." Again, since conduct norms vary from one community to the other, it is also recognized that crime is a social construction. There is also the belief that God is the absolute defender of the society's moral order. Yet, maintenance of law and order is the responsibility of the "patriarchs, living-dead, elders, priests, or even divinities and spirits who are the daily guardians or police of human morality" (ibid.). Nevertheless, God punishes evildoers in this life. God can also postpone the punishment for another lifetime when the evildoer reincarnates, hence peoples' misfortunes are interpreted as punishment for moral wrong either committed in the present life or the one before. One's enemies can also be responsible for his or her misfortunes.

It is believed offenders harm more than the individual victim, for they also harm the community. Offenders, it is recognized are also harmed by their own actions. African societies view themselves as a collective, hence responsible for the well-being of its members, including victims and offenders. Crime represents lack of respect, not only for the direct victim, but also the entire community. As Mbiti (1970:214) states, "I am because we are, and since we are, therefore I am." Above all, violations are believed not only to create fear and distrust, but also undermine community bonds and harmony. In this respect the conflict resolution process seeks to attend to the wounds and feelings of the victim, and to restore the community to its former position. Crime is believed to disrupt community bonds and harmony.

To accomplish the above, the offender is actively involved in the process of conflict resolution. The offender, the victim, and the community see themselves as stakeholders in the justice process. Together, they all seek solutions which promote repair, reconciliation and reassurance. The road to repair and reconciliation begins when the offender acknowledges that his/her behavior is a violation of people and other relationships, and that violations create obligations to make things right. An offender's expression of remorse and responsibility over the consequences of his/her behavior is a key to peace. Reparation to the victim is further negotiated in an atmosphere devoid of symbols of power and intimidation. The process is educational with the participants involved in the analyses and definition of societal values. Offenders' competence is greatly enhanced in the process. It is noted that when offenders are actively involved in the decision making process that they are more likely to be in accord with the decisions reached.

People convicted of crimes in Afikpo are either fined and or made to compensate the victim. As previously mentioned, other punishments include reprimand, ridicule, exposition and the use of the offender's name in songs. In high crimes like the unmasking of masquerades and other offenses against the Ogo cult, the culprit's property, both movable and immovable, including that of his or her family and the entire village are looted and destroyed. However, looting is a last resort, and carried out if the culprit refuses to pay the imposed fine and provide the necessary materials for the expiation processes.

It is also important to note that when an individual is accused of stealing or murdering another person through sorcery and witchcraft, the offender is given the opportunity to prove his or her innocence. The offender in the justice process is not required to plead guilty or not guilty. The onus is on the accused to prove his or her innocence. Sometimes the evidence provided is not conclusive either to convict or exonerate the accused. Traditional judicial process demands that the determination of the facts in a case require that all parties to the case be heard. Eyewitness testimony is generally preferred to testimony based on hearsay. Hearsay and circumstantial evidence are considered, but only when the evidence was supported. The credibility of the witness is very important. Evidences obtained through threats or by duress are generally disqualified. Defendants are allowed to interrogate the plaintiff and his/her witnesses. It is also the right of the plaintiff to do the same. The defendants give their own evidence and call witnesses in support of their defense.

Where the evidence provided is not overwhelming to convict the individual accused of theft or witchcraft, for example, the tribunal may decide to administer an oath. The administration of oath is very central to the resolution of conflict in the community. Both the plaintiff and the defendant may seek to use oath swearing to substantiate their innocence and truthfulness. Oath swearing derives from the general belief in the community that the supernatural will acquit the innocent and convict the guilty. This is the standard way of resolving conflicts where the facts of the matter are not so clear and opinions of litigants seem contradictory. Oath swearing works like the polygraph test used to determine truth or falsity in the West.

Imprisonment was never part of indigenous punishments in African societies. Execution was sometimes used in very rare cases where the offender was considered a major threat to life and property in the community. Decisions to impose capital punishment, like every other decision of the indigenous institutions of conflict resolution, must be reached through a consensus of participants present at tribunal. Generally, punishments are geared towards the re-establishment of equilibrium and harmony in the community. The communities are close-knit such that judges of the tribunal often know offenders well enough. As such, punishments are guided by the love ethic that is at the center of the justice system, hence offenders are leniently treated since it is realized that offenders, as members of the community also have good and redeeming qualities.

The healing of offenders begins with their reconciliation with their victims. Since offenders and victims are often accompanied and supported by their family members and well-wishers throughout the court processes, the reconciliation must include them. The healing sometimes must require sacrifices to the earth goddess, if the offence, like the killing of a kinsman, is an abomination. For harmony to be completely restored in the community, reconciliation of the victim, offender, their families and well-wishers, and the angered spirits must take place. It is important to emphasize that when an individual is accused of a crime bordering on abomination, no individual must be seen to show outward support to him or her. The individual must account for his or her actions to the angered spirits alone. People are careful

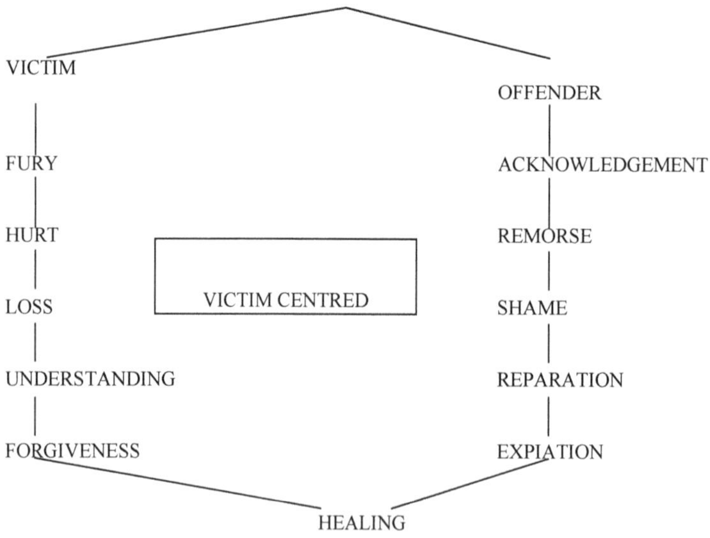

Figure 8.3. Crime and Damage to Victims.
Source: (Brown 1995: appendix)

not to incur the wrath of the deity by supporting an accused who might well be guilty of the offence against the deity. The diagram above illustrates the expectations from offenders in the Afikpo indigenous justice process.

VICTIMS

Victims of crime in Afikpo, like the offender, are actively involved in the conflict resolution process. Victims are involved in the definition of harm and the search for solutions. Above all, the system provides opportunity for the victim to express his/her anger and for the offender and the community to validate his/her loss. The African system of conflict resolution is victim-centered. Nsereko (1992) points out that victims and the community are central to African indigenous justice systems. Further, he observes that under African customary justice system, victims are, cared for by the community. He notes that "many precolonial African societies aimed less at punishing criminal offenders than at resolving the consequences to their victims." It is also recognized that victims have many needs and that not all the needs, can be met by justice. The system provides opportunities for victims to tell their stories in a conducive atmosphere. The victim is supported both by family members, friends and the community without judgment. The victim comes out feeling validated and vindicated.

Sanctions were compensatory rather than punitive, intended to restore victims to their previous position (Nsereko (1988) as cited in Van Ness/Strong 1997:9). Restitution by offenders to victims is, also recognized as a symbolic apology by the offender and his/her family. Victim care is a priority because of strong social solidarity and a prevailing spirit of good neighborliness in the society. It is a serious offense in Afikpo for an adult male not to respond to the distress calls of a kinsman. For a society where very few insure their lives and property, community members come to the rescue of other community members who lose their property through theft, arson and other misfortunes. When a family breadwinner dies or is incapacitated, relatives and community members see it as their obligation to provide for the widow and orphans. African communities grieve with their own who are victims of crime or other misfortunes.

The following case from the village-group traditional courts illustrates the Afikpo justice principles discussed above. The case was, delegated to the Chief-in-Council by the State High Court in Afikpo. However, it is treated as cases adjudicated by the village-group courts because all members of the Chief's Cabinet and the Chief are judges of the traditional courts. Two members of the Afikpo Town Welfare Association, an association of Afikpo youths, are incorporated into the Cabinet in an attempt to represent youths in decision-making. The Chief-in-Council is guided by the same principles that determine cases at the traditional courts. The relationships between litigants are given due consideration in the resolution of a case. Every effort is made to restore the relationship to its former position as much as possible. The responsibility of a community member towards another who is a victim of crime or other misfortunes is also highlighted in the case. Not giving necessary assistance to a community member who is a victim of crime or other misfortune is a violation of the African communalism[8] spirit and a sanctionable offence in Afikpo. The interventionist aspect of Afikpo peoples' culture is also emphasized. A community member will be failing in his/her responsibility towards another if he/she fails to intervene if they are convinced that the community member is involved in behaviors that are potentially harmful to either the actor or other community members. The case exemplifies the relationship between State institutions of social control and Afikpo indigenous institutions of social control. The case is reproduced below verbatim.

Some judgments of, the Afikpo traditional courts are rejected by the litigants or one of the litigants to the case. Litigants may also appeal the judgments of the traditional courts to any of the State Courts in the area. However, where the litigants refuse to appeal the case to the State Courts, the judges of the traditional courts are authorized to enforce the judgment. Acceptance to have one's case tried in the traditional courts also indicates the litigants agreement to abide by the decisions of the courts. The judgments of the traditional courts carry high moral authority, consequently, only few people will reject the judgments of the courts. Judgments like, the case above is not amenable to enforcement. The judges of the courts believe it is their moral responsibility to intervene and bring peace amongst feuding relatives. The refusal of some litigants to accept the judgments of the courts does not threaten or affect the moral authority of the courts to administer justice in the community. The system remains very popular. As the above case illustrates, Afikpo people residing outside the town are likely to bring their conflicts home for resolution if they fail to resolve the conflict amongst themselves.

Non-indigenes from other towns bring cases against Afikpo people in those towns to the courts. These are often cases where the Afikpo businessmen failed to honor business agreements they entered into with others. As earlier stated the Afikpo traditional courts are most effective in recovering debts. Some of the cases of debt recovery are brought by the non-indigenes of Afikpo doing business in the community. It is reiterated here that when convicted offenders are judged incapable of compensating their victims, that the families and village members of the offenders are held responsible.

Fig. 8.4 Case Note (Arbitration in a Civil Matter)

ARBITRATION IN A CIVIL MATTER

(SUIT NO. HAF/20/83)

BETWEEN:

Patrick Agha Uche— Plaintiff

AND

Patrick Uwa Okokpa— Defendant

On 29th August, 1984, the Senior registrar I of the High Court, Afikpo addressed a letter No. HAF/20/83/20 to Ezeogo Otuu Oyim I, the Omaka-ejali of Ehugbo (Afikpo) requesting him "to look into the above-mentioned suit and find possible means to settle the misunderstanding among the parties in the above mentioned Civil Suit pending in this High Court." (A copy of the letter is annexed as Appendix A).

In part, the ORDER OF COURT (also annexed as Appendix B) states:

" . . . I APPOINT EZEOGO OTUU OYIM I, OMAKA-EJALI OF EHUGBO AND AGHA UCHE AND ANY OTHER PERSON OR PERSONS THEY MAY LIKE TO CO-OPT AS ARBITRATORS."

In obedience to the High Court's order and in compliance with the provisions of the Imo State Chieftaincy Institution, and in consonance with the rules and regulations guarding the Omaka-ejali-in-council, the following were summoned to constitute the Aribtration panel:

Ezeogo Otuu Oyim	-	the Omaka-ejali
Esaa Emerson A. Uche	-	Palace Secretary
Esaa (Omezue) N.M. Agada	-	(Nkpghoro) Cabinet Leader
Esaa Nnachi Enwo (Snr.)	-	(Itim) Cabinet Member
Esaa Alu Ezeali	-	(Ugwuegu) Cabinet Member
Esaa Azu Alum	-	(Ozizza) Cabinet Member
Esaa D. O. Egwu	-	(Ohaisu) Cabinet Member

Nze L. E. Oko (Afikpo Town Welfare Association (ATWA) National President) Ex officio

Mr. G. A. Agwo (ATWA National Secretary)—Cabinet Member.

SITTINGS:

On the first day, Saturday (Eke) 29th September 1984 Patrick Uwa Okokpa (Defendant) and three of his witnesses were present while Patrick Agha Uche and his witnesses were absent. The arbitration was put off (after over an hour's waiting) to Saturday, 20th October, 1984.

On 20th October, 1984 all the Arbitrators as named above were present. The two parties were present as follows:-

Patrick Agha Uche	-	Plaintiff
Patrick Uwa Okokpa	-	Defendant

The witnesses were named as follows:-

For the Plaintiff: Irem Obiahu, Akpu Anwara, Oka Otu, Raphael Oko Alu, Lucia Egwu, Teresa Aghaisuoti, Lawrence uche, Uche Alu and Daniel Oko Ibiam.

For the Defendant were: Grace Okokpa, Raphael Oko Alu, Nkiriuka, Johnson Okokpa (absent) and Evelyn Uro Uche.

During the hearing, the Plaintiff stated his case and called FOUR witnesses. The defendant stated his own, and called three witnesses and tended two documents in support of his claims as Agha Uche's in-law.

The detailed proceedings are contained in the Omaka-ejali's official records book which is available on demand. Following is the

SUMMARY OF THE FINDINGS AND DECISION

From the evidences brought before the arbitrators and supported by individual and personal knowledge of the two parties in dispute, the arbitrators have established that:

1. Patrick Agha Uche (Plaintiff) and Patrick Uwa Okokpa (Defendant) are in-laws in every aspect of Ehugbo tradition and custom. Patrick uche's deceased elder brother, Uzor Egwu, was the father of Grace Enya Okokpa (nee Enya Uzor) i.e. Patrick Uwa Okokpa's wife. In Ehugbo tradition and custom, Patrick Agha Uche is now the father-in-law of Patrick Uwa Okokpa. Thus in the absence of Uzor Egwu, Agha Uche could stand in loco parentis and collect Bride price on the Defendant's wife.

   Because of this relationship Patrick Uwa Okokpa could not even pay the customary Bride Price on his wife, grace Okokpa without due consent and or presence of Agha Uche.

2. For over four months Agha Uche lived happily as an in-law in Uwa Okokpa's house at Abuja at no extra costs. During that period Agha Uche was well treated as a Contractor in search of contract work at Abuja. He was looked after and treated like the father of the household at Abuja.

3. Uwa Okokpa became displeased with Agha Uche when he, Agha uche, continued importing free women and noisy visitors to their house against his (Uwa's) expressed wishes.

4. This source of annoyance reached a breaking point on the day an agreement was to be signed and sealed between the Defendant and a boy being apprenticed to him (Defendant) as a draughtsman.

The plaintiff was invited and on going took along a "strange girl" to the Defendant's house. The Defendant expressed his displeasure and told the Plaintiff such an action was capable of corrupting his (defendant's) loyal wife. The Plaintiff did not take kindly to that observation as reflected in the libation speech.

As the elderly man in the occasion, the Plaintiff was given the 'hot drink' meant for libation. Instead of praying for their success and long life, the Plaintiff Agha Uche poured out curses saying inter alia "those who do not want me to move along with the women I like should not see any good thing in life. They should go to blazes." The Defendant, of course, was angered by this and felt the purpose for the libation was defeated. In a reaction, he, Defendant, poured out and served the drink indiscriminately even to uninvited passers-by.

5. When Agha Uche finally settled down in his own quarters, he did everything to run down Uwa in the way of character assassination—branding him a man without any visible means of livelihood and one who was incapable of associating with people from his own home town.

6. The height of the bitterness against the Plaintiff was reached when the Defendant's brand new peugeot saloon car was seized from him by armed robbers outside his house about 6 a.m. on 16th february, 1983. Agha Uche, his close neighbour and a father-in-law heard the gun shots and the noise of the car driven away. He, Agha Uche never showed up for a moment to sympathise with Uwa even when he Agha Uche, knew that the Defendant's wife was hit on the thigh by a stray bullet from the armed robber's rifle.

7. **Apart from Agha Uche having acted as a bad neighbour he contravened Ehugbo Customary way of life by failing in his duty to run to the aid of a fellow indigene especially in a strange land.** Besides, up to date he has not asked Uwa about it, even on the road. It was inhuman for Agha Uche to send for Uwa and his wife at the time when near and distant neighbours and well-wishers flooded their house to sympathise with the family on the armed robbery incident. Agha Uche's apparent care of Uwa's children and his wife when Uwa was away at the Police station, was very casual (emphasis added).

8. No convincing evidence has been aduced to show that Uwa ever accused Agha Uche of either being the thief of his car or planning for the theft. If Uwa ever suspected Agha Uche he could have named him as a suspect to the Police at Abuja where the incident took place.

9. Raphael Oko Alu, who incidentally stood in as a witness to both parties, is a very slippery and unreliable character. Most of the misunderstanding that led to the court case at home probably arose from his activities and utterances. It is possible he misrepresented one party before the other and therefore caused the mischief.

The fabricated story of Raphael Oko Alu that Agha Uche was responsible for the car theft led to his (Agha Uche) suing Uwa to Court. He denied ever telling Agha Uche so.

DECISION

Having patiently listened to the two parties and their witnesses, and carefully studied the evidence aduced before the arbitrators, the unanimous decision is that:

1. Agha Uche has not proved his case beyond reasonable doubt that Uwa Okokpa accused him of being responsible for the theft of his car.

2. Uwa Okokpa's main source of annoyance and complaint against Agha Uche his father-in-law, is that he (Agha Uche) has failed to show sympathy towards him (Uwa) for the loss of his three month's old car to armed robbers at Abuja.

3. Agha Uche is hereby advised to withdraw the case from Court but Uwa Okokpa is to refund half of the summons charges to Agha Uche.

4. **Both Plaintiff and Defendant are hereby called upon to resort to the Ehugbo traditional way of reconciliation by:**

   (a) **Offering of handshake to each other and**

   (b) **Exchanging of drink from a cup** (emphasis added).
   Before us here and now.

5. Raphael Oko Alu is hereby seriously reprimanded for his mischievous role in the whole matter.

   Signed and sealed under our hands this day, Friday (Nkwo) 23rd November, 1984 in the year of our Lord.

Ezeogo Otuu Oyim I	-	the Omaka-ejali
Esaa Emerson A. Uche	-	Palace Secretary
Esaa (Omezue) N.M. Agada	-	(Nkpghoro) Cabinet Leader
Esaa Nnachi Enwo (Snr.)	-	(Itim) Cabinet Member
Esaa Alu Ezeali	-	(Ugwuegu) Cabinet Member
Esaa Azu Alum	-	(Ozizza) Cabinet Member
Esaa D. O. Egwu	-	(Ohaisu) Cabinet Member

Nze L. E. Oko (Afikpo Town Welfare Association (ATWA) National President) Ex officio

Mr. G. A. Agwo (ATWA National Secretary)—Cabinet Member.

The recordings were made by Mr. G. A. Agwo on behalf of the Palace Secretary. The contents were read out to the Omaka-ejali-in-Council in both English Language and Ehugbo dialect of Igbo language. All appeared to understand everything and adopted same as correct proceedings throughout the duration of the arbitration hence the office seal as shown above.

Footnote:

When the findings and decision were read out to the Plaintiff and the Defendant, Agha Uche (the Plaintiff) rejected the decision while Uwa Okokpa (the Defendant) accepted the findings and decision.

As a result of Agha Uche's rejection of the decision, the traditional reconciliation recommended in (4) a & b above was not carried out.

The cost of producing the entire document was borne by Mr. G. A. Agwo as his personal contribution towards justice and fair play in the Society.

Signed

E. A. Uchay

Palace Secretary.

However, the Afikpo indigenous system of conflict resolution is faced with many challenges. These include the economy, urbanization, state institutions, the youth and Christian religious elites. The next section briefly examines the series of challenges facing the Afikpo indigenous system of conflict resolution.

CHALLENGES FACING THE AFIKPO INDIGENOUS SYSTEM OF CONFLICT RESOLUTION

The Afikpo indigenous system of conflict resolution is plagued with many challenges. Chief among the challenges facing the system is the co-existence of Christian and Moslem communities, demographic changes, and economic factors. The above seems to be the general view of most of the interviewees regarding the Afikpo indigenous justice system and culture. Some of the responses of one of the elders illustrate these points:

> **Question:** Chief, do you believe there is a future for the Afikpo traditional system of conflict resolution and culture in general?
>
> **Elder:** I believe there is.
>
> **Question:** Where do you base your hope, considering most of the traditional institutions are disintegrating and some of them are becoming almost extinct.
>
> **Elder:** Regarding justice making for instance, there do not seem to be a better alternative yet. People are gradually realizing that our system is effective and that there is need to return to it. The fact that some of you in academics are taking interest in our system is a good indication and that further raises my hope that the system has a future.

Question: What do you consider to be the major threats to Afikpo culture?

Elder: I will argue that the biggest threat to the Afikpo culture is the economy. This is because the system depends on the people for its survival. Afikpo economy is not expanding enough to keep youths at home. Look around the villages, you notice all you see now are old men and women who are retired. Knowledge about our culture are passed from one generation to the other through oral history and learning through the participation of the people in cultural activities. Further, the Afikpo town is rapidly urbanizing and that also could introduce some stress to the system.

Question: How about the activities of the Christian Churches—of recent there have been reports of clashes between Christians and traditionalists. Don't you find that problematic—perhaps the system needs to be more accommodating of divergent views and values.

Elder: The incidents you referred to are quite isolated. People have exaggerated the implications of the conflict. You must first note that the Catholic and Presbyterian Churches have been in Afikpo since 1907 or thereabouts and there have not been any noticeable disagreement between the Churches and the Afikpo people. What we are noticing now is the overzealousness of the few new generation Churches -the so called born-agains. For some reason, they believe that their militancy against the tradition of Afikpo is what they need to demonstrate that they have come of age in their new found faith. It's unfortunate but nothing that should bother anyone. They have already realized the fruitlessness of their actions. Besides, we know those who are sponsoring them.

Question: How about the influence of foreign culture on the system?

Elder: I believe the system is opening up—that is accommodating some values that the people find useful for its survival. The system is not static—it is also changing and so there is no need to fear about changes.

The issues raised in the discussion will be better appreciated when situated within the socio-economic and historical context of the society. Afikpo economy is agro-based. A sizable number of Afikpo people especially the elderly are engaged in subsistence farming. Other Afikpo people living along the Cross river and the big lakes are involved in fishing. The farming culture is encouraged by the communal land ownership system that makes land available to people interested in farming. That most lands are owned communally and by the lineages rather than individually does not mean that land is equitably distributed to every member of the community. Some lineages had long ago acquired larger and more fertile portions of the farming land. Lineages with more land than they can cultivate in one farming season do lease part of it out to families and individuals who require more land for farming.

Agricultural economy is labor intensive. Men with many wives and children have more chances of success as farmers. There are quite a few Afikpo people who were compelled to sell their labor power. Afikpo people are rather proud and will find it problematic working for a fellow villager. Most of my interview respondents concur with this view. There also exists cultural hatred for the alienation of one's labor among the Afikpo people. As such farm hands were mostly obtained from seasonal immigrant laborers from neighboring towns. Extra labor could be obtained from one's age grade and fellow villagers. Age-grades and villagers take turns to work on each other's farms. The economic system and activities reinforced the egalitarian values of Afikpo people. Support also came from villagers in many ways. Apart from providing labor and farm crops to one another, it was also villagers who came to the rescue of village members whose crops were destroyed by sudden calamity. Relatives and fellow villagers were ever ready to provide both material and moral support to their own afflicted by natural or other disasters. Further, if the entire village was in distress, villagers moved to live with their kinsmen in another area where food was not scarce.

The Marxist[9] perspective that the mode of production of material life conditions the social, political and intellectual life process in general is very evident in Afikpo. The major basis of the Afikpo wealth was agricultural cultivation with its dependence on human capital, hence an heightened appreciation of community. Community allegiance was very strong and transcended class proclivity. People mattered a great deal and every individual's contribution to the economy was valued, hence no individual was considered expendable. The economic system is arguably partly responsible for the humane and community centered conflict resolution model in Afikpo. As Eteng (1985:80) points out, the "Igbo traditional social welfare and humane living were inseparable phenomena directly linked with the prevailing production and distribution scheme . . ."

The Afikpo economic system is threatened on several fronts. This threat began in 1902 when the Afikpo was, conquered by the British colonial authorities. Subsequently an alien political, social, educational and economic system, were imposed on Afikpo people. The introduction of taxes forced villagers to seek paid labor or sell their farm products to raise the colonial tax. No doubt, the colonial tax was very much detested and resisted since Afikpo people hated the alienation of their labor or farm products. Many were therefore forced to seek paid jobs from the colonial government. Some relocated to other towns to work in plantations and other manufacturing industries. Others took to trading on palm fruits and kernel. The discovery of oil in Nigeria further undermined the local economy. Many Afikpo people with education and other transferable skills left home for Nigeria's bigger urban cities to seek employment. The result of this shift is that the agricultural economy suffered. Oil accounts for over ninety percent of Nigerian's export. With Nigeria's economy now dependent on oil, agriculture that used to be the primary base of the national economy is neglected. As such Nigeria has to import food to feed its teeming population. Massive importation of agricultural products further affected the value of local agricultural products. The result is that few could make a decent living through subsistence agriculture.

Further, Western education took youngsters away from the farm and other communal activities. It was through farming and other cultural activities that cultural values were passed from one generation to the other. Some indigenous institutions in Afikpo provided youths with recreational and educational opportunities. Values emphasized by these institutions included the respect for group and constituted authority, patience, deferred gratification, sacrifice and teamwork. With fewer and fewer people taking to farming and getting involved in community activities, values that formed the basis of the Afikpo judicial system are slowly replaced by alien values.

Further, the new elites of the community derive their economic dominance from their access to Nigerian government institutions that have sole control of the oil wealth. As such the source of the new elites' wealth is no longer the efforts and input of the extended family members. The modern elites have now moved to new suburbs outside their family homes of origin. They build houses following western housing patterns. Modern houses are clearly set out to accommodate the nuclear family and exclude the extended family. Some elites have in the process completely detached themselves from the commitments to members of the extended family. Individualism runs contrary to the communal spirit and further creates a gap between one generation and the other. These changes have serious implications for the indigenous system of conflict resolution. Some of my respondents believe that certain aspects of modernization, such as individualism and the extended role of money in human relations is understood to be destroying communal spirit and cohesion.

The role of Afikpo elites in the survival and progress of Afikpo culture is somewhat contradictory. The elites have a tendency to romanticize the culture and resist change. They sponsor cultural activities as part of their strategy to revive cultural practices that may be becoming extinct. However, the elites are likely to be working outside the town and only visit home on weekends and during other cultural ceremonies, hence are rarely susceptible to the oppressive aspects of the culture. Their allegiance is both to African culture and borrowed Western values. They bear no affinity to either African indigenous culture or to the moral standards of the borrowed culture, hence are not accountable to any. The behavior of the Afikpo elite in marriage illustrates this point. He marries one wife according to Christian values, but makes no bones about chastity. When conflict arises between him and his wife over an extra marital affair, he seeks the mediation of indigenous systems of conflict resolution. Here the mediators fail to sanction him since his behavior does not violate traditional polygynous marriage norms. The elite is well aware that he is taking advantage of the system since polygynous marriages and extra-marital affairs are not the same thing. African cultures approve of polygynous marriages but disapprove of unfaithfulness in marriages.

Demographic changes are also a source of worry for Afikpo people concerned about the future of the culture and traditional means of resolving conflict. About forty-five percent of the Nigerian population, are below fifteen years of age. This should also be the case in Afikpo. These youths have a different cultural orientation from that of their parents. Youths are deeply immersed in Western education and culture, and the cultural gap between generations is widening. Primordial attachments are weakening, as is the authority of elders upon whom the survival of customs depends. Eteng (1985:64) captures these phenomena succinctly:

> In the immediate and extended families, the kingroup, the neighbourhood and the community, those folkways and mores whose rigid observance traditionally bound individuals and groups to one another and to the community at large, now appear totally descrated and impotent. Elders and various 'significant others' who hitherto wielded authority, defined social norms, and accordingly inducted members into the Igbo 'cultural givens' now seem to have forfeited a significant proportion of their customary socializing functions, obligations and responsibilities to foreign 'cultures' and strange institutional arrangements.

In addition, youth delinquency is a major challenge to the Afikpo system of conflict resolution. Youth violations tend to occasion violence. There are now frequent cases of armed robbery threatening life and property in the community. Youths have also tended to question and sometimes outrightly challenge the cultural practices. For example, certain cultural activities that affected the movements of women and that of non-initiates into the Ogo culture are now regularly questioned and resisted by youths. The issue is not so much youth involvement in more serious violent crimes as so much that the Afikpo system of social control is not effective with the control of youths. The Afikpo system of social control uses persuasive rather than coercive mechanisms to enforce conformity. This works well with adults who depend on the community for their social and economic survival.

All the Afikpo indigenous systems of social control also provide both economic and social support to community members. This support is one of the bases of the Afikpo indigenous system's legitimacy. The age-grade system provides interest free loans to members. Another source of capital drawn upon was the revolving credit scheme operated by community members. The system also has medical revolving loans which members can tap into when needed. Labor needed in farmwork and other projects are sometimes, provided by members of the age-grade, extended family members and other villagers. Non-conformity is therefore very costly. Failure to comply to community norms can lead to ostracization and denial of other needed support. Few youths find the communal support network important and useful. Youths in Afikpo like other societies have limited economic interest. They have no farms nor are they involved in other business undertaking that requires the kind funding or cooperative labour exchanges provided by the community. His or her social support network is sometimes also outside the community.

As a result of these factors, controlling youths who go against the custom of the land has been difficult. Most villages have had to administer corporal punishment to erring youths. One of the few cases I witnessed involved youth gangs who stole chickens, goats and other materials. On conviction, they were publicly flogged. Sometimes, their parents are persuaded to take responsibility for the behavior of their children. For more dangerous offenders, the community hands them over to the local police. The community has no effective way of dealing with delinquent youths.

The eighties witnessed several incidents of conflict between members of the Christian church and other Afikpo people actively involved in the community's cultural activities. The conflict led to the destruction of houses, household property and livestock of the church members directly involved in the conflict. This conflict was almost a replica of the wave of violence that greeted the Moslem community when they first erected their Mosque and made aggressive moves to convert indigenes in the fifties. Incidentally, Christian churches of the Catholic and Protestant denomination have been in Afikpo since the turn of the century without significant conflict between them and Afikpo traditionalists.

Many blame the conflict on the insensitivity of adherents of the new generation churches. The Churches have not hidden their distaste for the Afikpo culture which they label heathenish. They made it a major objective of theirs to save the "lost souls" by converting them to Christianity. They have also refused to participate in communal activities like the clearing of village common playgrounds and footpaths. They refuse to pay development levies and openly desecrate village cultural shrines. The most provocative of their activities have been the demasking of village cultural masquerades. The demasking of masquerades in Afikpo is a treasonable offense with penalties ranging from fines to extensive expiation rites. Failure to perform these rites can result in the destruction and looting of the property of culprits and that of his or her paternal lineages.

The Christian churches on their part blame the conflict between Christians and traditionalists in Afikpo on the encroachment of traditionalists on their religious activities. Some of my respondents blame Afikpo men for forcefully seizing their members and initiating them into the Ogo cult. It is noted that for any man in Afikpo to play any active social and political role in the community, the man must be initiated into the Ogo cult. A man who has not been initiated into the Ogo cult cannot marry in the traditional manner. Similarly, women who have not undergone female circumcision are not expected or allowed to enter into the matrimonial state. Christians believe these practices offend their religious beliefs and have vowed to resist any attempts to coerce their members to go through these initiation rites. Afikpo Council-of-Elders view Afikpo men who do not fulfill these rites of passage as deviants and outlaws and have refused them certain rights—such as community farm and residential lands. Afikpo Christians also find the oath swearing practice inimical to their beliefs. Oath swearing as we have seen is very central to Afikpo indigenous processes of conflict resolution.

The conflict between the new generation churches in Afikpo and the Afikpo traditional authorities is the most overt attempt to resist the authority of the community by a group of people. The conflict has led to State government intervention through the appointment of the Ogo/Church Peace Committee headed by a prominent member of the Catholic Church. Peace seems to have returned into the community with the decisions of the committee for both sides of the conflict to respect the rights of the other to perform their own religious activities without interference. Church members are now allowed to enter into marriage with or without initiation into the Ogo cult. Further attempts are also underway to integrate Christian and traditional religious practices by doing away with vexing practices that polarize the two religions.

The activities of state institutions also weaken indigenous authority and operations. The Nigerian state has failed in its onerous duty of providing adequate security for its citizens. Nigerian police as we have seen are not only corrupt but, grossly incompetent and ineffective. As violent crimes and armed robbery spiral in the community, the community has resorted to the setting up of vigilante groups. The police, rather than encouraging and supporting these self-policing measures, feel their authority is threatened and have acted to undermine the community's efforts in this regards. We are not oblivious of the dangers of vigilante groups, but believe the police cooperation and respect of community initiatives will be more productive.

CONCLUSION

The indigenous justice system of Afikpo (Ehugbo) was examined from a restorative, transformative and communitarian principles. Since 1902 when the British colonial authorities conquered Afikpo and imposed their rule on the community, the traditional Afikpo system assumed a secondary position. The Afikpo indigenous system of conflict resolution in post-colonial Nigeria functions as an alternative system of conflict resolution. As such only Nigerian state agencies of social control have jurisdictions over serious and violent crimes. Cases handled by the Afikpo indigenous institutions of social control are mostly of civil nature such as dowry, divorce and remarriage matters. The Afikpo indigenous institutions of, social control popularity in the recovery of debts has been increasing in recent times. Minor criminal offenses like theft, assaults and failure of persons to contribute, to communal projects or to perform communal labor are handled by the indigenous courts. The indigenous courts have no authority over murder and armed robbery cases. However, murder through sorcery and witchcraft are handled by the indigenous systems of social control since state courts do not recognize crimes of sorcery and witchcraft. Incest cases are also heard in the indigenous courts.

White-collar crimes are not heard in the indigenous courts, unless they are cases of corruption and embezzlement involving officers of the traditional courts or other indigenous institutions. Delinquent and other youth offenses are also not suitable for the indigenous courts. Youths are better restrained through their families or by their peer groupings. Where youth behaviors pose a danger to the community, they are handed over to the State police who are better equipped to deal with violent offenses. If the youth behaviors are minor, their parents can be fined or the community can administer corporal punishment on the erring youths.

There are many institutions for conflict resolution in Afikpo. Some of the indigenous institutions of conflict resolution such as the family, patrilineal and matrilineal groupings apply mostly mediative approaches to conflict resolution. Since these are primary groupings, the goal of the justice process is social solidarity and the restoration of harmony within the group. Fines are rarely imposed. The institutions are also major agents of socialization and resocialization. The traditional justice process is an exercise in counseling. The purpose of counseling is to bring about positive change in the offender and also to protect and restore group harmony. The process is participatory, negotiative and geared towards enhancing understanding and the healing of the victim and the offender.

The age-grade institution is another major agent of conflict resolution and social control in Afikpo. It is a peer group which is very effective in dispute settlement and social control. It is also a major agent of resocialization. The age-grade institution wields a lot of authority among their members. Such authority derives partly from the economic and social support provided to members. Other institutions for the resolution of conflict and social control in Afikpo are the village courts and village-group courts. These institutions are more formal than the ones earlier mentioned. Nonetheless, the process is democratic and participatory. Again, the goal of justice is social solidarity and the restoration of harmony within the group. The institutions are also major agents of resocialization. Judicial proceedings provide opportunities for the review of societal norms. Further, since most of the indigenous institutions of social control are also institutions for social and economic activities, they are very effective in crime prevention.

The Afikpo indigenous system of conflict resolution is victim-centered. Victims, offenders, and their families, as well as the general community are involved in the definition of harm and resolution. All parties acknowledge the emotional and material loss of the victim. Offenders and their families are held responsible for the victim(s) injury and loss. Offenders are persuaded to pay restitution to victims. They also apologize to the victim, his/her family and the community. In sum, the goal of justice is therefore the reparation of harm done to victims and communities by offenders. Appropriate support is accorded to victims and their families by the, community. Above all, the victim is provided an opportunity and support to express his/her anger and sense of loss in order to seek understanding of his/her victimization. Healing for victims is enhanced through confronting their victimizers, understanding of their victimization and the ability to forgive the offender. The victim is not only empowered by his/her participation in the process, the victim comes out feeling vindicated and validated. Furthermore, the victim's safety in the process is guaranteed.

The Afikpo indigenous systems of conflict resolution and social control, is human centered and emphasizes social solidarity. This theme is reflected in its treatment of offenders. Strenuous efforts are made not to alienate the offender, and arbitration cannot proceed if family members of the offender are not involved. Offenders are therefore supported and treated with respect in the justice process. The offender is engaged in dialogue to re-educate him or her. Counseling is to bring about positive changes in the offender. A possible outcome of the process is the offender's acknowledgment of wrongs done. The offender expresses remorse, shame and reparation. Some offenses demand expiation ceremonies as part of the general healing process of the victim, the offender and the entire community.

Furthermore, community members are actively involved in the justice process. Participation in justice making is an extension of community responsibility. Residents are not paid for involvement as such they are genuinely interested in the well-being of the community. As primary stakeholders in the community, residents are sincerely mindful of the intended and unintended outcomes of their response to crime and victimization. There is a renewed sense of empowerment when community residents are actively involved in the justice process. A feeling of equality is fostered amongst participants in the justice process. A major check against the abuse of power is the fact that all residents participate in decision-making. Decisions are reached through consensus of participants. Further, all residents are cognizant of the fact that they or other members of their families could be in a position where others sit over judgment. Describing decision-making in stable egalitarian societies, Coleman (1974:95–96) rightly points out that: "Natural limits are imposed on the exercise of self-interest by the recognition that one is himself sometimes likely to be in a position comparable to that of the person who is the object of his contemplated action."

Responsibilities are shared through partnerships for action. Since crime is a violation of people and interpersonal relationships, the community as much as the victim is harmed and need restoration. The community realizes that crime is a small part of a larger conflict. As such a larger, holistic view, rather than narrow understanding is taken. Sentences are acknowledged as a small part of the solution since a sentence does not resolve conflict. The focus is on the process, rather than the result or outcome of responses, since it is appreciated that process shapes relationships of all parties.

A major feature that has contributed to the uniqueness, effectiveness and success of the Afikpo indigenous system of conflict resolution is the compact and well-organized structure of the villages. This structure not only has made deviance transparent but has also reinforced an egalitarian view of life and social conscience. Further reinforcing the cooperativeness and inter-dependence of the community is the economic system. The basis of local wealth is subsistence agriculture and fishing. Labor is, mostly provided by family members and fellow villagers. Farms and yam barns are centrally located outside the settlement areas such that villagers interact with one another. The common use of toilet facility and common taps and streams where water is drawn also enhances cooperativeness and interdependence. Life is very much in the open. The age-grade and the extended family system enhance community allegiance thereby militating against class consciousness and its divisive effect. As Ottenberg (1972:110) points out, " . . . the consensus systems of leadership at Afikpo makes for a sort of contradiction: men should be personally ambitious, but without disturbing the principle of group control."

Appendix
Research Methods

> *When researchers treat persons as objects, they learn only about their physical movement as physical objects. When researchers treat persons as organisms, they learn only about their basic needs and their reflexes. However, when researchers treat those whom they research as persons, then they are more likely to uncover understandings which are relevant to the human condition and therefore contain practical value.*
>
> —*Hunt (1992:114) as cited in Sommers (1995:9).*

A review of the methods employed in the gathering of the data for this book is undertaken here to shed light on the culture that informs and sustains the Afikpo indigenous justice system. Several ethnographic research techniques were employed in this study. The underlying reason for employing this research strategy is the belief that a social or political process such as democracy or justice must be studied in intimate detail. In this respect, Uchendu (1995) notes that the observer must immerse him/herself in the situation, which he calls the idiographic approach. The researcher seeks to have a first-hand knowledge of the process. Uchendu argues that the nomothetic[1] significance of the study is not lost, for the study is always guided by, universal laws and concepts. In support, Griffiths (1996:206) observes that to do justice to a study of a culturally-derived, holistic system of conflict resolution, several research methods may have to be employed.

> . . . community-based, restorative justice initiatives provide non-adversarial forums for responding to criminal behavior, increase community participation in and control over the response to crime, and provide a *holistic context* within which the causes as well as the consequences of criminal behavior for victims, offenders, and the community can be addressed [emphasis added].

Combining several research methods is preferred over other approaches, because each approach has limitations that can be partially compensated for by other approaches. Employing several methods in research is known as triangulation. Babbie (1995:106) notes the value of this approach: " . . . each research method has particular strengths and weaknesses, there is always a danger that research findings will reflect, at least in part, the method of inquiry. In the best of all worlds, your research design should bring more than one research method to bear on the topic."

Given the complexity of the issues examined in this study, several research methods were employed to obtain data, including participant observation, in-person and focus group interviews, oral history and archival research. No quantitative data on crime and conflict in Afikpo were obtained. As indicated in the previous chapter, there are several indigenous institutions in Afikpo for the resolution of conflict. Some of these institutions operate as ad-hoc tribunals and do not keep records. Even in the more established and permanent courts, detailed records are kept only in some cases, specifically those that might be appealed to the state courts. The Nigerian state police in the area would also not allow me access to their records of crime in Afikpo. Information on records of crime, I was told, is collected nationally and can only be obtained from the National Police headquarters. Information from police headquarters was also not useful for the study.

PARTICIPANT OBSERVATION

Participant observation was the method used to acquire a major part of the data for this study. One major advantage of participant observation is that it affords one the opportunity to observe the power dynamics in the group, which may not be appreciated from interviews or through reading the reports of the court proceedings. The researcher enters the field with no preconceived ideas, as the subjects dictate issues that are important and relevant, and the processes they follow in their deliberations. Another important aspect of observation is that the researcher can also draw meanings from gestures, nonverbal as well as verbal behaviors. Further, the approach enabled the researcher to observe how the community residents think and act in their natural habitats. While listening to the debates was certainly the most important means of obtaining data for this study, observing the physical structure and surroundings of the conflict resolution institutions was quite useful. Bailey (1996:70) explains,

> At the start of your research, you have the almost overwhelming task of observing everything . . . However, as your research progresses,

> as your understanding grows, and as your goals become specific, your observations will become more focused. Decisions about what to observe are part of the researcher's daily reflective process, and these decisions are affected by the social relationships in which the researcher takes part.

The observational study was *covert*[2] since most of the people involved in the conflict resolution systems were unaware that they were being studied. One important reason for this approach is that I am an indigene of the Afikpo community, and, as well, most of the traditional institutions of conflict resolution in Afikpo are open to the public, since all their proceedings are conducted in the open. Like all adult males of Afikpo, I belong to several groups that are involved in conflict resolution in the community. For example, I participated in the village trial of several cases ranging from theft to adultery. In these institutions, I was also a participant observer.

Identifying the institutions of conflict resolution in Afikpo for participant observation was not difficult. Based on my personal knowledge of and experience in Afikpo community, I knew which institution handled which kind of conflict. Moreover, my field trip coincided with the election of candidates for the Chairmanship of the local government. Afikpo people showed keen interest in this election and the indigenous institutions of conflict resolution were fully employed in the process. This presented a rare opportunity for me to witness a session of the Afikpo General Assembly.

For purposes of this study, I observed the proceedings of the Traditional Courts between January and April 1996. I also observed the proceedings of the Government-sponsored Customary Court in Afikpo within this period. I also participated in most of the village and village-group meetings besides that of my age-grade during this period. To further explore the social phenomenon under study, and also do a follow-up to my earlier study, I visited Afikpo again in December 1997 and January 1998 for four weeks. In this second field trip, I further observed the Traditional Courts and met and crosschecked information with some of my key interviewees.

INTERVIEWS

Unstructured questionnaires were administered to the key players in the conflict resolution institutions of Afikpo. Unlike surveys, researchers do not construct standardized questions in advance for unstructured interviews. Oral interviews were used since the majority of the key[3] players in the system have little or no education. Palys (1996:164) notes that open-ended interviews are appropriate for exploratory studies: "open-ended questions are clearly superior if the researcher is interested in hearing respondents' opinions in their own words—particularly in exploratory research, where the researcher isn't entirely clear about what range of responses might be anticipated." Again, unstructured interviews are useful where the interviewer does not know in advance appropriate questions to ask, especially the wording of the questions. Here, concerns about threatening and ambiguous questions are addressed by, raising issues relevant to the study and allowing interviewees freedom to digress. Unstructured interviews are relaxed and natural, like conversations, only more inquisitive. Interviewees hardly know they are being interviewed as the issues to be discussed seem decided on the spot. Hence, the interviewer is also able to probe further the issues raised by the interviewee, utilizing words which are familiar to the interviewee, according to Berg (1989: 17–22).

The basis for selecting people for interviews depended very much on my personal knowledge of their involvement in the indigenous conflict resolution systems or lack thereof. In all, fifty-five adults (40 men and 15 women) were interviewed for this study. Five of the men and five of the women interviewed were known active members of the Christian churches in the community. The reason for singling them out for interviews was their refusal to take their cases to any of the indigenous institutions of conflict resolution. They have also in the past been known to campaign against their members' involvement with any of the indigenous institutions of conflict resolution on the grounds that the institutions derive from heathen religions and practices.

Five of the respondents (three men and two women) were non-indigenes of Afikpo doing business in the area. Some of the respondents were identified from their involvement in the traditional courts, either as litigants or judges. However, over fifty percent of the data from oral interviews were obtained from three male elders in the community. These men are very active in the social and political activities in the area. Again, they are regular contributors to the "Afikpo Today" Magazine. Most of their writings hinge on Afikpo culture, development and changes. I spent about twenty-five hours with these elders and reviewed some of their writings that are relevant to my study with them. Their writings were mostly descriptive of the Afikpo historical, social and cultural practice and process, with no indication of any ideological preferences.

To get a broad-based view and opinion of the Afikpo indigenous institutions of conflict resolution, the following individuals and groups were interviewed both individually and in groups:

- male elders in their sixties with University education

- male elders in their sixties with little or no education (persons in group 1 and 2 are judges of the 1st traditional courts)
- female elders from about fifty years or above (most community leaders come from this age group)
- adult females with University education
- male elders in their fifties with University education
- male elders in their fifties with little or no education (persons in group 5 and 6 are judges of the 2nd traditional courts)
- women political activists in the community
- other adults (male/female)
- members of the Afikpo Christian organization—members of this Christian organization are known to be opposed to the Afikpo cultural practices on the grounds that the culture derives from a heathen religion
- Non-Afikpo indigenes in the community—the choice of non-indigenes was to appreciate how those who did not grow up in the system understood the system. Some of the non- indigenes may have lived all their life in Afikpo but rarely participated in the cultural activities of the people. I singled out non-indigenes who have brought their cases or were defendants in the traditional courts.
- offenders and victims of crime—this category of people were believed to have perspectives of the system different from that of the judges.

Ninety percent of the interviews were conducted in the respondents' homes. Some of the interviews were conducted in my home or other public places like schools and government office buildings. It is customary for a host to provide some kind of entertainment for his/her guests in the Afikpo community. Again, if you ask people a favor, you are expected to provide some kind of tangible present as a mark of appreciation and goodwill. Most of the interviewees provided drinks, kola-nuts and food when the interviews were conducted in their homes. I also took gifts of alcoholic beverages to some of the elderly respondents. When the interviews were conducted in my home, I provided drinks, kola-nuts and sometimes food to my respondents. Most of the interviews were tape-recorded. I took notes where tape-recording the interviews was not possible. None of the respondents objected to my tape-recording or taking notes during the interview. All my respondents seemed enthusiastic about participating in the interview and seemed pleased with the study and were quite supportive. Some interviewees, however, raised concerns with my reporting some aspects of our culture that might throw them in a bad light. I countered this by assuring them that every culture has both good and bad aspects, but that such judgments largely depended on the perspective of the observer.

FOCUS GROUPS

Focus group discussion is, in many ways, like open-ended interviews, except that many people are involved. Griffiths and Wood (1993: 6) note that "focus groups are a widely-used, cost-effective technique for obtaining information from various groups within a community. Focus groups bring together individuals who share a common attribute, be it age (adult/youth); gender (male/female); or experience (victim/offender)." Here the researcher interviews and moderates the groups' discussions. The researcher directs the discussion to issues relevant to the study. Participants in the group discussion are often people with experience and opinions on the subject at hand.

Using focus groups as a primary data collection method helped to highlight the community group dynamics. For example, most of the in-person interviews later turned into a focus group discussion. In one scheduled interview at one of the elder's home, the interview started at 7 a.m. as scheduled. We were about 30 minutes into discussion when visitors started arriving to see the elder. These were also adults in the community whose views were found relevant to the study. We ended up reconstituting the group into a focus group discussion. This happened several times with other interviewees. The advantages accruing from focus group discussions were more visible when one or more participants tended to recall issues better than others, since some of the events under discussion may have happened some time in the past. Since some of the businesses examined at the traditional courts are not an everyday occurrence, the more people involved, the better it is to recall events. With the focus group discussion, some who were either eyewitnesses or participants in some events could present the issues better with others supporting or interjecting the stories with their own versions of the incident.

Focus group discussion also provided an avenue for crosschecking information. Often a participant would be asked to address a particular issue of his involvement one way, or the other with the incident. Some participants would also on their own raise an issue that they believed relevant to the study, thereby acting as a catalyst to the generation of further information. Focus groups proved to be the most useful and effective method for obtaining information for this study. As Field and Morse (1995: 31–32) have observed:

> One premise related to the use of focus groups is that attitudes and perceptions are not developed in isolation but through interaction with other people . . . In selecting participants for a focus group, the researcher selects a relatively homogenous group because the goal in using this technique is to encourage individuals to share their ideas and perceptions. A group is typically composed of 7 to 10 participants who are selected because they are knowledgeable about the topic that is focal to the research. Because the purpose for using focus groups is to produce self-disclosure, homogeneity is seen as reducing perceived risk to the informants. For this reason, several focus groups are generally used within a research project to increase the range of beliefs and values that will be represented in the population under study, with the aim to have heterogeneity between the groups.

A total of eleven focus group discussions were held. Only four of the focus groups were initially constituted as such, and these discussions took place in my home. The other focus groups evolved from in-person interviews in the respondents' homes. The situation was such that during interviews, neighbors or visitors from within or outside the village arrived in my interviewees' homes. This seemed difficult to avoid. Besides, their presence did not disrupt or affect the discussion in any way. Initially, the visitors just sat and listened, while sharing in the drinks, kola-nuts and food provided by my host or that I brought with me. Before long, they interjected with their own views or just introduced other ideas they believed relevant to the discussion. Their participation was very much encouraged. This proved quite useful and saved me a lot of trouble and time, which I otherwise would have needed in order to arrange for interviews to set up time that was suitable for several people at the same time. Such is life in Afikpo community. You are hardly alone. The level of social interaction is very high.

The number of people in the focus groups ranged from four to eleven. Two of the focus groups were composed entirely of women. The rest were constituted entirely of men, except in two instances where two women sat in and actively participated in the discussion. The ages of the participants were quite diverse. The discussions were quite frank and lively. Sometimes, the discussions were argumentative, but constructive. Most times I allowed discussions on issues to run its logical course, or I asked a question to redirect the line of discussion.

All the focus group discussions were tape-recorded. No one objected or expressed any reservations to the recording of the discussions. The only drawback to focus-group interviews is that it is sometimes difficult to sort out multiple voices from the recording. Again, no issues were considered taboo or too sensitive for discussion. Some of the participants in the focus group discussion went the extra mile to inform me of relevant articles or theses written by other Afikpo scholars that they believed to be relevant to my study. Some either asked me to come by their place to pick up the materials, dropped them off, or sent somebody to drop them off at my place for me to photocopy and return to them. The assistance I received from members of the Afikpo community was incredible and very supportive, for which I will forever remain grateful. In return, many requested that I make a copy of the book available to the local library for the benefit of other students and other researchers and general interest readers.

My opening question to the participants in the focus group discussion was how much they were involved in the community's institutions of conflict resolution. I also sought to know from participants the basis for defining certain behaviors a crime or problem. Further, the inquiries sought answers to the following issues:

- behaviors that are defined as crimes or problems in Afikpo
- the institution/s with authority to determine and define behaviors either crime or otherwise
- when killing constitutes murder or manslaughter
- the processes and institutions involved in conflict resolution
- incidents of incest and punishments
- processes and goals of socialization in the community
- incidents of suicide and community attitudes towards suicide
- role of satire as a tool of social control
- age grade organization and functions of the age grade institution in the community
- what remedies, if any, are there for victims of crime
- the community's concept of justice—when justice is done or miscarried
- in the absence of prisons, the punishment and control of offenders.

ARCHIVAL RESEARCH

There is no known criminological work done in the Afikpo area. Furthermore, the records of the Afikpo indigenous institutions of conflict resolution were insufficient for my purposes. However, I found some of the anthropological works done within the Afikpo area quite useful. For example, this study relies heavily on the extensive anthropological works of Simon Ottenberg in Afikpo. Extensive use was also made of the records and minutes of the court proceedings that I inherited from a past Secretary of the Afikpo traditional courts. These records date back to the 1950s when he started keeping records of the court proceedings. These materials were studied and evaluated in line with the stated objectives of the study.

Other archival research techniques were employed in this study to complement other methods of information gathering. In this respect, all the copies of the Afikpo Magazine published from 1980 were reviewed. Other relevant government publications, such as panel reports and white papers on social disturbances in the area, as well as state newspapers, were also reviewed.

ORAL HISTORY

While the above records were useful for the study, they were not adequate, and so did not do justice to the issues. Until recently, most of the social history of Afikpo was largely unwritten, hence the recourse to oral history. Afikpo people have, through oral history, passed information from one generation to another. Grele (1996) defines oral history as "the interviewing of eye-witness participants in the events of the past for the purposes of historical reconstruction" (as cited in Perks and Thomson 1998: ix). Haley (1998) notes that people in societies without a writing culture develop their historical skills through oral history. People develop skills that enable them to sift and select evidence and make informed decisions. Listening, questioning, talking and arguing skills are important ingredients of story telling and oral history, and many societies without a written text have used oral history as a method of education and information dissemination. Community members gifted with story telling and oral history skills provide such valuable information when needed. Perks and Thomson (1998:2), observe that "oral history recording taps into a vast, rich reservoir of oral traditions sustained through family, community and national memories." Oral history narrators give their own interpretation to events as they recall the past. The narrator can be the historian as well as the source of history.

Critics of oral history question the accuracy and reliability of oral history. Cutler (1970) questions the validity of oral history. Memories are not very reliable, and other influences, including the cultural milieu, can further undermine the validity of oral history (as cited in Grele 1998). Oral history is likely to reflect the views of the interviewees which are not representative of the whole community. Bornet (1955) further observes that while "oral history is probably to be ranked above contemporary hearsay evidence," [oral history] cannot rank with an authentic diary, with a contemporary stock report, or with an eyewitness account transcribed on the day of the event" (as cited in Grele 1998:41). Oral history without the support of related written materials should not be relied upon. There is also the fear that oral history can be abused or used to serve narrow political interests.

Palys (1996) observes that oral history is a credible method of information-gathering since such stories are often recounted in the public fora and are open for rebuttal or support. Palys argues that oral history technique is particularly useful for research involving marginalised people. Palys, (1996: 160) citing Reinharz (1992), notes that "oral history . . . is useful for getting at people less likely to be engaged in creating written records and for creating historical accounts of phenomena less likely to have produced archival material." Fontana and Frey (in Denzin and Lincoln) (1994: 368) insist that "oral history does not differ from the unstructured interview methodically, but in purpose."

Thompson (1998) argues that through oral history the scope of history is enlarged and enriched. The experience of people hitherto hidden, from history are recorded. The view-points of leaders as well as the experiences of ordinary people are noted, hence, Thompson insists oral history has democratized the study of the past. Thompson (1998:26) posits that through oral history,

> the chronicle of kings has taken into its concern the life experience of ordinary people. But there is another dimension to this change, of equal importance. The *process of writing history changes with the content.* The use of oral evidence breaks through the barriers between the chroniclers and their audience, between the educational institution and the outside world. (emphasis added).

Through oral history, ordinary people and minority groups acquire a voice and their experiences and interpretations are recorded and become part of history. The community as well as individual and minority groups are empowered by oral history. Community members get to assert their interpretation of the past, thereby influencing not only the process of knowledge formulation, but also its outcome.

DOING RESEARCH AS AN "INSIDER"

It is important to address my position as "insider" in this research. Field researches are either conducted by "outsiders"/"strangers," or "insiders." The "insider" describes a situation where "the person who conducts research on the cultural, racial, or ethnic group of which he himself is a member," (Jones 1988:30). The issue is that the "insider" researcher enjoys several privileges, including access to the research subjects, trust and a better understanding of the phenomenon under study. Secondly, the validity of the research findings is enhanced.

Being an indigene of Afikpo was definitely an added advantage in many respects. First, access into the community and to the indigenous institutions of conflict resolution was guaranteed. Secondly, I am sufficiently acquainted with the gate-keepers and practitioners[4] of the system and knew from the onset who was useful to me for this research. This saved a lot of resources, time and money. Other advantages of being an insider include "immeasurable advantage of trustworthiness, authentically revealing precisely the elusive intimate thoughts and sentiments of the native, who spontaneously reveals himself in these outpourings" (Boas cited in Jones 1988:32). As an insider, I also have the advantage of knowing thoroughly the language of the Afikpo people, which an outsider might not.

Being an insider also has limitations. According to Jones (1988), research subjects may take it for granted that you already know some things and so fail to volunteer vital information to you, which may not be the case where a non-indigene is concerned. Research subjects may assume it unimportant discussing everyday affairs with somebody who is part of the community, but will readily grant this information to an "outsider." This was the case with me, where it was assumed I was familiar with the practices and processes of the community's system of conflict resolution. While this was true in most cases, still there were issues where my knowledge was scanty. At the time I was growing up in Afikpo, our teachers and Church leaders discouraged us from participating in most of the Afikpo cultural activities, except those with sporting values. This was apparent from the manner of responses from my interviewees when I asked certain questions. Some issues and events were assumed commonplace, which every adult in the community should be familiar with. Respondents were sometimes persuaded to go into considerable detail, which may not have been necessary for an "outsider." It is experiences like these that led Jones (1988:32) to conclude that "the crucial point is that insiders and outsiders may be able to collect different data; they also have different points of view which may lead to different interpretations of the same set of data."

Further, there remains the danger of information distortion by both the insider and outsider (Jones, 1988). In this case, the outsider approaches the research with certain assumptions, which lead to certain types of conclusions. The outsider is more critical of his/her research subjects than of his/her perspectives, and this may likely affect the research outcome. On the other hand, the insider's identification with research subjects, sentiments, and his/her commitment to positively represent his/her people, according to Jones, can also affect the research outcome. Outsiders, he argues, may likely detect phenomena, which an insider may overlook. Jones (1988:36–7), citing Jarvie, illustrates this point,

> To observe a way of life best, it seems, involves living that way of life. This assumption invites two criticisms, each of which has both a theoretical and a practical aspect. First, is "the insider" a privileged observation point? There is nothing especially privileged about the observations of a parade made by those in it. Spectators may be in a better position, television viewers in a still better one. Which vantage point you choose must surely be a matter of what you want to observe and why.

ETHICAL ISSUES

There were no crucial ethical problems anticipated in this study of the Afikpo traditional system of conflict resolution. Participation in the interviews and focus group discussions were voluntary. Participants were all informed of their rights to refuse participation or to withdraw their participation at any time. No minors were involved in the research. The research did not in any way pose any health, right to privacy or financial risks to any of the participants. Further, there were no access problems of any kind to the institutions under study. All my requests for interviews were granted. The main reason for this is that I am an indigene of the Afikpo community. The enthusiastic support I received from the community may also have to do with the fact that I have a fairly good standing in the community. The Afikpo people's satisfaction with the extensive anthropological works of Ottenberg[5] and others in the community may also have added force to their trust and support. Further, most of the traditional institutions of conflict resolution in Afikpo are open to the public, with proceedings conducted in the open.

The only access problem I had, if I can call it a problem, was with the study of the institutions of conflict resolution operated by women. Here, adult males are not expected to be present during their deliberations. Besides, if the women allowed me to sit in their deliberations, I believe my presence would affect the dynamics of the meetings. However, I had no difficulties having access to the minutes and records of the proceedings of their meetings. And since my interest in observing the women's association meetings was to observe the verbal and nonverbal behavior of the proceedings, I could not utilize the services of a proxy. I did not find a suitable assistant who could perform such functions for me. I also believe I could rely on my memory, for as a teenager I used to record the minutes of a number of the meetings of the women in my village. At the time, there was no female member of the meetings available who could write.

The institutions run by women are the same as those of the men. There are associations based on the age grade system and the central body comprising of all the married women. The latter is called the village women's welfare group. The women dealt with issues of concern to them, either as women or just members of the community. In this organization, the women can take far-reaching decisions to challenge the authority of men. In my village, for example, there is a known case where the village women's welfare group took a decision not to sleep with their husbands for a given period. This decision was a form of protest against what they observed as wayward behavior by the men. Most of the men in the village had been keeping late nights, and spending longer time in the beer parlors and restaurants. This behavior started shortly after the men took agricultural loans from the governments. By the time the conflict was resolved, there was no birth in the village for three years.

Notes

NOTES TO THE PREFACE

1. Ifemesia (1978) describes Igbo societies as humane. A humane living according to him is a "way of life emphatically centered upon human interests and values, a mode of living evidently characterized by empathy, and by consideration and compassion for human beings. ... Igbo humanness is deeply ingrained in the traditional belief that the human being is supreme in the creation, is the greatest asset one can posses, is the noblest cause one can live and die for " (as cited in Iro 1985:4).

NOTES TO CHAPTER ONE

1. Tradition and Indigenous are terms used interchangeably throughout this study to convey the same meaning. Their use is not intended to denote lack of progress or a phenomenon that is static or unchanging. We accede to Makang's (1997:324–325) perspective which views " . . . human traditions as processes and as historical phenomena which occur everywhere and in all stages of societies' development. Traditions are not frozen in time, but are in continual development, adapting themselves to new historical circumstances. It is therefore, unduly that the notion of tradition is set in opposition to those of modernity and progress."
2. The following institutions are major agents of socialization and resocialization in indigenous Igbo societies. There are "the family in the first instance; the neighborhood; the peer groups; the kingroup; affines; nursemaid; town crier; patrilineal daughters (umuada); non-kinship groups such as age set/grade; various occupational associations of hunters; blacksmiths; herbalists; potters; midwives; rain-makers; craftsmen; fishermen; titled associations; secret societies; and various social institutions (economic, politic-juridical, religious, expressive and recreational, etc.)" (Eteng 1985:69). He further identifies the contents of Igbo traditional socialization as including: "folkways, customs and usages, folklores, techniques and skills, riddles and conundrums, traditional myths,

rituals, traditions, basic health habits, taboos, adages, philosophies of life, cosmological beliefs, food habits, social positional roles and corresponding norms, body adornments, work habits, games, etc." (ibid).

3. Until December 12th, 1991, Lagos was the national capital of Nigeria.
4. For our purpose, culture is defined as "an historically created system of explicit and implicit designs for living, which tends to be shared by all or specially designated members of a group at a specified point in time" (Kluckhohn and Kelly 1945 as cited in Kluckhohn 1967:75). Kluckhohn (1967) observes that culture is learned and derives from the "biological, environmental, psychological, and historical components of human existence" (ibid.). Culture is structured, dynamic and variable. Culture is that "complex whole which includes knowledge, belief, art, morals, law, custom and any other capabilities and habits acquired by man as a member of society" notes Edward B. Tylor (1871) as cited in Kluckhohn (1967:74).
5. The reforms put in place to address this anomaly include victim impact statement programs and financial restoration programs whereby victims sue their offenders at the civil courts for financial compensation. Others include community service work order programs. Crime victims can also contact the parole board and/or correctional officials for information relating to the timing and specifics of any release of their victimizer. Victims in some jurisdictions in Canada can also observe parole hearings and express their concerns to correctional authorities and/or the parole board (See Griffiths and Cunningham 2000).

NOTES TO CHAPTER TWO

1. There are two dominant conceptions of the state. Marx and Engels (1967:82) define the state as "a committee for managing the affairs of the whole bourgeoisie" (cited in Ratner et al 1987:85). The second perspective conceives of the state as a "political organization whose rule is territorially ordered and which is able to mobilize the means of violence to sustain that rule" (Giddens 1989:20). The latter definition stems from the Weberian perspective. However, for our purposes, the state is as represented by governmental system and all its paraphernalia such as the executive, legislature, judiciary, military and police.
2. Herman Bianchi, an anti-prison advocate, points out in a 1997 CBC interview that not every conflict or crime is suitable for restorative justice system. Violent crimes should be handled by the state run retributive justice system, which is equipped to deal with violence. Society needs to be protected from violent criminals. Violent criminals need institutionalization for society's protection. Offenders who fail to acknowledge their wrongs and express remorse are also not suitable for restorative justice systems. He states: "So there are two types of prisons that will remain necessary forever: prisons, for very, very dangerous people and prisons for those people who have received the opportunity to do penitence, to come to reconciliation, to settle the dispute, and refuse, refuse, refuse. Then there is no other solution

than a prison. Those are the two types of prisons. All the rest should be abolished" (p.3).

NOTES TO CHAPTER THREE

1. Rwezaura (1992) defines living law as the "unwritten irregular, that is flexible and highly negotiable, representing the law governing the actual social life of the people in their day to day lives often changing in response to changing conditions" (cited in Armstrong et al 1993: 19).
2. Austin defines law as a "rule laid down for the guidance of an intelligent being by an intelligent being having power over him" (cited in Elias 1962: 37).
3. The United Nations Organization was formed in London in 1945. Its objective is to check and promote human rights agenda all over the world. It is also to guide against a repeat of the reckless abuse of human rights witnessed during the Second World War.
4. The African Charter on Human and Peoples' Rights came into force on October 21, 1986 upon ratification by a simple majority of member states of the Organization of African Unity (OAU). It is also referred to as the Banjul Charter because the final draft was adopted in Banjul, the capital of Gambia. The Charter was first adopted in 1981 by the 18th Assembly of Heads of State and Governments of the, Organization of African Unity (OAU). The African Commission on Human and Peoples' Rights, known as commissioners, are eleven in number, and are elected by the OAU secret ballot for a six-year term and serve in their own personal capacities, and are the sole implementing organ of the Charter. OAU is now called African Union (AU).
5. Some traditional Igbo societies have constitutional monarchy. Uchendu (1965) lists the Onitsha, Agbaja, and the Aro-Chukwu as few of the Igbo societies that were not completely acephalous. However, the villages in these communities remained autonomous and leadership was exercised through the Council of Elders. Further, the participatory democracy and egalitarian outlook of the people were not affected by the hierarchical socio-political arrangement. It is noted however, that at certain levels of political discourse, women and children were not allowed full participation.

NOTES TO CHAPTER FOUR

1. It is imperative to distinguish underdevelopment from undevelopment. Undevelopment describes a situation where a nation's natural and human resources are not fully exploited for national benefit. Underdevelopment, on the other hand, describes a situation whereby resources are being exploited often from the dependent states for the benefit of the dominant states.

   A country is said to have developed when the country successfully reduces societal problems that are generally associated with underdevelopment, such as poverty, the high incidence of disease, unemployment, ignorance, poor infrastructure and technological backwardness.

2. Ferraro (1997: 3) distinguishes dependency theory from the Marxist theory of Imperialism. The Marxist theory of Imperialism tends to explain dominant state expansion, while, on the other hand, dependency theory explains underdevelopment. Ferraro notes that "Marxist theories explain the reasons why imperialism occurs, while the dependency theories explain the consequences of imperialism."

NOTES TO CHAPTER FIVE

1. Legend has it that the founder of Ehugbo was Igbo Ukwu, and that subsequent settlers had to swear oath of allegiance to Igbo Ukwu before settling. According to Aja (1988), settlers were made to swear to settle with the permission of Igbo, which translates to "Na-Eha-Igbo," later shortened to Ehugbo.
2. The policy establishing the Customary Court falls within the regulatory policy typology. Hill/Bramley (1986:14) define regulatory policy as government action to prevent and control individual activities. This category includes policing and law enforcement. Other types of policy are distributive, redistributive and constituent policy.
3. In 1984 when Nigeria operated a 21 state federal government structure, Afikpo was in Imo State. Presently, there are 36 states in Nigeria, with Afikpo in Ebonyi State. However, the Customary Court Edict is still operational in the Igbo speaking states.
4. Sharia Courts serve the interests of people within the Moslem faith. The Customary Courts on the other hand serve the interests of people with interests in customary matters.
5. Perham defines indirect rule "as a system by which the tutelary power recognizes existing African societies and assists them to adapt themselves to the functions of local government" (1937: 346).
6. The proponent of Negritude is Leopold Senghor. Negritude as a concept advances the view that the African outlook on life is humanist. It is also a movement for the restoration of the African identity and self-esteem destroyed by the inhumane experiences of slavery and colonialism. Ujama as articulated by Julius Nyerere also promotes the African humanist outlook on life. It is an alternative approach to socio-political development that is group oriented and eschews individualism. It also opposes the Western capitalist views that emphasize profit motive (cited in Elechi 1996: 354).
7. Incrementalism or "muddling through" according to Lindblom "relies heavily on the record of past experiences with small policy steps to predict the consequences of similar steps extended into the future" (1959: 79). Incrementalism unlike the rational model argues that information and knowledge are rarely adequate for a complete policy program. Policies are developed in stages, with series of adjustments.
8. There is a list of Igbo customary law drawn up by Dr. S. N. C. Obi. It is titled the "Customary Law Manual of Igboland." According to Okere

(1986) the laws set out in the paper have been described by the Commissioner for Law Revision and a team of law officers as "current, well established customary laws." There is no indication however that the customary laws listed carry the force of the law. I assume they provide more theoretical than legal guide.

NOTES TO CHAPTER SIX

1. Afikpo culture being interventionist oriented, mediators in conflict do not hesitate to intervene when necessary, pointing out to parties to a conflict where they erred and suggesting solutions. However, parties to the conflict are actively involved in the process and generally encouraged to resolve the conflicts on their own. The belief is that conflicts not addressed or resolved will likely be blown out of proportion and might spread. Further, a victim whose needs are not addressed is a potential offender.
2. Two brothers cannot belong to the same age grade. The spacing of childbirths in the society is one way of guiding against two brothers belonging to the same age grade. It is an offense in Afikpo for a woman to get pregnant before she completely weans her latest child—which takes at least two and a half years. However, two half brothers from the same father can belong to the same age grade.
3. Any boy or man of Afikpo not initiated into the Ogo cult is not considered matured. In judicial matters in Afikpo, he is a minor. If he violates any of the Afikpo laws, he is subjected to corporal punishment rather than fines and so on. It must be borne in mind, however, that all Afikpo males go through the initiation before their 20th birthday at the latest.
4. Oath swearing is illegal and unconstitutional in Nigeria. One cannot be forced to swear an oath. However, many are prepared to do it to either establish their innocence or for the interest of peace or good neighborliness. Still, some challenge it on the ground that it violates their belief system.
5. The Igbo week is four days, namely Eke, Orie, Afor and Nkwo.
6. The court may halt further proceedings if a member dies, or if a more pressing business is introduced on the agenda.
7. My respondents were of the view that women litigants are not allowed into the courthouse because of their emotional and quarrelsome dispositions. However, Ottenberg (1971) observes the real reason is because the elders do not want to be contaminated by women who might have either given birth to twins or are menstruating. Birth to twins used to be an abomination in Igboland in pre-colonial times. Women under menstruation had also restricted public roles, since they are considered unclean.
8. The Afikpo Town Welfare Association (ATWA) is a grouping of Afikpo Youths—mostly professionals and the new elites. This association has branches in other Nigerian cities with a sizable population of Afikpo people. The associations reflect village family meetings. They provide economic, social, cultural and moral support to their membership. Above all, the associations constitute tribunals to resolve conflicts that may arise

among their membership. Many have observed that these associations are common among African egalitarian communities. And that it is their way of adapting to urban life. As Parkin 1966:92–3 notes: "migrants from egalitarian tribes adapt to the urban 'class' system by using traditional social units and arranging them in some hierarchy by formalizing certain of their activities through associations" (as cited in Pratten 1996:51).

NOTES TO CHAPTER SEVEN

1. Perhaps separation rather than divorce is the appropriate word. It is not uncommon for women to leave their second husbands and return to their first husbands. Again, the grown-up son of the woman can and usually demands that his mother returns to his father's house. And seen against Mbiti's (1970) observation that the process of marriage is only complete after the woman passes a child-bearing age, then what obtains in Afikpo should be classified as separation rather than divorce.
2. Violence here refers to the means by which a man controls, dominates, and/or intimidates his female partner. It is important to recognize that violence takes different forms besides physical assault and that all forms can have devastating consequences. Violence here pertains to physical, sexual, and emotional abuse.

NOTES TO CHAPTER EIGHT

1. The Aro oracle no longer plays any role in the community's judicial processes hence it is not discussed in this study.
2. Similarly, Basden (1982) observes every conduct in Igboland is publicly regulated. He states: "They have rules for the regulation of conduct applicable to almost every detail of life. Habits are naturally engendered and developed; they are a subconscious part of the native's being and amongst the older generation, it is a rare thing to find one failing to observe the traditional rules of conduct (as cited in Iro (1985: 6).
3. To qualify as an ancestor when one dies, one needs to live to a ripe old age—not only having children, but also catering for them until they become independent. To die without having a child or leaving your children as young orphans is a bad death, and is not honored or mourned. People who committed crimes against the deities and who died as a result of that do not qualify for ancestoral status.
4. The reason for this limited belief in sorcery has to do with other beliefs in Afikpo. It is widely believed that if you practice sorcery against a kinsman, and partake in the sacred feasts performed during yam festivals, it will boomerang on the perpetrator. Further, any practice of sorcery is bound to catch up with the sorcerer if they share drinks, food etc. with their victims or any member of their family. As such, during social gatherings, one or two cups are used in sharing alcohol or other drinks. Hence, solitary individuals risk being accused of witchcraft.

5. Further discussions of rape are undertaken in the next section.
6. Abomination is not only a crime against the land, it is also a crime against the gods. It is a belief shared by all African societies. According to Amadi (1982:15), "an abomination, as conceived in Nigeria, is an offense against a deity, who is expected to deal with the offender unless certain rites are performed and fines paid." Efforts are made to reconcile people guilty of abomination with their victims and the earth goddess (ala or ali) for example. In this respect, sacrifices are performed to appease the deity to whom the offense was committed against too. The offender is therefore reconciled with both the spirit and everyday world.
7. There is a class dimension to this system today. If the deceased was rich, his adult dependants will strongly resist the involvement of the matrilineal lineage in the distribution of his wealth. In such a situation, they will seek the intervention of state courts that recognize father-son inheritance. But the reverse may be the case if the deceased is poor and the attending relatives rich.
8. Communalism is defined as the "doctrine or theory that the community (or, group) is the focus of the activities of the individual members of the society. This idea places emphasis on activity and the success of the wider society, not necessarily to the detriment of the individual, but rather to the well-being of every individual member of society" (Gyekye 1996:36). Here society is seen as an organism whereby what affects a part of the organism affects the whole. Further, there is the African spiritual communalism which Onwuachi (1977:17) describes as the " . . . spirit of kinship, respect for age and wisdom, economic cooperation, reverence for ancestral spirits, discipline and social justice, the fundamental collective responsibility for order, and the basic recognition of African dignity and respect for human personality."
9. Rusche and Kirchheimer (1939:362)'s research on the relationship between social structure and punishment support this Marxian thesis. They observe that "the transformation in penal systems cannot be explained only from changing needs of the war against crime, although this struggle does play a part. Every system of production tends to discover punishments which correspond to its productive relationships. It is thus necessary to investigate the origin and fate of penal systems, the use or avoidance of specific punishments, and the intensity of penal practices as they are determined by social forces, above all by economic and then fiscal forces."

NOTES TO THE APPENDIX

1. Nomothetic method refers to a study undertaken with the objective of formulating general principles. Individual events are studied not for their own sake but for their significance in the formulation of general principles. Idiographic method, on the other hand, studies its subject on case by case basis. Here, emphasis is placed on the complete understanding of individual case rather than seeking generalizations from the particular study (Uchendu 1995).

2. The consent of the judges and the administrative staff of the Customary Court was sought before this study. At the Traditional Courts, most of the key players were aware of the study. Some of them were also involved in the face-to-face and focus group interviews. It was not considered productive or necessary announcing to the general assembly that this study was in progress.
3. By key players is meant those who show keen interest in the community's conflict resolution practices and processes. This was determined by how regularly they participated as judges in the traditional courts, measured through their level of activity and how often they contributed to proceedings. Some were known spokespersons of their age-grades, and others were pointed out to me as knowledgeable persons of Afikpo culture.
4. It is noted that the Judges of the government sponsored Customary Court in Afikpo turned down my request for an interview. Since they gave no reasons for refusing me an interview and access to their records, I can only speculate they were suspicious of my intentions.
5. Most of the elders I interviewed remember fondly Prof. Ottenberg who carried out his anthropological research in the community in the early 1950s. Many Afikpo people have copies of the Ottenberg's books on Afikpo, which they believe is a balanced and accurate account of Afikpo culture and history. As indication of their appreciation, Ottenberg was honored with a Chieftaincy title in the community.

Selected Bibliography

Achebe, C. (2000). *Home and Exile.* New York, New York: Oxford University Press.

Adeyemi, A. A. (1992). Corruption in Africa: a case study of Nigeria. In *Criminology in Africa* by Tibamanya mwene Mushanga (ed.). Rome: United Nations Interregional Crime and Justice Research Institute (UNICRI).

Afikpo Today Magazine, Vol. 1, Nos.1 to 10 (1980–1999), published by Tagteam (Nigeria) Limited, 23 Mukandasi Street, Okota, Isolo, Lagos.

Agozino, B. (2003). *Counter Colonial Criminology: A Critique of Imperialist Reason.* London: Pluto Press.

Aja, R. O. (1988). *A Brief Socio-Political History of Ehugbo.* History Department, University of Port Harcourt, Nigeria.

Ake, C. (1989). *The Political Economy of Crisis and Development in Africa.* Lagos: JAD Publishers.

Alderson, J. (1984). *Human Rights and the Police.* Strasbourg: Council of Europe.

Amadi, E. (1982). *Ethics in Nigerian Culture.* Ibadan: Heinemann Educational Books (Nigeria) Ltd.

Amadiume, I. (1995). *African Matriarchal Foundations: The Case of Igbo Societies.* London: Karnak House.

Ancel, M. (1994). Social Defence (originally published 1954) in *Classics of Criminology* by Joseph E. Jacoby (ed.) Illinois: Waveland Press, Inc.

Apena, A. (1996). Female Circumcision in Africa and the problem of cross-cultural Perspectives in *Africa Update*—a Newsletter of the CCSU African Studies Program, Central Connecticut State University.

Aubert, V. (1989). *Continuity and Development—in Law and Society* . Oslo: Norwegian University Press.

Aubert, V. (1969). *Sociology of Law (Selected Readings).* Middlesex: Penguin Books Ltd.

Armstrong, Alice, Chaloka Beyani, Chuma Himonga, Janet Kabeberi-Macharia, Athalia Molokomme, Welshman Ncube, Thandabantu Nhlapo, Bart Rwezaura and Julie Stewart (1993). *Uncovering Reality: Excavating Women's Rights in African Family Law.* Women and Law in Southern Africa Working Paper No. 7, WLSA Harare, Zimbabwe.

Awa, E. (1985). Igbo Political Culture in (The Igbo Socio-Political System) Papers presented at the *1985 Ahiajoku Lecture Colloquium.* Owerri: Ministry of Information, Culture, Youth and Sports.

Ayittey, G. B. N. (1999). *Africa in Chaos.* New York: St. Martin's Griffin.

Babbie, E. (1995). *The Practice of Social Research.* 7th Edition. California. Wadsworth Publishing Company.

Bailey, C.A. (1996). *A Guide to Field Research.* Thousand Oaks, CA: Pine Forge Press.

Banks, C. L. (1990). *Women in Transition: A Study of the Status of Women in the Traditional and Introduced Systems of Social Control Control in Papua New Guinea.* M.A. Thesis. Burnaby. Simon Fraser University School of Criminology.

Basden, G. T. (1966). *Among the Ibos of Nigeria.* New York: Barnes & Noble, Inc.
Bazemore, G. and Umbreit, M. (1997). Balanced and Restorative Justice for Juveniles: A Framework for Juvenile Justice in the 21st Century. *Office of Juvenile Justice and Delinquency Prevention (OJJDP).* University of Minnesota.

Bazemore, G. and Walgrave, L. (1999). Restorative Juvenile Justice: In Search of Fundamentals and an Outline for Systemic Reform. In *Restorative Juvenile: Repairing the Harm of Youth Crime.* by Gordon Bazemore and Lode Walgrave (eds.) Monsey, New York: Criminal Justice Press.

Beccaria, C. (1994). On Crimes and Punishment (originally published 1764) in *Classics Of Criminology* by Joseph E. Jacoby (ed.). Illinois: Waveland Press, Inc.

Bentham, J. (1994). An Introduction to the Principles of Morals and Legislation (originally published in 1789) in *Classics of Criminology* by Joseph E. Jacoby (ed.). Illinois: Waveland Press, Inc.

———. (1995). Punishment and Utility (1823 edition) in *Punishment and Rehabilitation* (3rd Edition) by Jeffrie G. Murphy (ed.). Belmont, California: Wadsworth Publishing Company.

Berg, B. (1989). *Qualitative Research Methods for the Social Sciences.* Boston: Allyn and Bacon.

Bohannan, P. (1973). *The Differing Realms of the Law.* In the Social Organization of Law, by Donald Black and Maureen Mileski (eds.). New York: Seminar Press.

Braithwaite, J. (1989). *Crime, Shame and Reintegration.* New York. Cambridge University Press.

———. (1991). The Political Agenda of Republican Criminology. Paper to the British Criminological Society Conference, York, 27th July.

———. (1998). Restorative Justice: Assessing an immodest theory and a pessimistice theory. <http://ba048864.aic.gov. (March 5th).

——— and Parker, C. (1999). Restorative Justice Is Republican Justice. In *Restorative Juvenile Justice: Repairing the Harm of Youth crime.* by Gordon Bazemore and Lode Walgrave (eds.) Monsey, New York: Criminal Justice Press.

Brown, J. A. M. (1995). Background Paper on New Zealand Youth Justice Process. Being a paper presented at the Workshop on Putting Aboriginal Justice Devolution into Practice: The Canadian and International Experience. Simon Fraser University at Harbour Centre—July 5–7, 1995.

Burtch, B. (1992). *The Sociology of Law: Critical Approaches to Social Control.* Toronto: Harcourt Brace Jovanovich Canada Inc.

Busia, Jr. N. K. A. (1994). The Status of Human Rights in Pre-Colonial Africa: Implications for Contemporary Practices. In *Africa, Human Rights and the Global System* by Eileen McCarthy-Arnolds et al (eds.). Westport, Conn.: Greenwood Press, Pp. 225–50.

Carneiro, R. L. (1979). A Theory of the Origin of the State, in *The Politicization of Society* by Kenneth S. Templeton, Jr. (ed.). Indianapolis: Liberty Press.

Carnoy, M. (1974). *Education as Cultural Imperialism.* New York: David McKay Company, Inc.

———. (1984). *The State and Political Theory.* New Jersey: Princeton University Press.

Carter, M. (1994). *The Call to Context, the Phenomenology of Adjudication and Sentencing Circles: Preliminary Thoughts.* Paper prepared for Crim. 840, Simon Fraser University.

Cayley, D. (1998). *The Crisis in Crime and Punishment and the Search for Alternatives.* Toronto: House of Anansi Press.

Chambliss, J. W. (1979). Contradictions and Conflicts in Law Creation. In *Research in Law and Sociology* Vol. 2, pp. 3–27, JAI Press Inc.

Chamlin, M. B. and Cochran, J. K. (1997). Social Altruism and Crime. *Criminology.* Vol. 35, No. 2.

Christie, N. (2004). *A suitable amount of crime.* London: Routledge-Taylor and Francis Group.

———. (1981). *Limits to Pain.* Oslo: Universiteteteforlaget.

———. (1973). *Criminological Data as Mirror for Society.* Oslo: Institute for Criminology and Criminal Law Stencilseries No. 15.

———. (1976). *Conflict as Property.* Oslo: Institute for Criminology and Criminal Law Stencilseries, No. 23.

Clifford, W. (1974). *An Introduction to African Criminology.* Nairobi: Oxford University Press.

Cockcroft, J. D., Frank, A. G., & Johnson, D. L.: *Dependence and Underdevelopment: Latin America's Political Economy.* Anchor Books, Doubleday & Company, Inc. Garden City, New York 1972.

Cohen, S. (1985). *Visions of Social Control: Crime, Punishment and Classification.* Cambridge: Polity Press.

Coleman, S. J. (1974). *Power and the Structure of Society.* New York: W. W. Norton and Company Inc.

Collins, P. H. (1991). *Black Feminist Thought: Knowledge, Consciousness, And The Politics of Empowerment.* New York: Routledge.

Constitution of the Federal Republic of Nigeria 1999: http://nigeriaworld.com/focus/ Republic/constitution/constitution.html (12/10/1999).

Cragg, W. (1992). *The Practice of Punishment: Towards a theory of Restorative Justice.* London: Routledge.

Customary Courts Edict, 1984: Imo State of Nigeria Gazette No. 21, Vol.9.

Customary Courts (Amendment) Edict, 1986. Supplement to Imo State of Nigeria Gazette No. 21, Vol. 11, dated 9th October 1986.

Customary Courts (Amendment) Edict, 1987. Supplement to Imo State of Nigeria Gazette No. 16, Vol. 12, dated 16th July 1987.

Customary Court Rules, 1989. Supplement to Imo State of Nigeria Gazette No. 13, Vol. 16, dated 30th May 1991.

Diamond, L., Linz, J. J., & Lipset, S. M. (eds.). (1988). *Democracy in Developing Countries—Africa*. London: Adamantine Press Ltd.

Diamond, S. (1973). The Rule of Law Versus the Order of Custom in the *Social Organization of Law* by Donald Black and Maureen Mileski (eds.). New York: Seminar Press.

Dike, C. P. (1986). Igbo Traditional Social Control and Sanctions in (Igbo Jurisprudence: Law and Order in Traditional Igbo Society). *Ahiajoku Lecture (Onugaotu) Colloquium*. Owerri: Ministry of Information and Culture.

Donaldson, Peter: *Worlds Apart: The Development gap and what it means*. Penguin books, Middlesex, England 1986.

Donnelly, J. (1989). Universal Human Rights in Theory and Practice. Ithaca, N.Y.: Cornell University Press.

———. (1984). Cultural Relativism and Universal Human Rights. In *Human Rights Quarterly 6*.

Dunn, W. (1994). *Policy Analysis: An Introduction*. Englewood Cliffs, New Jersey: Prentice Hall.

Durkheim, E. (1966). *The Division of Labour in Society*. Translated by G. Simpson. Toronto: Collier-Macmillan.

———. (1969). Types of Law in Relation to Types of Social Solidarity in *Sociology of Law* by Vilhelm Aubert (ed.).

Dye, T. R. (1978). *Understanding Public Policy*. New Jersey: Prentice Hall.

Ebbe, O.N.I. (1985). Power and Criminal Law: Criminalizing conduct norms in a Colonial regime. *International Journal of Comparative and Applied Criminal Justice* 9(2):113 -122.

Eboh, C. (2005). "Obasanjo says Nigeria police torture, kill suspects" Reuters South Africa (http://za.today.reuters.com/news/NewsArticle.aspx?type=

Ekeh, P. P. (1975). Colonialism and the Two Publics in Africa: A Theoretical Statement. *Comparative Studies in Society and History*, Vol. 17.

Elechi, O. O. (2004). "Women and (African) Indigenous Justice Systems" in *Pan-African Issues in Crime and Justice* by Kalunta-Crumpton, A. and Agozino, B. (eds.). London: Ashgate Publishing Limited.

———. (1999). Victims Under Restorative Justice Systems: the Afikpo (Ehugbo) Nigeria Model. *International Review of Victimology*, Vol. 6, pp. 359 -375. Great Britain: A B Academic Publishers.

———. (1996). Doing Justice Without the State: The Afikpo (Ehugbo) Nigeria Model of Conflict Resolution. *International Journal of Comparative and Applied Criminal Justice*. Fall, Vol.20, No.2.

———. (1991). *Alternative Conflict Resolution in (Ehugbo) Afikpo*. Oslo: Institute for Criminology and Criminal Law, Stencilseries, No. 67.

Elias, T. O. (1956). *The Nature of African Customary Law*. Manchester Press.

Elias, R. (1993). *Victims Still: the Political Manipulation of Crime Victims*. Newbury Park, CA: Sage Publications Inc.

El-Wathig, K. and Kursany, I. (1985). *Corruption as the "Fifth" Factor of Production in the Sudan*. Research Report No. 72; Scandinavian Institute of African Studies, Uppsala.

Einstadter, W. & Henry, S. (1995). *Criminological Theory: An Analysis of its Underlying Assumptions*. Toronto: Harcourt Brace College Publishers.

Ericsson, K. (1982). *Alternative Konfliktlosning*. Oslo: Universitetsforlaget.

Eteng, I. (1985). Relations of Production and Contemporary Igbo Patterns of Socialization in (The Igbo Socio-Political System) Papers presented at the *1985 Ahiajoku Lecture Colloquium*. Owerri: Ministry of Information, Culture, Youth and Sports.

Fanon, F. (1963). *The Wretched of the Earth*. New York: Grove Press.

———. (1968). *Black Skin White, White Masks*. New York: Grove Press.

Farrell, D. M. (1995). The Justification of General Deterrence in *Punishment and Rehabilitation* (3rd Edition) by Jeffrie G. Murphy (ed.). Belmont, California: Wadsworth Publishing Company.

Fattah, A. E. (1995). Restorative and Retributive Justice Models—A Comparison. In Hans Kuhne (ed.) *Festschrift fur professor Koichi Miyazawa*.

———. (1998). A Critical Assessment of two Justice paradigms: Contrasting the Restorative and Retributive Justice Models in *Support for Crime Victims in a Comparative Perspective: A Collection of Essays dedicated to the memory of Prof. Frederic McClintock* by Ezzat Fattah and Tony Peters (eds.) Leuven: University Press.

Feld, C. B. (1999). Rehabilitation, Retribution and Restorative Justice: Alternative Conceptions of Juvenile Justice. In *Restorative Juvenile Justice: Repairing the Harm of Youth Crime* by Gordon Bazemore and Lode Walgrave (eds.) Monsey, New York: Criminal Justice Press.

Ferraro, V. (Dependency Theory: An Introduction). *http: //www.mtholyoke.edu/ acad/intrel/depend.htm*. Accessed 04 March 1998.

Field, P.A., and Morse, J. M. (1995). *Qualitative Research for Health Care Professionals*. California: Sage Publications, Inc.

Fischer, F. (1995). *Evaluating Public Policy*. Chicago: Nelson-Hall.

Frank, A. N.: *The Development of Underdevelopment*. In Dependence and Underdevelopment: Latin America's Political Economy, by Cockcroft, J. D., Frank, A. G., & Johnson, D. L.: Anchor Books, Doubleday & Company, Inc. Garden City, New York 1972.

Freeman, M. (1995). Are there Collective Human Rights? *Political Studies*. XLIII, 25–40.

Fontana, A. and Frey, H. J. (1994). Interviewing: The Art of Science, in *Handbook of* Qualitative Research by N. K. Denzin and Y. S. Lincoln (eds.). Thousand Oaks: Sage Publications.

Foucault, M. (1977). *Discipline and Punish*. Translated from the French by Allan Sheridan. Middlesex: Penguin Books Ltd.

Fuller, J. R. (1998). *Criminal Justice: A Peacemaking Perspective*. Boston: Allyn and Bacon.

Gibbs, Jr., J. L. (1973). Two Forms of Dispute Settlement among the Kpelle of West Africa. In *The Social Organization of Law* by Donald Black and Maureen Mileski (eds.). New York: Seminar Press.

Giddens, A. (1989). *The Nation State and Violence*. London: Polity Press.

Gilsinan, J. F. (1991). Public Policy and Criminology: An Historical and Philosophical Reassessment. *Justice Quarterly*, Vol.8, No. 2, June 1991.

Gluckman, M. (1969) The Judicial Process among the Barotse of Northern Rhodesia (orginally published 1955) in *Sociology of Law* by Vilhelm Aubert (ed.).

Grele, J. R. (1998). Movement Without Aim: Methodological and Theoretical Problems in *The Oral History Reader* by Robert Perks and Alistair Thomson (eds.). New York: Routledge.

Griffiths, C. T. (1996). Sanctioning and Healing: Restorative Justice in Canadian Aboriginal Communities. *International Journal of Comparative and Applied Criminal Justice*. Fall 1996, Vol. 20. No. 20.

——— and Wood, D. (1993). *Crime, Trouble and the Delivery of Criminal Justice Services to the Canim Lake Band, Canim Lake, British Columbia: A Needs Assessment*. Simon Fraser University.

———, Kennedy, C. M. and Mehanna, S. (1989). Social Change, Legal Transformation, and State Intervention: Youth Justice in the Arab Republic of Egypt in the *State as Parent: International Research Perspectives on Interventions with Young Persons* by Hudson, Joe and Burt Galaway (eds.).

——— and Cunningham, A. (2000). *Canadian Corrections*. Scarborough, Ontario: Nelson: a division of Thomson Learning.

Gyekye, K. (1996). *African Cultural Values: An Introduction*. Accra, Ghana: Sankofa Publishing Co.

Hale, M. S. (1990). *Controversies in Sociology*. Toronto: Copp Clark Pitman Ltd.

Haley, A. (1998). Black History, Oral History and Genealogy, in T*he Oral History Reader* by Robert Perks and Alistair Thomson (eds.). New York: Routledge.

Hall, A. J. (1987). Classical Liberalism and the Modern State. *DAEDALUS—Journal of the American Academy of Arts and Sciences*, Vol. 116, No. 3.

Harris, M. K. (1989). Alternative Visions in the Context of Contemporary Realities in *Justice: The Restorative Vision: New Perspectives on Crime and Justice*. Occasional Papers of the MCC Canada Victim Offender Ministries Program and MCC U.S. Office of Criminal Justice. Issue No. 7. February.

———. (1987). Exploring the Connections between Feminism and Justice. *The National Prison Project Journal*. Fall. Pp. 33–35.

Hartwell, R. M. (1979). Introduction, in *The Politicization of Society* by Kenneth S. Templeton (ed.). Indianapolis: Liberty Press.

Hedlund, S. and Lundahl, M. (1989). *Ideology as a Determinant of Economic Systems: Nyerere and Ujamaa in Tanzania*. Uppsala: Scandinavian Institute of African Studies.

Hoebel, E. A. (1967). *The law of Primitive Man: A Study in Comparative Legal Dynamics*. Cambridge, Massachusetts: Harvard University Press.

Howard, R. (1993). Cultural Absolutism and Nostalgia for Community. *Human Rights Quarterly*. Vol.15. US: John Hopkins Univ. Press.

——— and Donnelly, J. (1986). Human Dignity, Human Rights and Political Regimes. In *Hastings International and Comparative Law Review 80*. pp.801 807.

Hutchison, W.T. (ed.). (1968). *Africa and Law: Developing Legal Systems in African Commonwealth Nations*. Madison: The University of Wisconsin Press.

Iro, M. (1985). Igbo Ethics and Discipline in (The Igbo Socio-Political System) Papers presented at the *1985 Ahiajoku Lecture Colloquium*. Owerri: Ministry of Information, Culture, Youth and Sports.

Isichei, E. (1983). *A History of Nigeria*. London: Longman.

Iweriebor, I. (1996). Brief Reflections on Clitorodectomy in *Africa Update*—a Newsletter of the CCSU African Studies Program, Central Connecticut State University.

Iwuagwu, A. O. (1980). The Ogu Corpus and the Igbo Concept of the Moral Law. *The 1980 Ahiajoku Lectures Colloquim*. Owerri, Nigeria: Ministry of Information and Culture.

Jackson, M. (1994). Aboriginal Women and Self-government in Crim. 840 Casebook Compiled by Joan Brockman, S. F. U.

Jones, D. J. (1988). Towards a Native Anthropology: In *Anthropology for the Nineties: Introductory Readings*. by J. B. Cole (ed.). New York: The Free Press.

Kamalu, C. (1990). *Foundations of African Thought: A Worldview Grounded in the African Heritage of Religion, Philosophy, Science and Art*. London: Karnak House.

Kant, I. (1995). On the Right to Punish and to Grant Clemency in *Punishment and Rehabilitation* (3rd Edition) by Jeffrie G. Murphy (ed.). Belmont, California: Wadsworth Publishing Company.

Kashagama, Dan (2001) (e-mail exchange of May 29, 2001).

Kirby, S. and McKenna, K. (1989). *Experience, Research and Social Change: Methods from the Margins*. Toronto: Garamond Press.

Kluckhohn, C. (1967). The Study of Culture (originally published in 1951) in *The Study of Society: An Integrated Anthology* by Peter I. Rose (ed.).

Lauren, P. G. (1998). *The Evolution of International Human Rights: Visions Seen*. Philadelphia: University of Pennsylvania Press.

Lindblom, C. E. (1959). The Science of "Muddling Through" *Public Administration Review* pp.79–88.

———. (1979). Still Muddling, Not Yet Through *Public Administration Review* pp. 517–526.

Lloyd, D. (1964). *The Idea of law*. Baltimore, USA: Penguin Books.

Macionis, J. J., Clarke, J. N., & Gerber, M. L. (1997). *Sociology*. Scarborough, Ontario: Prentice Hall Allyn and Bacon Canada.

Magstadt, M. T. (1991). *Nations and Governments—Comparative Politics in Regional Perspective*. New York: St. Martin's Press.

Mahmoud, S. (1993). The State and Human Rights in Africa in the 1990s: Perspectives Prospects. *The Human Rights Quarterly*. Vol.15. US: John Hopkins Univ. Press.

Maine, H. (1969). From Status to Contract (originally published in 1917), in *Sociology of Law* by Vilhelm Aubert (ed.).

Makang, J. (1997). Of the Good Use of Tradition: Keeping the Critical Perspective in African Philosophy, in *Postcolonial African Philosophy: A Critical Reader* by Emmanuel C. eze (ed.). Blackwell Publishers.

Marx, K. (1994). Class Conflict and Law (originally published in 1844) in *Classics Of Criminology* by Joseph E. Jacoby (ed.). Illinois: Waveland Press, Inc.

Matias, A. S. (1996). Female Circumcision in Africa in *Africa Update*—a Newsletter Of the CCSU African Studies Program—Central Connecticut State University.

Mazrui, A. A. (1974). *World Culture and the Black Experience*. Seattle: University of Washington Press.

Miller, W. B. (1973). Ideology and Criminal Justice Policy. In the *Journal of Criminal Law and Criminology* Vol. 64, No. 2, pp. 141–162.

Milner, A. (ed.) (1969). *African Penal Systems.* London: Routledge & Kegan Paul.

Montclos, de M. A. P. (1997). <http:www.monde-diplomatique.fr/en/1997/08–09/afpol. html. (August–September 1997 edition).

Moore, D. B., & McDonald, J. M. (1995). Achieving the 'Good Community': A local police initiative and its wider ramifications in *Perceptions of Justice: Issues in Indigenous and Community Empowerment* by Kayleen M. Hazlehurst (ed.). Aldershot: Avebury.

Moore, S. M. (1995). The Moral Worth of Retribution in *Punishment and Rehabilitation* (3rd Edition) by Jeffrie G. Murphy (ed.) Belmont, CA.: Wadsworth Pub. Co.

Moore, S. F. (1978). *Law as Process: An Anthropological Approach.* London: Routledge & Kegan Paul.

Morley, F. (1979). State and Society, in *The Politicization of Society* by Kenneth S. Templeton, Jr. (ed.). Indianapolis: Liberty Press.

Morris, H. (1995). Persons and Punishment in *Punishment and Rehabilitation* (3rd Edition) by Jeffrie G. Murphy (ed.). Belmont, CA.: Wadsworth Pub. Co.

Morris, R. (1999). *7 Steps From Misery Justice To Social Transformation.* Toronto: Rittenhouse, A New Vision.

———. (1995). *Penal Abolition: The Practical Choice.* Toronto: Canadian Scholars' Press.

Motala, Z. (1989). Human Rights in Africa: a Cultural, Ideological, and Legal Examination. *Hastings International and Comparative Law Review* 12, 373–410.

Murphy, G. J. (1995). *Punishment and Rehabilitation.* 3rd Edition. Belmont, CA.: Wadsworth Publishing Comompany.

———. (1995). Getting Even: The Role of the Victim in *Punishment and Rehabilitation* (3rd Edition) by Jeffrie G. Murphy (ed.). Belmont, CA.: Wadsworth Publishing Company.

Mutua, M. W. (1992). The African Human Rights System in a Comparative Perspective: the need for Urgent reformation. *Legal Forum.*

———. (1995). The Banjul Charter and the African Cultural Fingerprint: An Evaluation of the Language of Duties. *Virginia Journal of International Law 35,* 339–380.

Nader, L. & Harry, F. (eds.) (1978). *The Disputing Process: Law in Ten Societies.* New York: Columbia University Press.

Njaka, E. N. (1974). *Igbo Political Culture.* Evanston: Northwestern University Press.

Nkrumah, K. (1970). *Consciencism.* New York: Monthly Review Press.

Nsereko, D.D.N. (1991). Extenuating Circumstances in Capital Offences in Botswana. *Criminal Law Forum.* Vol.2, No.2, Winter.

———. (1992). Victims of crime and their Rights. In *Criminology in Africa* by Tibamanya mwene Mushanga (ed.). Rome: United Nations Interregional Crime and Justice Research Institute (UNICRI).

Nsugbe, P.O. (1974). *Ohaffia: A Matrilineal Ibo People.* Clarendon: Oxford University Press.

Nzegwu, N. (1995). Recovering Igbo Women's Tradtions for Development: The Case Of Ikporo Onitsha, in *Women, Culture and Development* by Martha Nussbaum And Jonathan Glover (eds.) Oxford University Press.

Ogbaa, K. (1999). *Understanding Things Fall Apart.* London: Greenwood Press.

Ogundipe-Leslie, M. (1993). African Women, Culture and Another Development, in *Theorizing Black Feminisms: the Visionary Pragmatism of Black Women* by S. M. James and Abena P. A. Busia (eds.). New York: Routledge.

Okere, T. (1986). Law-Making in Traditional Igbo Society, in Igbo Jurisprudence: Law and Order in Traditional Igbo Society. *The 1986 Ahiajoku Lectures Colloquium.* Owerri—Nigeria: Ministry of Information and Culture.

Okereafoezeke, N. (2001). *Africa's Native Versus Foreign Control Systems: A Critical Analysis.* Unpublished Manuscript presented at the 10th Annual Pan-African Conference, organized by the Centre for African Peace and Conflict Resolution, California State University, Sacramento, May 1–5, 2001.

———. 2002. *Law and Justice in Post-British Nigeria: Conflicts and Interactions Between Native and Foreign Systems of Social Control in Igbo.* Westport, Connecticut: Greenwood Press.

Okereke, O. G. (1993). Public Attitudes Toward the Police Force in Nigeria. *Police Studies.* Vol.16 No.3, Fall, pp.113–1121.

Olowu, D. and Erero, J. (1996). Governance of Nigeria's Villages and Cities through Indigenous Institutions. In *African Rural and Urban Studies (ISSN 1073–4600).* Volume 3, Number 1, pp. 99–121.

Olujinmi, A. (2004) *Agenda for Reforming the Justice Sector in Nigeria.* Abuja, Nigeria: Federal Ministry of Justice, Federal Secretariat, Abuja, Nigeria.

Opolot, J. (1976). *Criminal Justice and Nation Building in Africa.* Washington, D.C.: University Press of America.

Otuu, M. O. (1977). *Afikpo (Ehugbo) Age-Grade Organization (A Study in Continuity and Change).* Unpublished B.Sc. Thesis, June 1977. University of Nigeria Nsukka.

Ottenberg, P. V. (1959). The Changing Economic Position of Women among the Afikpo Ibo, in *Continuity and Change in African Cultures* by Bascom, W. R. and Herskovits, M. J. (eds.). Chicago: The University of Chicago Press.

Ottenberg, S. (1971). *Leadership and Authority in an African Society: The Afikpo Village-Group.* Seattle: University of Washington Press.

———. (1968). *Double Descent in African Society—the Afikpo Village Group.* Seattle: University of Washington Press.

———. (1972). Humorous Masks and Serious Politics among Afikpo Ibo. In *African Art and Leadership* by Douglas Fraser and Herbert M. Cole (eds.). Madison: The University of Wisconsin Press.

———. (1965). Inheritance and Succession in Afikpo. In *Studies in the Laws Of Succession in Nigeria* by J. Duncan and M. Dekkett. London: Oxford University Press.

Pal, L. (1992). *Public Policy Analysis* (2nd Edition). Toronto: Nelson.

Palys, T. (1995). Lectures and Papers Presented to Class of Crim. 862, 10/03/95. Simon Fraser University.

———. (1997). *Research Decisions: Quantitative and Qualitative Perspectives.* 2nd Edition. Toronto, Canada: Harcourt Brace.

Parrinder, G. (1969). *Religion in Africa.* Baltimore, Maryland: Penguin Books.

———. (1970). *African Traditional Religion.* Westport, Connecticut, Greenwood Press, Publishers.

Parnell, C. P. (1988). *Escalating Disputes: Social Participation and Change in the Oaxacan Highlands.* Tucson: the University of Arizona Press.

Peil, M. (1982). *Social Science Research Methods: An African Handbook.* London: Hodder and Stoughton.

Peoples, E. E. (2000). *Basic Criminal Procedures.* New Jersey: Prentice Hall.

Perham, M. (1937). *Native Administration in Nigeria.* London: Oxford University Press.

Plato (1995). Punishment as Healing for the Soul (fifth- fourth Century B.C. publication) in *Punishment and Rehabiliation* (3rd Edition) by Jeffrie G. Murphy (ed.). Belmont, California: Wadsworth Publishing Company.

Pospisil, L. (1978). *The Ethnology of Law.* Menolo Park California: Cummings Publishing Co.

Pranis, K., Stuart, B., & Wedge, M. (2003). *Peacemaking Circles: From Crime to Community.* St. Paul, Minnesota: Living Justice Press.

Pratten, D. T. (1996). The Intermediary Role of Sahelian Associations. In *African Rural and Urban Studies (ISSN 1073–4600).* Volume 3, Number 1, pp.99–121.

Rapoport, A. (1975). *Theories of Conflict Resolution and the Law.* In *Courts and Trials:* A Multi-Disciplinary Approach by M. L. Friedland (ed.) Toronto: University of Toronto Press.

Rattray, R.S. (1929). *Ashanti Law and Constitution.* Clarendon: Oxford University Press.

Report of Proceedings from the Tradtional Courts and Chief in Council Court Cases and other Afikpo Indigenous Institutions of Conflict Resolution.

Reuters Limited—http://www.nairaland.com/nigeria/topic-3247.0.html)

Roberts, S. (1979). *Order and Dispute: An Introduction to Legal Anthropology.*

Rock, P. (1995). The Opening Stages of Criminal Justice Policy-Making. In *British Journal of Criminology* Vol.35, No.1.

Rodney, W. (1974). *How Europe Underdeveloped Africa.* Washington, D.C.: Howard University Press.

Ross, R. (1996). *Returning to the Teachings: Exploring Aboriginal Justice.* Toronto: Penguin Books.

Ruby, J. (1992). Speaking for, speaking about, speaking with, or speaking alongside: An anthropological and documentary dilemma. *Journal of Film and Video.*44.1–2. Spring-Summer.

Rusche, G. and Kirchheimer, O. (1994). Punishment and Social Structure (originally published in 1938) in *Classics of Criminology* by Joseph E. Jacoby (ed.). Illinois: Waveland Press, Inc.

Shaidi, L. (1992). Traditional, Colonial and Present Day Administration of Criminal Justice. *United Nations Interregional Crime and Justice Research Institute (UNICRI).* Rome: UNICRI Publication No. 47.

Schwartz, R. D. and Miller, C. J. (1973). Legal Evolution and Societal Complexity in *The Social Organization of law* by Donald Black and Maureen Mileski (eds.).

Shell-Duncan, B., Hernlund, Y. (eds.) (2000). *Female "Circumcision" in Africa: Culture, Controversy, and Change.* London: Lynne Rienner Publishers.

Stake, R. E. (1994). Case Studies, in *Handbook of Qualittative Research* by N. K. Denzin and Y. S. Lincoln (eds.). Thousand Oaks: Sage Publications.

Stangeland, P. (1985). Informal Modes of Conflict resolution: The Norwegian Experience. *Institute for Criminology and Criminal Law Stencilseries*. Oslo.

Stern, V. (1999). Alternatives to Prison in Developing Countries. In *Punishment and Society*. Vol. 1 Nr. 2.

Stevens, J. (2000). *Access to justice in sub-Saharan Africa: the role of traditional and Informal justice systems*. United Kingdom: Penal Reform International.

Sommers, K. E. (1995). *Voices from Within: Women Who Have Broken the Law*. Toronto: University of Toronto Press.

Toby, J. (1967). Is Punishment Necessary? In *The Study of Society: An Integrated Anthology* by Peter I. Rose (ed.). New York: Random House.

Tribune (2005) Tribune Nigerian Newspapers of December 15, 2005 (http://www.tribune.com.ng/151205/news07.htm)

Tunbridge, L. (1998). Vancouver Sun (Wednesday, March 25th).

Thompson, P. (1998). The Voice of the Past: Oral History, in *The Oral History Reader* by Robert Perks and Alistair Thomson (eds.). New York: Routledge.

Uchendu, V. C. (1965). *The Igbo of Southeast Nigeria*. New York: Holt, Rinehart and Winston.

———. (1995). Ezi na Ulo: The Extended family in Igbo Civilization. *The 1995 Ahiajoku Lecture*. Owerri, Nigeria: Ministry of Information and Social Development.

Umozurike, U. O. (1981). Adjudication Among the Igbo, in Perspectives on Igbo Culture. *The 1981 Ahiajoku Lectures Colloquium*. Owerri, Nigeria. Ministry of Information and Culture.

United Nations (1985). Declarations of Basic Principles of Justice for Victims of Crime and Abuse of Power.

Uwazie, E. E. (1994). Modes of Indigenous Disputing and Legal Interactions Among the Ibos of Eastern Nigeria in *Journal of Legal Pluralism and Unofficial Law* 34, 87–103.

Van Ness, D. & Strong, H. K. (1997). *Restoring Justice*. Cincinnati, Ohio: Anderson Publishing Co.

Van Ness, D. (1989). Pursuing a Restorative Vision of Justice, in *Justice: The Restorative Vision*. Occasional Papers of the MCC Canada Victim Offender Ministries Program and the MCC U.S. Office of Criminal Justice. February 1989 Issue No. 7.

Walgrave, L. and Bazemore, G. (1999). Refelctions on the Future of Restorative Justice for Juveniles. In *Restorative Juvenile Justice: Repairing the Harm of Youth Crime* by Gordon Bazemore and Lode Walgrave (eds.) Monsey, New York: Criminal Justice Press.

Weitekamp, E. G. M. (1999).The History of Restorative Justice. In *Restorative Juvenile Justice: Repairing the Harm of Youth Crime*. By Gordon Bazemore and Lode Walgrave (eds.). Monsey, New York: Criminal Justice Press.

Wilson, A. R. (1986). Customary Marriage and Divorce in IgboSociety. In Igbo Jurisprudence: Law and Order in Traditional Igbo Society. *The 1986 Ahiajoku Lectures Colloquium*. Owerri, Nigeria. Ministry of Information and culture.

Wiredu, K. (1997). Democracy and Consensus in African traditional Politics: A Plea for a Non-Party Polity. In *Postcolonial African Philosophy: A Critical Reader* by Eze, E. C. (ed.). Cambridge, Massachusetts: Blackwell Publishers.

Wolfgang, M. E. (1994). Victim-Precipitated Criminal Homicide (originally published in 1957) in *Classics of Criminology* by Joseph E. Jacoby (ed.). Illinois: Waveland Press, Inc.

Wright, M. (1996). Victims Meet Offenders in an English Urban Community. *International Journal of Comparative and Applied Criminal Justice*, Fall, Vol. 20., No. 20.

Zehr, H. (1989). Stumbling Toward a Restorative Ideal. *In Justice: the Restorative Vision: New Perspectives on Crime and Justice.* Occasional Papers of the MCC Canada Victim Offender Ministries Program and the MCC U.S. Office of Criminal Justice, Issue No. 7, February.

———. (1990). *Changing Lenses: A New Focus for Crime and Justice.* Waterloo, Ontario: Harald Press.

———. (2002). *The Little Book of Restorative Justice.* Intercourse, PA: Good Books.

Zellerer, E. (1996). *Violence Against Inuit Women in the Canadian Eastern Arctic.* Ph.D. Dissertation. Burnaby: Simon Fraser University School of Criminology.

Index